y&
ilds

IT skills for
e-Quals
Level 1

Protocol

Hodder & Stoughton
A MEMBER OF THE HODDER HEADLINE GROUP

City & Guilds name and logo and e-Quals are the registered trade marks of The City and Guilds of London Institute and are used under licence. © The City and Guilds of London Institute 2003. All rights reserved.

Orders: please contact Bookpoint Ltd, 130 Milton Park, Abingdon, Oxon OX14 4SB. Telephone: (44) 01235 827720. Fax: (44) 01235 400454. Lines are open from 9.00 - 6.00, Monday to Saturday, with a 24 hour message answering service. You can also order through our Website: www.hodderheadline.co.uk.

British Library Cataloguing in Publication Data
A catalogue record for this title is available from the British Library

ISBN 0 340 859148

First Published 2003
Impression number   10 9 8 7 6 5 4 3 2 1
Year   2008 2007 2006 2005 2004 2003

Copyright © 2003 Protocol

All rights reserved. No part of this publication may be reproduced or transmitted in any form or by any means, electronic or mechanical, including photocopy, recording, or any information storage and retrieval system, without permission in writing from the publisher or under licence from the Copyright Licensing Agency Limited. Further details of such licences (for reprographic reproduction) may be obtained from the Copyright Licensing Agency Limited, of 90 Tottenham Court Road, London W1T 4LP.

Typeset by Pantek Arts Ltd, Maidstone Kent.
Printed in Italy for Hodder & Stoughton Educational, a division of Hodder Headline Plc, 338 Euston Road, London NW1 3BH.

e-Quals
Contents

UNIT 003   **SPREADSHEETS**   **55**

UNIT 004   DATABASES   88

e-Quals
Introduction

Welcome to e-Quals

Whether you are an experienced IT user or a complete novice, this reference book for Level 1 IT Users is designed to support you by providing easy to understand and comprehensive information for all the modules covered within the City and Guilds e-Quals Level 1 – Certificate for IT Users. The book has been produced in co-operation with, and is fully endorsed by, City and Guilds.

The e-Quals suite of qualifications has been designed in consultation with business and training professionals, combining the use of common IT applications with a range of study levels. This multi-layered approach has ensured its relevance to business and future IT users. The programme of study offers achievable goals, progression, and the confidence that your achievements today will be recognised tomorrow.

Designed with flexibility in mind, the programme allows you to study and learn within the work or home environment. It also allows you to complete the programme as quickly or as slowly as is convenient to you.

This reference book has been designed to provide you with the knowledge and practice to assist you in achieving the e-Quals Level 1 certificate. There are tasks throughout that will test your knowledge as you progress through the units. In addition, the book has been designed to be used as a quick reference point. This facility means that you will be able to consult and search for information in a format you are already familiar with, whenever you require reminders or hints regarding the e-Quals applications.

Keep your e-Quals reference book by your computer and learn the skills required for tomorrow's IT professional.

Course requirements

The e-Quals Level 1 qualification is divided into 8 units. For the award of a full certificate, candidates must successfully complete the assessments for the core unit plus two optional units. Candidates will also receive a certificate for each individual unit achieved.

The 8 units offered, and covered in this book, are.

Core unit
001 IT Principles
Optional units
002 Word processing
003 Spreadsheets
004 Databases
005 Using the internet
006 Presentation graphics
007 Email
008 Desk top publishing

e-Quals
Acknowledgements

Screen shots reprinted by permission from Microsoft Corporation.

This Product has been developed by Hodder & Stoughton Limited, is intended as a method of studying for the e-Quals qualifications and the content and the accuracy are the sole responsibility of Hodder & Stoughton Limited. Therefore the City and Guilds of London Institute accepts no liability howsoever in respect of any breach of the intellectual property rights of any third party howsoever occasioned or damage to the third party's property or person as a result of the use of the Products.

e-Quals
UNIT 001
PRINCIPLES OF I.T. (INFORMATION TECHNOLOGY)

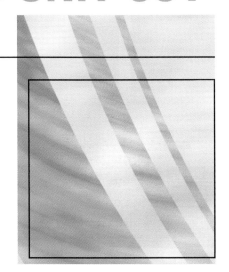

Information Technology in the modern world involves accessing, modifying and exchanging information via computers. This information might be, for example, written text, photographs or other pictures, or radio or television programmes. Computers allow this information to be transmitted locally, nationally or internationally to other computers, usually within seconds or minutes. The following text explains in principle how this is done, and gives some indication of how it is achieved in practice. The text is arranged under, and covers the following sub-headings: Hardware, Software, The Operating Environment, Files and Directories, Information Networks, Health and Safety Requirements and Exercises.

HARDWARE

As the name suggests, hardware is hard – you can physically touch it.

The computer, in a unit or case that usually sits on a desk (a desk-top) or stands on the floor under or behind a desk contains, amongst other units, wires and frames; the **hard disk** or **hard drive** (the internal storage facility permanently installed in the computer by the manufacturer which holds nearly all the instructions, programmes and data required by the user and the computer in order to function. Although referred to as a singular disk, the unit actually holds several rigid disks, like a stack of records or CD's, revolving around a central spindle. Both surfaces of each disk are able to store data. To locate any particular data, the surfaces are 'read' by 'heads' moving across, but not touching, each disk surface as the disks rotate);

The **CPU** (Central Processing Unit – the 'brain' of the computer – processes (combines, separates, calculates) all data accessed and/or required by the user. The electronic circuitry of the CPU is usually located on a 'chip' (a small silicon body a few centimetres long by one centimetre wide with metal contacts ('legs') extending from both long sides. Today, materials other than silicon are used to make chips so 'microchip' is a more accurate name than silicon chip). With modern miniaturisation the CPU might be entirely held on a single chip and known as a 'microprocessor'. Processor types are usually distinguished by their commercial names e.g. the Pentium processor made by Intel, with each successive model identified by increasing numbers (Pentium 5 for example) is a well-known type);

1

The **VDU** (Visual Display Unit i.e. the screen and the plastic cabinet holding it);

The **keyboard** (the range of 'buttons' or 'keys' that can be pressed by your fingers, similar to a typewriter); the mouse (a small, curved plastic case which fits into the palm of your hand and when moved, moves a pointer on the screen. Buttons on the mouse can be pressed or 'clicked' to change things on screen) and

Printers (which produce 'hard copy' on paper or other media as explained below);

and any other piece of computer-ware that you can touch, are all hardware.

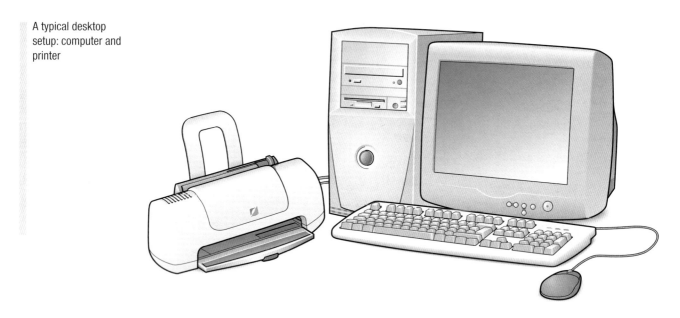

A typical desktop
setup: computer and
printer

The hardware uses other hardware to perform its functions.

Storage Devices

For example, a 'floppy disk' is a small (3.5ins square), thin, hard plastic casing protecting a very thin and 'floppy' plastic disk coated with a magnetic film. Floppy disks slot into a 'disk drive' on the computer casing and can be used to store files and/or directories of data. These 'floppies' and the data they hold (which can be both 'read' and 'written to'), can then be taken away for use on other computers (not just those connected by a 'network' to the original computer – see page 17 for an explanation of networks) or held as 'backup' i.e. a copy, in case some irreparable damage occurs to the computer. Floppies cannot, by modern standards, store much data (a maximum of 1.44 Megabytes – see page 7 for an explanation of megabytes).

The same functions can be performed by Magnetic Tape which can also be 'written to' or 'read from' but store much more information than floppy disks (usually between 10 – 2100 Mb). To utilise tape, computers need 'tape drive' slots where tape cartridges can be inserted.

All magnetic media must be handled and stored carefully to prevent corruption or deletion of the data they hold. Magnetic and electric fields from TVs and other electrical appliances, and spillages of food or drink can corrupt or destroy data stored magnetically, as can physical damage.

CD-ROM's (Compact Disk Read Only Memory) and their drives (a different and slightly larger slot on the computer casing) are the technical equivalent of CD music disks and players. The data is not stored magnetically but optically and is read by a laser beam. This allows the data to be stored much closer together and hence CDs can store much data – usually around 600 MB. Whilst CDs should still be protected from physical damage, they are not susceptible to the other risks magnetic media are prone to as mentioned above. 'Read Only Memory' means just that: the data stored can only be 'read' by the computer. It cannot be 'written to' i.e. added to or altered in any way. Some modern computers have an additional facility called a CD re-writer, which does allow data to be 'written to' the CD.

Following the same trend as home entertainment, DVDs (Digital Video Disks) store even more data than CDs and commonly hold films and television programmes. Computer DVD drives also read these disks and although not yet common, will soon be able to write to them.

The Scanner

A scanner acts like a photocopier (and some may be used as such) but instead of producing hard copy i.e. a piece of paper with the copied image or text on it, an image or text is sent to the computer where the user can alter and/or store the image and/or text.

Computer with
scanner connected
(on right)

The Printer

The printer uses other hardware such as paper, cartridges (holding inked or carbon ribbons) or toner (holding powdered ink), all of which run out after a while and are therefore known as 'consumables'. Adequate stocks of spare consumables are advisable to prevent avoidable delays when a component runs out. Obviously, the printer needs to be kept supplied with paper or if appropriate, other 'media' such as envelopes, card, transparencies etc.

Printer cartridge

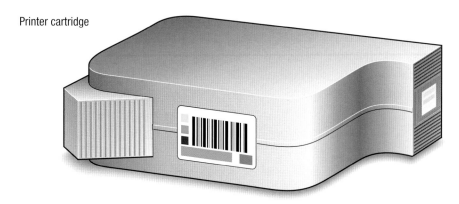

Different types of printer are available. The speed and quality of printing required usually determines which is used.

A 'dot-matrix' printer makes individual pins in the printer head strike against an inked ribbon positioned in front of the paper, producing a pattern of dots corresponding to the letter or symbol required. The matrix or grid of a 9-pin head cannot produce a high resolution of print but can print quickly. Some dot-matrix printers 'double print' by repeating the print with the head offset just slightly downwards or sideways to fill in the gaps between the dots to produce a better image – but reduce printing speed. Alternatively, a 24-pin head produces NLQ (Near Letter Quality) text. Dot-matrix printers are inexpensive and can be very fast but they are noisy when printing and even the best do not produce very high quality text.

An 'Ink-jet' printer holds a number (typically 64) of very fine ink tubes or nozzles in the print head which spray tiny dots onto the paper as the head moves back and forth horizontally over the paper. As each character is formed from hundreds of these dots within a matrix or grid the quality of text is very good. The printing is quiet but the speed relatively slow – only about 200 characters per second at a maximum rate.

Laser printers use a laser beam controlled by an internal microprocessor to write characters and graphics to a rotating internal drum which picks up powdered ink (toner) in the pattern of the text or image on the drum. The individual characters are still formed on a matrix or grid and each dot is called a 'pixel'. At a standard 14 000 pixels per cm^2. top quality print is produced at a minimum rate of about 8 pages per minute and very quietly. Laser printer prices have been relatively high but are falling quite rapidly.

Ink-jet and laser printers are now the most common printers in use in both home and office and, if suitable hardware and software (see page 6 for explanation of software) is provided can produce colour images and text.

laser printer showing paper feed

ink jet printer showing
paper feed

With such a wide range of media available for use, the user must 'tell' the printer via the computer what medium it must print on. 'Printer Settings' in the computer will control how and in what way the printer prints. Prior to printing anything for the first time, it is a good idea to initiate a 'self-test' for the printer, which will ensure that the computer can 'talk to' the printer and that the required font (shape and size of letters and symbols) can be printed. Click Start, Settings, Printers, select the printer to which you wish to test, right-click the mouse button and select Properties from the pop-up menu. Click the Print Test Page button, click OK to confirm the test page was printed, or click Troubleshoot for help on why it may not have printed.

TASK

Print out a test page from your computer (assuming that you have a printer connected).

Physical adjustments to paper guides and feed trays should also be made if necessary to ensure problem-free printing. Although usually a standard A4 size paper is required, modern printers can accommodate a wide variety of paper and envelope sizes. An enormous range of variously sized labels is also available. These labels are usually self-adhesive and attached to acetate backing pages with a standard number of labels to a page, which the printer must be set to accommodate.

Attempting to print without consideration of the above procedures can produce unwanted hard copy or, perhaps, nothing at all e.g. attempting to print without any paper in the printer feed tray will not produce any hard copy but will produce an 'error message' on screen telling you the printer is out of paper.

All hardware is concerned with accessing, editing, creating or presenting data. Each item either has data put into it or it puts data out. So each item acts as either an input or output device.

Input Devices

Input devices include the keyboard, the mouse, scanner and, not mentioned above, barcode readers (used, for example, in supermarkets, libraries, airports and warehouses), magnetic stripe readers (used, for example, to read all sorts of plastic cards such as credit or debit cards), touch screen (such as information systems in museums and town centres), light pen (a hand-held stylus used to 'write' on screen) and tracker balls (as used on some lap-top computers to move the pointer instead of a mouse).

Output Devices

Output devices include VDUs, printers and, not mentioned above, plotters (used to draw accurate graphs, diagrams, maps, plans and 3-dimensional drawings) and voice synthesisers for people unable to speak but able to use a keyboard.

EXERCISE QUESTIONS

1 Name 3 input devices

2 Name 3 output devices

3 Name 3 consumables

4 Name a processor type

5 What does the CPU do?

6 True or false?

    A printer can only print on paper.

    A hard disk is just that – a hard, single disk.

    A dot-matrix printer prints the highest quality text.

7 What does a scanner do?

8 Why is a floppy disk called floppy?

9 What is the storage capacity of a CD?

10 What is ROM?

SOFTWARE

All the hardware mentioned above is of no use unless it understands and obeys instructions to perform its functions. These instructions are given by software – computer programs. There are two types of software: systems software and applications software. Before we look at the distinctions between these types of software, we shall see what is common to both.

At the most fundamental level, there are only two states in which any electric or electronic circuit can be: 'current on' or 'current off'. All and anything a computer can do depends on instructions coded into patterns of 'current on' or 'current off'. A communication system comprising of only two states is required, hence the use of a binary system of two digits; 1 and 0. Usually 1 represents 'current on' and 0 represents 'current off'. 'Binary digit' is contracted to 'bit' and a bit is 1 or 0. Any equipment using a binary digit system is known as 'digital'.

It would take too much space to explain in detail how patterns of 1s and 0s (patterns of 'current on' and 'current off') are used to make computers work but the principle is as follows. If you numbered the letters of the alphabet 1-26, you could write messages or instructions using sequences of numbers instead of letters (e.g. 3, 4 would stand for CD). The number base we use when writing 1 to 26 is base 10 (0–9 then 10, 10–99 then 100, etc.).

There are ways of translating base 10 numbers into base 2 (binary) numbers. Hence, it is possible to write messages or instructions in binary i.e. in 'bits', a language that the electric and electronic circuits in a computer can respond to.

According to the particular computer, its manufacturer and its purpose, a particular number of bits represent each character or symbol. Usually 8 bits represent a single character, which is known as a 'byte'. So, each letter or symbol on screen is a byte and each is coded for by 8 bits e.g. the letter A is represented by 01000001, B by 01000010, C by 01000011, D by 01000100 and so on. Hence when the computer reads '0100001101000100' it displays 'CD'.

You can see that thousands if not millions of bytes are involved when dealing with pages of text or images. So units are required to enable us to deal with such large numbers without having to manipulate enormous numbers.

1 Kb (kilobyte) stands for about 1000 bytes (exactly 1024)

1 Mb (megabyte) stands for about 1 000 000 bytes (exactly 1024Kb)

1 Gb (gigabyte) stands for about 1 000 000 000 bytes (exactly 1024Mb)

You will often see these units describing the data storage capacity of floppy disks, CDs etc.

Systems software controls the internal functioning of the computer, all the tasks that have to be completed in general for any type of job rather than those associated with particular applications. One of the most important jobs for systems software follows from what we have just been reading about: translating the 'high-level' language as typed on the keyboard by the user to the binary digits (the 'machine code') the computer understands. Systems software also controls the computer when 'booting up' after the user switches it on, the performance of the computer and the screen displays, for just a few examples. Some of the systems software is held in ROM (Read Only Memory). This is installed by the manufacturer and is not accessible to the user because the instructions it holds are fundamental to the computer's operation, and if altered would cause problems. This ROM is essential for the computer to work, unlike the other ROM we encountered with CD-ROM, which is optional and 'extra' information for use with a particular application.

At this point it would be appropriate to explain a similar term – RAM. This stands for Random Access Memory and is used to store data actually in use for any particular application (see page 8 for details on applications). This allows the data to be immediately available without the user having to wait while the hard drive locates and loads it for use. It is accessed randomly and probably differently each time the computer is used. When the computer is shut down the contents of RAM are lost (for some purposes a special type of RAM called static RAM can retain the data between power down sessions). Memory that is lost with power down is 'volatile' whilst that which is retained is 'non-volatile'. To view the available RAM that your system has, double-click the My Computer icon (picture) on the desktop (initial Start up screen). Click Start, Settings, Control Panel, double-click the System icon the resulting screen will display system information including RAM.

TASK

View your computer's system information.

Another very important part of the systems software is the operating system. This is the set of 'master' programs and instructions that control the orderly and meaningful execution of the user's commands in conjunction with the computer's hardware and applications software (see below). It decides on how the CPU will 'time-share' between different tasks the user has given the computer and automates many necessary but, if the user had to do them, time-consuming jobs e.g. checking the availability and state of input and output devices and the transfer of data between them. There are a number of operating systems available, one of the most common being Microsoft Windows.

To find out which operating system you are using, double-click the My Computer icon on the desktop, right click on the C: drive and select Properties from the pop-up menu this will result in displaying an information box with the version you are using.

Now we have a functional computer system with appropriate hardware, governed and made functional by systems software, we are ready to use the computer for a particular job, a particular application.

Applications Software

Applications software allows us to do this. Today, different applications software is available, depending on what we need to do. For business applications there are software packages to deal with accounting and payroll (spreadsheets), writing letters and reports (word processing) and providing computer-based displays to customers and colleagues (presentation graphics); for research applications (mathematical and design software) and for home use (games, money management, creative art and music software). The biggest software suppliers such as Microsoft and Apple Macintosh give names to these packages e.g. Microsoft's spreadsheet package is called Excel, its word processor package is called Word and its presentation graphics package is called PowerPoint. Use of various applications software is explored in the following two sections. To view the applications that you have loaded onto your machine, click Start and then Programs, the menu displayed will show the applications installed.

> **TASK**
>
> **Make a note of the applications that you have on your computer.**

THE OPERATING ENVIRONMENT

When the computer is switched on, it 'boots up' (because it is making itself work without any external help, it was historically compared with and referred to as 'pulling oneself up by one's own bootstraps'). After a minute or two it presents a screen displaying the options immediately available for use. Older systems would present a flashing cursor (a short vertical line) waiting instructions to be typed using the keyboard. Once work had begun on some application, it was necessary to use the arrow keys on the keyboard to move the cursor around the screen and locate it where editing or action was required. However, people found this a somewhat awkward and unfriendly 'operating environment'. Most workers, prior to computers, had a variety of folders or ledgers etc. on or around their desks ready for use. Therefore the computer showed the equivalent software on a screen 'desktop' as little pictures or images – 'icons' – to represent familiar items such as wastebaskets, files and filing cabinets. An arrow replaced the cursor, and could be moved around the screen by a hand held 'mouse'. Pointing and clicking with the mouse selected a particular option, some of which would make a rectangular box appear on screen (a 'window') displaying further options. These operating environments are known as WIMP ('Window, Icon, Mouse, Pointer') or a Graphical User Interface (a GUI – pronounced 'gooey'). Users preferred this easy-to-use and friendly operating environment which has been developed by Apple Macintosh, IBM and Microsoft. Microsoft called its product 'Windows'. GUI's and in particular Microsoft's Windows is the most common operating environment for PCs (Personal Computers) in use today.

Whilst the mouse is most commonly used, nearly all of its functionality is duplicated by keys or combinations of keys or function keys (the numbered F keys along the topmost row of the keyboard which can be programmed to execute particular functions). The keyboard is also, of course, essential for the entry of letters, numbers and symbols. In addition it can do a few other things the mouse cannot e.g. take the cursor straight to the beginning or end of a document, impose a scroll lock (preventing a page moving off screen) and other functions.

At the foot of the screen a task bar might also be shown displaying more icons and 'buttons' – which reveal a menu of further options when clicked.

Desktop screen showing task bar

Icons can be created and deleted. They can also be moved around the screen by clicking on them with the left mouse button and, while holding the button down, dragging the icon to a new position on the desktop. Clicking the right mouse button reveals other options including renaming and pasting icons. Double clicking the left mouse button activates the function represented by that icon and usually displays a window on-screen.

As more than one window can be opened at one time it is sometimes convenient to resize or move windows. Usually at the top right corner (at the far right of the title bar) are three little buttons:

one shows an x and clicking on it will close the window completely and terminate its particular function. Another shows a single horizontal black line. Clicking on this will cause the window to disappear (minimise) and a button (labelled the same as the window was) to appear on the task bar at the foot of the screen.

Clicking on this button restores the window to the screen. This saves having to reselect all the options that produced the window and keeps the user's work ready for immediate access.

The other button shows two little rectangles, one overlapping the other. Clicking on this reduces a full screen window to a smaller window filling only a portion of the screen and allowing other windows and/or the desktop to be seen. The new, smaller window will no longer display the icon with overlapping rectangles but, instead, a button with a little black square. Clicking on this will maximise the window.

You needn't be overwhelmed by the quantity and variety of buttons, for applications make it easy to learn and remember the function of a button. If you hover the mouse pointer over any button on any toolbar and pause for half a second (do not click!), Access displays the button's name on a yellow 'sticky label' type note called **ToolTip** that pops up next to the button.

TASK

Open the My Documents window by double-clicking on the icon on the desktop and practise moving, minimising, restoring, viewing tooltips and closing.

Any window can be dragged to any part of the screen or resized by positioning the arrow over a window border, where it will change to a double-headed arrow. Holding the left mouse button down and moving the mouse will move the border as required, the window contents adjusting to the new size automatically when the mouse button is released. Click on the blue border and drag to move the window to a new location.

Illustration displaying overlapped windows, notice the active window has the blue border,

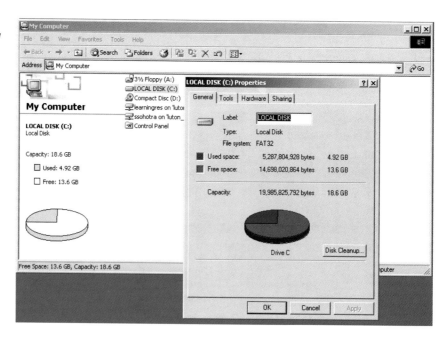

Sometimes more than one application is required to be in use at one time (or more than one file of a particular application e.g. two letters being edited under the software application Word) and each needs to be viewed as a full screen window. Opening each application or file will display the last opened as a full screen. Clicking on the 'Window' button on the Menu bar will display a drop-down menu of all the applications or files open at that time. Clicking on any one will display it as the window to be worked on.

One of the usual icons on the desktop is called 'My Computer'. When selected, various other icons are displayed which give access to any connected equipment, allowing times, settings and configurations to be set for printers, modems (see section 'Information Networks' for explanation), cameras and any other hardware connected to the computer.

Once an applications icon has been selected, the new screen shows, usually at the top of the screen, a title bar with a description of the application selected and the particular file in use. Just underneath it, a menu bar with written text (e.g. File, Edit, etc.) shows various options. Immediately underneath the menu bar is a tool bar showing various icons that in many cases represent options also available within the text buttons of the menu bar but act as a 'short-cut' i.e. the ability to select an option by the fewest clicks. Bars can be customised by a user to reflect his/her preferred way of working and the functions most frequently used. When the screen displays data that extends beyond the screen boundaries, scroll bars allow the user to move the display horizontally or vertically to view the rest of the data.

TASK

Open the Word Processing application by clicking on the Start button (bottom left of the screen), Programs, Microsoft Word.

Although this example shows the word processing software many of the features are replicated within the other Microsoft packages.

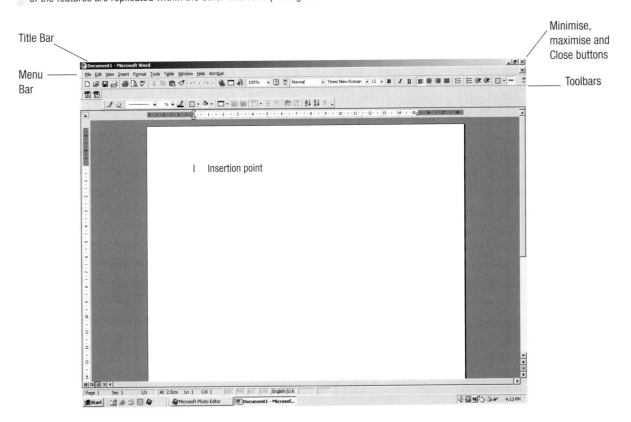

If the toolbar you want isn't there, one way to see them is to select View (Alt+V), Toolbars (t) and then highlight the one you want and press Enter, or simply click on it.

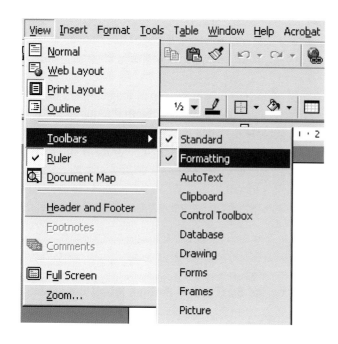

All toolbars that are showing will have a tick next to their name.

If a toolbar is showing which you don't want to see, access the toolbars in the same way and remove this tick by highlighting it and pressing Enter or clicking on it.

When work is completed and saved, the user should close each window until they return to the desktop. Here, usually in a menu revealed by clicking on a screen button, is an option to shut the computer down. It is better to use this option rather than simply switching the power off. This ensures that data is not corrupted or deleted due to power surges or sudden loss of power (such uneven electrical flow could also cause a binary pattern of instruction to be changed with potentially far-reaching consequences). If the user has forgotten to close any particular window the system will do this or, if necessary, ask the user for decisions concerning any open window, by displaying questions or error messages in 'dialog boxes' displayed on screen (error messages and screen prompts, in this or other contexts, should always be responded to by a user to ensure trouble-free operation). The screen will then display a message similar to 'The computer can now be switched off'. A dialog box is a screen that needs to have dialogue between you and your computer, you will be prompted for criteria.

Tip:

The triangle ▶ next to the Toolbars option indicates a sub-menu, and is a standard feature

Tip:

You can press the Tab key to move around in the dialog box or Shift and Tab to move in the opposite direction. As you move around, either the value is highlighted showing that you can change that one or, if it's a button, a dotted line will appear informing you that this is the one that would be selected if you pressed Enter at that point. These buttons are said to be in focus when the dotted line is around them. Here the Cancel button is in focus:

EXERCISE QUESTIONS

Find out what these icons do and write them down in the space provided. The first one has been done for you.

Icon	What it does	Keyboard equivalents via menu	via short cut keys
	Creates a new blank document	File:New	Ctrl+N

1   In computing terms, what is a window?

2   What is 'Windows'?

3   Are you a WIMP user?

4   What would you use to point and click?

5   Are the following true or false?

       Once a window is opened it cannot be resized

       Only one window must be open at any one time

       The arrow head pointer changes to other symbols according to function

6   What would you maximise and minimise and why?

7   What is a desktop in computing terms?

8   What is the purpose of software?

9   What are the two major types of software?

10   What does digital mean?

11   Why do computers work digitally?

12   Name one function of software held in ROM

13   What is an operating system?

14   What is Excel?

15   What is Word?

16   What is PowerPoint?

17   What are the above three items all types of?

18   Where is software stored?

19   What is the safest method of keeping valuable data?

So we now have computer hardware, being operated by systems software so that we can use particular applications software, which we access using a Windows operating environment.

TASK

Choose Help from the menu bar and select Microsoft Word Help.

e-Quals

Help

The Microsoft applications include an extensive, context-sensitive on-line **Help** system, with interactive tutorials and examples that demonstrate how to use the program and its many features. You can obtain help from the application no matter what you are doing at the time – entering data, selecting options from a dialog box, selecting a command, reading an error message, entering an expression or even asking for help. Help is available on every aspect of the application: commands, functions, macros, Toolbar buttons, etc. On-line help uses a cross-referencing system that enables you to jump to a related topic by simply clicking on a highlighted word in the help text. There are several ways to get help:

- The **Office Assistant** [?] shows tips about the mode you are working in, offers advice as to how to use the program features or the mouse more effectively or how to use keyboard shortcuts. You can ask the Assistant specific questions. For example, to get Help on how to create a table, type "How do I create a table". You can also choose an Assistant and options that match your personality and the way you work. As the Assistant is shared by all the Office programs any options you change in one application will affect the Assistant in all other Office programs as well.

- If the correct topic doesn't appear in the Assistant balloon, click **None of the above** and look for more help on the Web at the bottom of the list of topics. You will get suggestions on how to phrase a question to the Office Assistant or how to narrow your search by using keywords.

- The Assistant automatically provides Help topics and tips on tasks you perform as you work, before you even ask a question. For example, when you design a letter or report, the Assistant automatically displays topics for helping you create and design a letter or report.

- The Assistant also displays tips on how to use the features in the Office programs more effectively. Click the light bulb next to the Assistant to see a tip.
  You can also select a different Assistant and set it to operate so that it matches your personality and the way you work. For example, if you prefer using the keyboard to using the mouse, you can have the Assistant display tips on shortcut keys. 💡

- Press the [?] button to obtain immediate, context-sensitive help. Pressing these buttons will bring up on your screen the applications general Help menu from which you can select the item on which you require help.

- Click **Microsoft ****** (depends upon the application your using) **Help** on the **Help** menu. If the Assistant is turned on, it appears. If the Assistant is turned off, the Help window appears. To type a question in the Help window, click the **Answer Wizard** tab. To scroll through a table of contents for Help, click the **Contents** tab. When you want to search for specific words or phrases, click the **Index** tab.

- **ScreenTips** show information about different screen elements. To see a ScreenTip for a menu command, toolbar button, or screen region, click **What's This** ▶? on the **Help** menu. Your mouse pointer will change to a pointer with a question mark, indicating that you are in the tip mode. Point and click any command, menu, toolbar button or screen element and when you release the mouse button, help will appear on the required item. To see a ScreenTip for a dialog box option, click the question mark button [?] (top right hand corner) and then click the option.

TASK

Use the different ways of getting help to find out about:

- **Moving a toolbar**
- **Customising a toolbar**
- **Setting up a new printer**
- **What is a background?**
- **What is screen resolution?**

15

Spell Checking

Another process that is generic to all the Microsoft applications is the spell checker.

The easiest way to check a document for spelling errors is to use the Spelling and Grammar icon in the Formatting toolbar: .

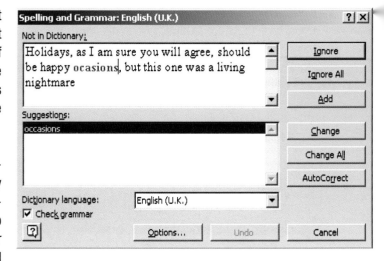

The Spelling and Grammar dialog box will suggest alternative spellings and sometimes other words if it can. Highlight the word you want and select Change. If the same spelling mistake occurs more than once throughout your work, select Change All. If the word is correct – it could be an unusual name – select Ignore or Ignore All.

You can have the checker search only part of a document, down to just checking only one word by highlighting what you want to be checked **before** executing the spell checker or the whole file. Click OK to confirm the spell checker has completed the error checks. As a safeguard you should always proofread your document, the spell check will not identify wrong but correctly spelt words, for example, 'the rods are nice and clear today' instead of 'the roads are nice and clear today'.

FILES AND DIRECTORIES

Whatever application we use, we are likely to want to save the work we have done for future reference and, with time, will usually produce a lot of work of various sorts. Files and directories are the methods used to organise all of this work so that it can be readily found, edited and/or delivered. For the purposes of description examples of a word processing application will be used but the same applies to spreadsheets, presentations etc. The principle is identical to the use of traditional paper files and directories:

A particular letter or document is saved and stored as a file, with a label name chosen by the user. Files relating to a particular category e.g. correspondence with the Inland Revenue or Aunt Sally can be grouped together in a directory (known as a 'folder' in Word for example), with its label name chosen by the user. To allow for subdivision of categories, sub-directories can be created under any directory to form a hierarchical system. Files or directories can be created, deleted and/or renamed.

When a user finishes work on any particular application, they have the choice of discarding it or saving it. Saving the file to the computer's hard disk is a frequently used option and this is usually offered as the 'C' drive amongst others, including an 'A' drive (the floppy disk) or a 'D' drive (CD or DVD).

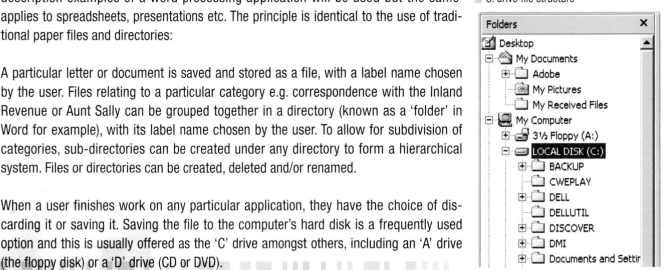
C: drive file structure

Once saved to any individual drive, files can be moved or copied to other drives or other directories either by repeating save procedures or by clicking and dragging files as displayed in a program called 'Windows Explorer'. In this program, drives appear on the left of the screen (the 'tree pane') while the contents of any highlighted drive (clicking on a particular label will highlight it by surrounding the text with a vivid, usually blue, background) appear as a hierarchy on the right (the 'details pane'). Any file can be dragged to any drive or moved or copied there.

Copies might be made for reasons (previously mentioned under the floppy disk section): Data on floppies, tapes, CDs or DVDs can be taken away for use on other computers (not connected by a 'network' to the original computer – see below for explanations of networks) or held as 'backup' in case some irreparable damage occurs to the computer. Sometimes the number of files and/or directories becomes very large. A 'find' function is available to save time. A user can enter the full name of a file or directory or only those details remembered and instruct the program to search for it, in particular places or anywhere in the system. The user can also search for particular items within files.

For this or any other function of applications software, help is available on screen. Either on the menu bar as 'Help' and/or as an icon on the tool bar, these buttons will, when clicked, provide a menu of options offering information, tips and explanations on all aspects of software loaded to the computer, to help the user find, operate, manipulate and output whatever is required.

EXERCISE QUESTIONS

1 True or false?

   Files contain directories to help organise data.

   A file is called a folder

   A file can be copied but not moved

   Once created, a directory can be renamed but not deleted

2 Why might you access files in Windows Explorer?

INFORMATION NETWORKS

We have just read how data can be taken from one computer to another by storing files on floppies, tapes, CDs or DVDs. Data could be transferred faster and more securely if it could be transferred directly to another computer without involving movable, corruptible, 'lose-able', hardware.

This is possible when the computers are physically connected to form a network. However, some adaptions have to be made to allow networks to function. Prior to networks, each person used an individual computer. Hence the computer's operating system e.g. MS DOS (until the late 1990s), was 'single-user'. Networks first appeared for military, and soon after, research and industrial use. These had a 'multi-user' operating system e.g. in the 1980s and early 1990s a system called UNIX became an industry-standard multi-user operating system. An individual

user was not switching the system on, or booting it, for their own exclusive use but accessing an already live and working system which other people might or might not be using. Hence the person 'logged on' to the system or network and 'logged off' the network when they had finished.

The network for a large company might also be large and hold either confidential information or information unnecessary for some workers. Therefore, a particular login name could restrict the options available to any individual user, allowing the person using that login to see only programs relevant to their work or responsibilities.

Once logged in, a user can open files and directories as before but now (provided the login name permits) has access to more drives i.e. those of the other computers connected to the network and labelled accordingly e.g. C1 drive, C2 drive etc. and more hardware e.g. other printers, again labelled accordingly.

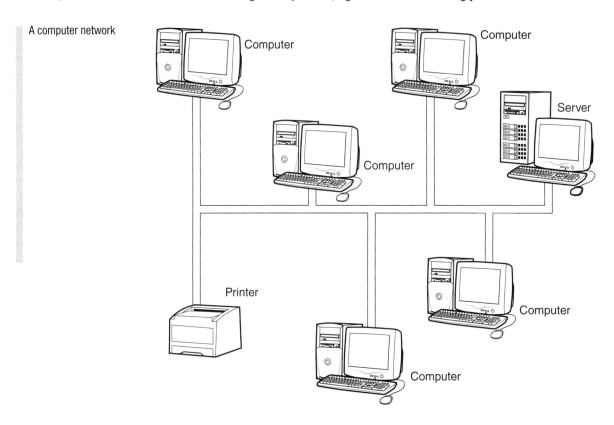
A computer network

Work on a file can be carried out as usual (providing both the login name and the file have the appropriate permissions e.g. a file might be 'read only') and saved, moved or copied as required around the network. Similarly, a file might be printed on any or all printers connected to the network. Alternatively, a message might be typed on screen sent to any or all other login names using electronic mail – email – and accessed by them whenever they logon to the network.

Small networks rely on wires for their connections. However, it was impractical and prohibitively expensive for most companies to connect their individual networks together if separated by long distances or even countries and oceans. So networks were connected to the already existing telephone networks and utilised the wires, cables and satellite/radio connections already available.

As we have seen, computers use digital communications ('current on/current off'). Telephone networks utilised analogue communications (a continuously varying electric current). Therefore it became necessary to translate between digital and analogue communication systems (although the telephone network is gradually being converted to digital communications, the task will take many years and a translating device allows us to use the benefits of global networks before this work is completed).

Analogue communications can be converted into digital communications and vice versa by a process known as modulation. After modulation the data need to be demodulated as before transmission. The device capable of doing this is a modem (a word formed from modulator demodulator). When the telephone network is completely digital, there will (in theory!) no longer be a need for modems. Modems used to be a box on a desk and connected to the computer and the telephone line. Today, modems still have the same connections but are now small 'modem cards' – small boards of electronic circuitry fixed inside the computer.

Use of the telephone network by the military and industrial computer networks opened the possibility of private homes with telephones and computers becoming connected to networks. PCs (Personal Computers) required developments in hardware (e.g. connectors and modems) and software – the operating system had to be able to communicate with others and adapt to the increased functionality and growth of networks in offices and homes. Hence MS DOS is now a multi-user operating system allowing the PCs which use it to access the global network called the internet and 'talk' to other computers connected to it. The other big manufacturer 'Apple' also provides such operating systems and both provide applications software to allow users full use of the global network e.g. email packages (allowing, amongst other facilities, an email address, chosen by the user according to criteria determined by the email provider – since a login name is no longer sufficient when communicating over many networks), internet browsers etc.

Internet browsers allow the user to browse the net i.e. explore the innumerable sites, pages and locations, known as 'web-sites' – holding, perhaps, still and moving pictures, sound and/or text on every conceivable human activity, interest or condition. Web-sites are so-called because they connect directly or indirectly with other sites on the 'world wide web' the addresses of which all begin 'www.'. A group, institution, individual or business might want a person browsing (known as a 'surfer') to find information on their product, service or activity, and create their own 'web-site' showing the details they want viewers to see or read about. The addresses of other related web-sites might be given and sometimes a 'link' – a button which when clicked, takes the surfer directly to that site.

Cameras and microphones have become so small as to sit unobtrusively on VDU's allowing images and sound to be sent globally via the net within seconds. Hence video conferencing became a useful tool for industry and academia, allowing individuals at different locations around the world to simultaneously discuss and resolve issues, exchange information or agree policy without the cost of air fares, accommodation and delays previously needed to get them all together at the same time.

The Internet, web-sites and email facilities also provide another way for business to sell its products or services. This is known as electronic commerce – 'e-commerce'. Surfers might discover or actively seek particular products on the net and take telephone or fax numbers or a postal address from the web-site. Alternatively, they might pay for the goods over the net using their credit/debit card numbers. This raises issues of security to prevent unscrupulous people or professional criminals from accessing such data and misusing it. Internet banks and other businesses continue to develop various security measures including passwords, PIN's and encryption (coding) to ensure safe transactions.

Financial security is not the only security issue raised by IT. With personal histories, medical records and all sorts of private or confidential information being held on computers, the security of such information is of prime concern. Hence new laws have been passed to ensure legislation exists to protect confidential information (e.g. Data Protection Act) and copyrighted material held on computers and/or storage media. However, it is prudent to make sure you are not careless with either the data you are responsible for (professionally or personally) or the passwords and PINs used to protect it.

As well as providing new crimes and new victims for criminals, global networks have also provided a new arena for people who make nuisances and irritations for others: computer viruses are programmes that reproduce themselves in any computer system they gain access to. The programs are varied and numerous and can cause irritating problems such as causing text to gradually or suddenly disappear or become jumbled, shut downs, deletion of files and directories etc. or major problems such as wiping the hard disk of crucial (or all!) data. Viruses can only gain access to a clean or healthy system by email or by arriving on disk and being loaded by an unsuspecting user. A virus checker is software that examines new emails or newly loaded data for viruses and warns the user if any are detected. As new viruses are being written all the time, virus scanners have to be up-to-date to ensure maximum protection. To date, viruses have not been written to be beneficial to the host system.

EXERCISE QUESTIONS

1 What is the significance of single-user and multi-user?

2 What was the problem connecting computers to telephone networks?

3 How is it currently overcome?

4 Will this situation change?

5 What is the Internet?

6 What is a web-site?

7 Name two security problems the Internet has brought with it.

HEALTH AND SAFETY

Health and safety of the computer is, obviously, important. However, the health and safety of the user is more important.

First ensure that the working environment is safe for you and others e.g. fire doors/exits and the paths to them must be kept clear and well marked. Electric supplies should not be through innumerable trailing gang sockets holding so many plugs as to exceed the safety limit of their electrical current capacity.

Operate the equipment to prevent injury or discomfort to yourself e.g. bad posture maintained for hours will cause pain or discomfort later and aggravate any existing problems such as back problems. RSI is Repetitive Strain Injury and results from repeating movements, such as mouse movements or typing, over many hours. Eyestrain can result from looking at screens for hours and the radiation from screens can have adverse effects on users. Take frequent breaks away from the screens and work in well-ventilated and naturally lit rooms. Position chairs, screens and keyboards to allow good posture (neck and back straight).

Operate the equipment according to the supplier's, manufacturer's and/or workplace requirements and recommendations. Observe and respond to any error messages displayed by the equipment (error messages on screen may indicate any of a variety of usually simple problems needing attention – no disk in disk drive, connections not made, printer out of paper etc). Where you are unable to safely rectify problems, report them according to established procedures.

It is a good idea to monitor and maintain simple physical aspects of the hardware such as broken or frayed cables, loose connections or trapped wires.

Prevention is better than cure, so keeping the apparatus clean can prevent problems. However, it can also cause problems if not conducted sensibly: with an electrical feed to most computer parts it is obviously dangerous to the computer and possibly yourself to use water or any liquid near or on a computer. If it is necessary to clean away marks and dirt, make sure you are using appropriate cleaning agents on a damp cloth or other applicator and that the power to the computer is switched off. Allow time for it to dry before switching on again.

Regular cleaning need only ensure the removal of dust from surfaces (be aware of the electric field of your vacuum cleaner if bringing it close to magnetic storage media).

Maintain safe-working practices at all times and you will ensure a rewarding and productive use of computers both professionally and personally, for yourself and others.

EXERCISE QUESTIONS

1   True or false?

It is best to use plenty of water when cleaning computers

RSI is caused by poor ventilation

A power point can be overloaded

2   Why should a user take frequent breaks away from the screen?

CONFIDENTIALITY AND COPYRIGHT

Confidentiality

Imagine the thousands of pieces of data that are held on computerised systems today. A large amount of this data is our own personal details such as our names, addresses, telephone numbers and even financial details. It is for this reason that legislation was put into place to protect us. This is called The Data Protection Act 1998 and is used to safeguard you and your personal data by enforcing obligations on data users who hold such information on their systems.

With the increasing use of passwords to get into systems, security of this information is getting safer. Certain people are given access rights and may only be able to access certain parts of your information.

Some applications (such as Microsoft Word) allow you to password protect your files. You become the only person that can gain access to that file. But you must remember the password! If it is lost, your data is irretrievable. Personal data is subject to misuse in the wrong hands. People called 'computer hackers' are able to 'hack' into data and obtain information. However, with increased security features, this can be prevented.

Copyright

The Copyright, Patents and Registered Designs Act covers Copyright. Copyright is a right of authors to prevent unauthorised copying or exploitation of their work for a limited period of time. The main areas affected by Copyright are: Literary Works (including Computer Applications in the UK); Dramatic Works; Musical Works; Artistic Works and Graphics Works.

Here in the UK a copyright is applied automatically when the work is created and lasts for the life of the author plus 70 years from the end of the calendar year from which the author dies.

Copyright is a right to protect unauthorised copying of an original work. All copyright work should be marked with the international copyright symbol © or with the word Copyright; the name of the owner/author and the date or year the work was carried out or created, for example:

e-Quals

© Made Up Plc 2002

In relation to the Internet and web sites containing graphics and text, copyright should be adhered to in the same way as other works, by displaying the copyright symbol and additional information as above. If a Company has been instructed to produce web sites for you, a suitable legal document could be produced to protect the copyright of the information on the Internet.

e-Quals
UNIT 002 WORD PROCESSING

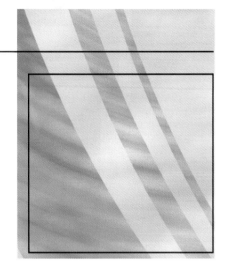

USING WORD PROCESSING SOFTWARE

Word processing makes producing documents so easy that you can fall into the trap of designing as you go along and this can sometimes actually take you more time and be an inefficient way to proceed.

Avoid the temptation of just beginning straight away without considering what type of document you want to produce, planning what you want it to look like and what you want it to achieve. Different documents contain different things – a business letter, for example, will be formally laid out, should show both the recipient's and the sender's address, the date, a formal salutation (Dear Sir or Dear Mr Jones) and a formal sign off (Yours faithfully or Yours sincerely). An advertising flyer will contain none of these but is likely to use simple language, be eye-catching and give just as much information to encourage people to find out more or purchase the item. A fax cover sheet will have space available for the fax number of the recipient, contact details of the sender, the date and how many pages there are altogether.

Some documents are best laid out as portrait

Some documents others may be better laid out as landscape.

Another thing you will need to consider is the font, font size and text enhancements (such as use of bold, italics, colour etc) you want to use to create maximum impact, and this will again depend on the purpose of the document and the audience it is targeted at. (You will soon create a couple of warning notices and it would be pointless if the font size was that which is used in a letter as it would be too easily overlooked).

Different paper sizes also lend themselves to different uses, but as size A4 is so commonly available, this is the one that tends to be most widely used. The smaller A5 is often used for flyers.

LAUNCHING YOUR WORD PROCESSING SOFTWARE

Click on the Start button at the bottom left of the screen. Choose Programs and then click on the program you wish to launch i.e. Microsoft Word.

Alternatively, you may have a 'shortcut' to the program on your computer's desktop. If you can see an icon representing the program on the screen, double-click on it.

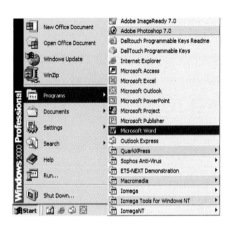

When you have opened Word, you will see a brand new document. You will see the title bar, which shows the name of the document (new ones by default are called document1, 2, 3 etc), the Menu bar and usually two toolbars (although these can be customised): the Standard toolbar and the Formatting toolbar:

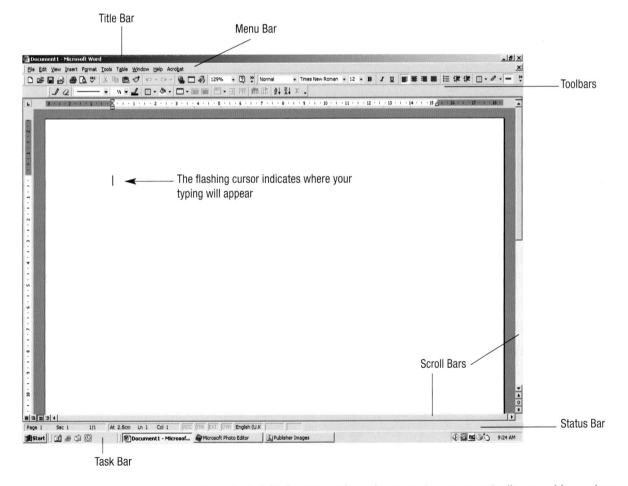

Once Word has opened, you are likely to be in Print Layout – where the computer screen actually resembles a piece of paper in that there is an edge on all sides. You can change the view by choosing View then selecting one of the other views, such as Normal, Outline or Web Layout. Alternatively, you can click on the icons in the bottom left corner:

25

Which view you use is entirely up to your preferred way of working. It is common for people to use different views as the need arises – you don't have to remain locked into using just one view.

TASK

Experiment with the different views. What is the difference between Print Layout and Normal view?

ADJUSTING THE PAGE

A number of characteristics in Word are supplied by default. You can change them if you want, but for many word processing purposes they are suitable and you probably won't need to. These characteristics include things like the margins and paper size. However, there may be occasions where you do want to change these, for example to change paper orientation from portrait to landscape, or to make the margins smaller so all the text will fit onto one page.

Everything you do in the Page Setup dialog box affects how each page will look when printed. Choose File, Page Setup.

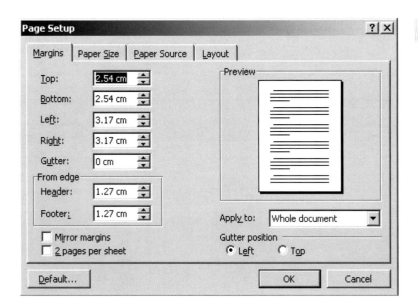

The Page Setup dialog box displaying the Margins tab.

The Page Setup dialog box has four tabs:

Margins – to alter the top, bottom, left and right margins. In the above dialog box, the measurements are in centimetres. Word can be configured to display inches if you prefer. If you make a change, the preview window shows you how the document will look.

Paper Size – to specify a paper size such as A4 or enter a custom paper size. To alter the paper orientation.

Paper Source – to specify which pages will be printed from a particular tray within a printer. These trays may contain different materials such as paper, transparencies or card.

Layout – used to alter the advanced features used within your document such as section breaks and line numbering.

Changing Page Orientation and Paper Size

By default, your document will appear as portrait. If you wish to change the paper orientation to landscape, choose File, Page Setup, click on the Paper Size tab and click the landscape button. Select the drop-down arrow and choose the paper size that you wish the document to print on to. Click OK to agree changes.

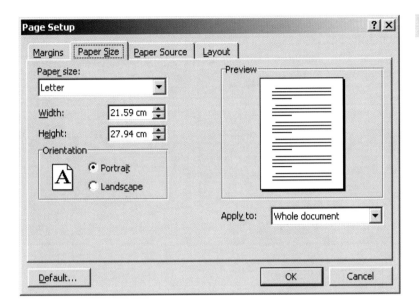

The Preview section displays how the paper will be displayed.

Changing Margins

A margin is the space between the edge of the paper and the beginning of the text. Default margins are originally set at 2.54 cm Top and Bottom and 3.17 cm Left and Right. However, these can be altered by choosing File, Page Setup, clicking on the Margins tab and using the spin buttons to adjust the margins. (The smaller the margin, the larger the work area and vice versa).

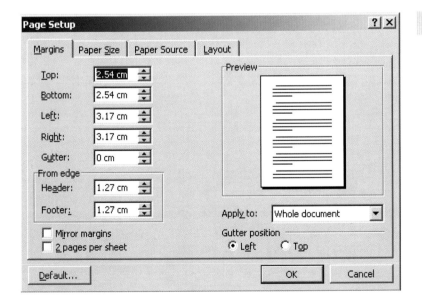

The Page Setup dialog box displaying the Margins tab.

INSERTING AND DELETING TEXT

Inserting Text

To enter text into a new document, the cursor (insertion point) must be flashing in the work area. The flashing cursor determines the exact location where text will be inserted or editing actions will be carried out.

To move the cursor to a new location within the document, move the mouse pointer to where you wish to start typing and double-click the left mouse button. The flashing cursor will appear in the new location ready for typing. However, this is not always the case depending on the version of software you are using.

Alternatively, press the Enter key on the keyboard to create extra blank lines, this moves the flashing cursor to a new line on each press.

Entering text is normally carried out via the keyboard.

Word processing uses a facility called 'Word Wrap'. On entering text there is no need to press the Enter key when you reach the end of the line, Word will automatically wrap the text onto the next line. This is unlike traditional typewriters where a new line has to be created manually.

Creating Paragraphs

Paragraphs break up the text in a document to make it visually stimulating and easier to read. To create a paragraph when typing, press the Enter key twice (leaving one clear line) to start a new paragraph.

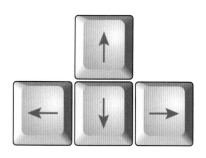

To create a paragraph within existing text, position the flashing cursor (using the arrow keys) where you want the blank line to appear and then press the Enter key twice.

Deleting Text

If mistakes are made when entering text use the Backspace and/or the Delete keys on the keyboard.

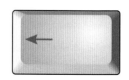

Backspace – deletes text appearing to the left of the cursor
Delete – deletes text appearing to the right of the cursor

TASK

Change paper orientation to landscape and the first document you will produce is a warning to people to use the other door! Type in 'Please use the other door'. Note the flashing cursor, which is informing you where the text will appear. If you use the mouse, note the symbol which looks a little like a capital I (sometimes called the I beam) as you move the mouse around.

Remember

Position the flashing cursor correctly before pressing the backspace or delete keys to avoid deletion error.

NAVIGATING AROUND A DOCUMENT

Using the Keyboard

To move around the text within a document, use the arrow keys on the keyboard to indicate the direction you wish to move (up, down, left or right). The arrow keys will only move around a document that contains data.

To move to the beginning of a line, press Home on the keyboard. To move to the end of a line, press End on the keyboard.

To move to the beginning of the document, press Ctrl+Home at the same time. To move to the end of the document, press Ctrl+End at the same time.

To move down one page, press Page Down on the keyboard. To move up one page, press Page Up on the keyboard. (Only active with documents containing more than one page).

Using the Mouse

To insert text into a blank section of a document, move the cursor to the new location and double-click the left mouse button (available with Office 2000 and newer). The flashing cursor will appear ready to type the new text.

To move up and down the page using the vertical scroll bar, click on the up or down buttons.

To move up one page using the vertical scroll bar, click on the Previous Page button.

To move down one page using the vertical scroll bar, click on the Next Page button.

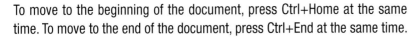

HIGHLIGHTING TEXT

If you wish to alter the appearance of text after you have typed it, you have to highlight the text you want to change.

There are several ways of highlighting text:

- Click and drag the mouse over the words.

- If it is only one word, double click the word.

- If it is a paragraph, triple click anywhere in the paragraph. (Word defines a paragraph as all text between one occurrence of Enter and another).

- If it is a sentence, press and hold the Ctrl key and click anywhere in the sentence.

- Move the mouse over to the left hand side of the page until it changes its shape from the I-beam and becomes an arrow pointing to 1 o'clock. Then click and drag vertically either up or down. Note that this method highlights complete lines.

FORMATTING TEXT

Formatting text allows changes to be made to text, to enhance the appearance of a document to make it easier to read. For instance, making specific words bold allows them to stand out from the rest of the text indicating to the reader that the emboldened words are important.

To change the font attributes after it has been typed, first highlight the text you want to change, then click Format, Font. This displays the Font dialog box:

The Font tab is displayed.

The Font, Font Style, Size, Font Color, Underline style/color and Effects can all be applied here. The Preview window displays the changes made. To accept these changes click OK.

Another way to alter font, font size and font style is to use the Formatting toolbar.

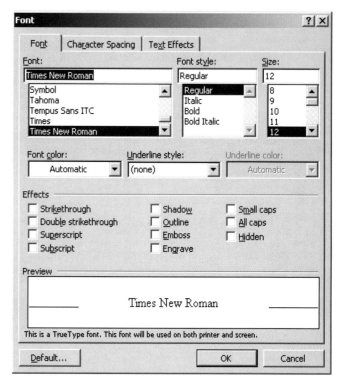

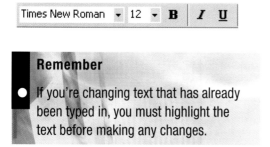

Remember

If you're changing text that has already been typed in, you must highlight the text before making any changes.

Tip

If you prefer, you can use the keyboard for some text styles;

- Ctrl+B will make the text bold
- Ctrl+I will make the text italic
- Ctrl+U will underline the text

If the text already displays such a font style, making the same selection again will turn the style off - in other words, they are toggle switches.

If you know what style or effect you want to apply **before** typing in the text, select the characteristics you want in exactly the same way as before and then type.

TASK

Change the text in your document to be font size 72 and try other fonts. Italicise the word 'Please'.

USING UNDO AND REDO

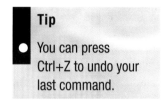

Tip

You can press Ctrl+Z to undo your last command.

The Undo command will 'undo' your last action. For example, if you do something you don't like, or delete something you didn't mean to, you can use the Undo button. Choose Edit, Undo or press the Undo button on the Standard toolbar.

The Redo command will 'redo' your last action. For example, if you have undone something by mistake, choose Edit, Redo or press the Redo button on the Standard toolbar to carry out the action again.

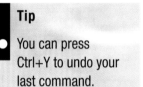

Tip

You can press Ctrl+Y to undo your last command.

If you wish to undo or redo more than one action, click on the drop-down arrow next to the button to open a list of your recent actions. Click on the action you wish to undo or redo and all actions back to that one will be undertaken.

PREVIEWING A DOCUMENT

If you are happy with your document you will probably want to print it. However, it is always a good idea to preview the document first to make absolutely sure it's right. Print Preview is a WYSIWYG package (pronounced *wizzywig*, which stands for 'What You See Is What You Get'). This means you can see the changes made to the document. If you make text bold or bigger, it actually looks bold or bigger on the screen. This means that there are no surprises when you come to print your document.

Print Preview

Before you print your worksheet, you may wish to view it as it will look when printed onto plain paper. To preview a document, Choose File, Print Preview or press the Print Preview button on the Standard toolbar.

Print Preview

The Print Preview screen will open. Your document is displayed as it will appear when printed and a new toolbar appears above the document.

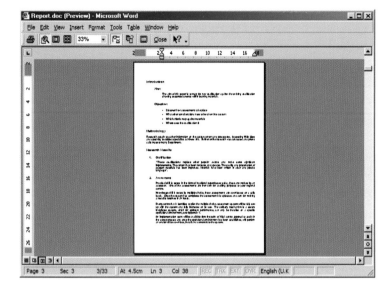

A document shown in Print Preview

At the moment, you are just being shown one page, but you can scroll up and down the document via the vertical scroll bar.

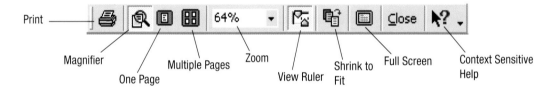

Print – will send the document to the printer.

Magnifier – is a toggle button to magnify the document (make it larger to see the text) or edit the document. The cursor shape will determine the tool you are using. If the cursor is an I-beam, you are in edit mode, if the cursor is in the shape of a magnifying glass, you are in magnifying mode.

One Page – displays a single page at a time.

Multiple Pages – displays multiple pages for document layout check.

Zoom – increases or decreases the display of the document (this does not increase or decrease the actual document or text size).

View Ruler – shows or hides the ruler depending on your preference.

Shrink to Fit – reduces the number of pages in a document by one so that you can prevent a small portion of a document spilling onto another page.

Full Screen – hides most of the screen elements so that you can view more of your document.

Close – closes the Print Preview screen and takes you back to your document.

Context Sensitive Help – useful if you've forgotten what a button does, click on the Context Sensitive Help button then click on the button that you wish to know more about. A helpful tip will appear, click on the page to close the help tip.

Viewing Multiple Pages

You can choose to see several pages by clicking on the Multiple Pages icon.

Press and hold the Shift key on the keyboard and use the arrow keys to select how many pages you want to see.

If you highlight too many pages, press and hold the Shift key on the keyboard and use the arrow keys to de-select the unwanted pages.

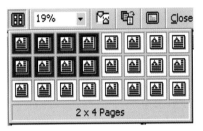

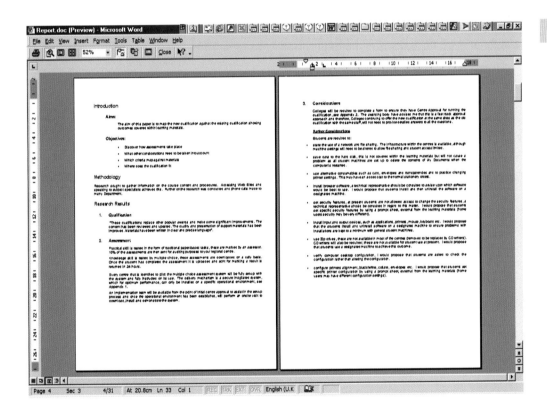

A multiple page preview screen.

View One Page

To see just one page either click on that page when the cursor looks like a magnifying glass, or click on the One Page icon.

One Page

Printing the Document

If you are satisfied with the document you can print it from here by clicking on the Print icon.

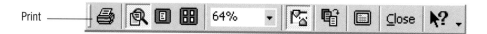

However, the print button will print the entire document not just the page(s) you are viewing.

To close the print preview screen and continue working on the document select the Close button.

SAVING DOCUMENTS

Using Save

If you wish to keep the document, so that you can use it again, you will need to save it. Saving your documents is important if you ever want to retrieve them later. You can also create a document, for example, a memo, which you can then use as the basis for all such documents in the future.

The first time you save a document you will be prompted to give the file a name and to choose which folder you wish to save it into.

Choose File, Save. The Save As dialog box will appear:

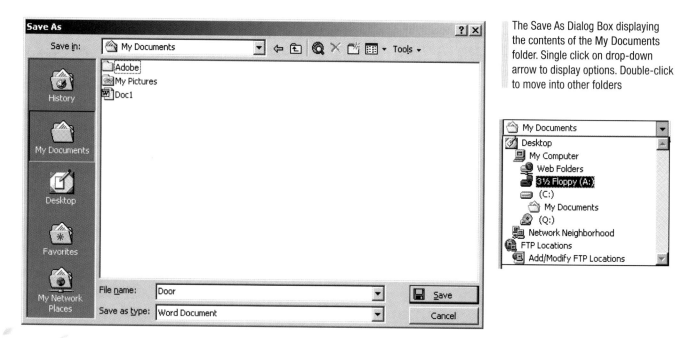

The Save As Dialog Box displaying the contents of the My Documents folder. Single click on drop-down arrow to display options. Double-click to move into other folders

Open the drop-down list by Save in and navigate to the folder that you wish to store your document in (folders are indicated by the yellow icon). Double-click on a folder to move into it, or use the Back or Up One Level buttons to move up out of a folder.

Tip

If you need to create a new directory in which to save your document, click on

— you do not have to go to Windows Explorer to create the directory.

Type a name for the document in the File name box and check that it will be saved into the correct format (under Save as type). Your filename can be up to 250 characters long – use an obvious name for your file so that you remember what you called it in the future! You do not need to type the .doc filename extension, as this will be added automatically. (The filename extension may not be visible if it has not been set in Windows Explorer). Click on the Save button at the bottom right of the dialog box.

Once you have saved the document, the name of the file will appear in the Title Bar across the top of the screen.

If you have previously saved a document, choosing Save will overwrite the previous version with the updated version. (It still has the same name and is stored in the folder that you initially put it in).

The Save button also appears on the Standard toolbar. You can click on this instead of choosing File, Save.

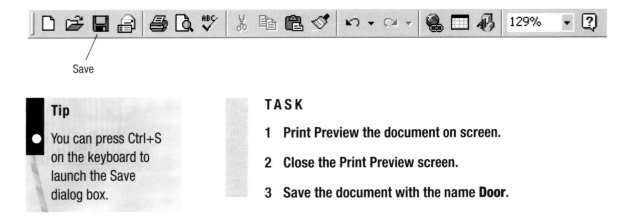

Save

Tip

You can press Ctrl+S on the keyboard to launch the Save dialog box.

TASK

1 **Print Preview the document on screen.**

2 **Close the Print Preview screen.**

3 **Save the document with the name Door.**

Using Save As

If you do not wish to overwrite a previously saved document, you can use Save As and give the new version a different name, or store it in a different folder. Choose Save As from the File menu.

CLOSING

Closing the Document

If you wish to remove the document from the screen, you need to close it. If you wish to keep the file on your computer, you must save the document before closing it.

Choose File, Close. If you haven't previously saved the document, the following message will appear on the screen.

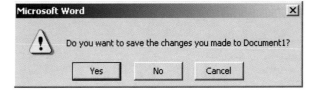

If you do wish to save the changes, click Yes. If you wish to close the document without saving, click No. Clicking Cancel will remove the dialogue box from the screen.

If you have already saved the document the document will close leaving a blank screen.

Closing the Application

If you wish to close down the application, you need to exit out of it. Choose File, Exit. Alternatively, click on the cross in the top right hand corner of the window. ☒

TASK

1   Close the Door document. Do not close the application.

OPENING EXISTING DOCUMENTS

You may need to retrieve saved documents, to view data, print or edit. Choose File, Open. The Open dialog box will appear.

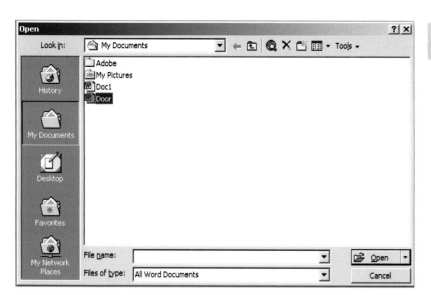

The Open Dialog Box displaying the contents of the My Documents folder. Single click on drop-down arrow to display options. Double-click to move into other folders.

Open the drop-down list by Look in and navigate to the folder that your document is stored in (folders are indicated by the yellow icon). Double-click on a folder to move into it, or use the Back or Up One Level buttons to move up out of a folder.   ⇐ 🔼

Locate the document you wish to open, click on it and then click on the Open button at the bottom right of the dialog box. (Alternatively, you can double-click on the file).

If you cannot see your document files in a folder, make sure the Files of type list at the bottom of the dialog box is showing the correct file types. Word recognises document files because they have a .doc filename extension. This filename extension may not be visible if it has not been set in Windows Explorer.

The Open button also appears on the Standard toolbar. You can click on the button instead of choosing File, Open.

Open

Tip

You can press Ctrl+O on the keyboard to launch the Open dialog box.

TASK

1 **Locate the file Door and open it.**

2 **Save the document with the new name Danger using Save As. (Note the Title Bar now shows the new name).**

PRINTING DOCUMENTS

Choose File, Print. This will open the Print dialog box

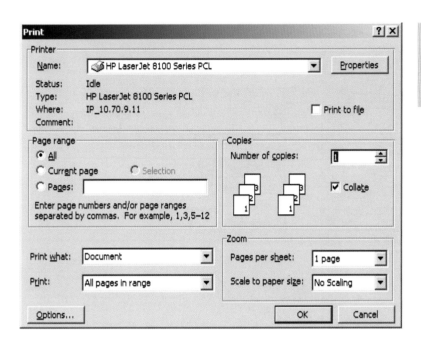

Print Dialog box displayed here indicates that the HP LaserJet 8100 Series PCL printer has been selected, the print range has been set to print all pages, number of copies is 1 and the document will be printed.

The Print dialog box offers much more versatility than the Print icon as you can select either a complete print out, just the current page or a range of pages. The Options button provides even more functionality, for example reversing the print order. The Properties button allows you to access your printer's controls.

Choose the Printer that you wish to print to. (Click on the down arrow to the right of the printer name and choose from the list of available installed printers).
Choose whether you want to print all the pages, current page or specific pages.
Choose the number of copies you want to print.

Click OK to send your document to the printer.

Tip

You can press Ctrl+P on the keyboard to launch the Print dialog box.

Alternatively, you can click on the Print button on the Standard toolbar. However, on each click of the button it will print one copy of all the pages within the document.

Print

TASK

1 **Print preview the document on screen.**

2 **Print one copy of the document.**

ALIGNING TEXT

Word enables you to align the text on the page. Ensure that the cursor is placed within the text that you want to align.

Choose Format, Paragraph.

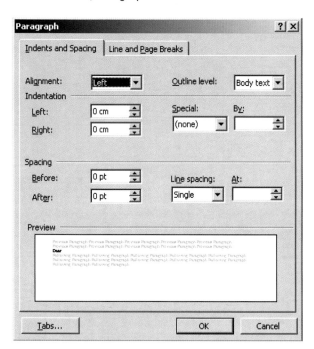

The alignment is shown as left.

Click on the drop-down arrow next to this for the available options:

Make your selection and then press Enter.

Alternatively, use the icons in the Formatting toolbar:

Left – text is positioned evenly against the left margin and jagged to the right of the page.
Centre – each line of text is positioned centrally on the page (jagged to the left and right of the page).
Right – text is positioned evenly against the right margin and jagged to the left of the page.
Justify – text is positioned evenly against the left and right margins.

TASK

1 **Select the text in the Danger document.**

2 **Press the Delete key on the keyboard.**

3 **Add the following text to the document.**

   Danger of Electrocution

4 **Centre the text on the page.**

5 **Save the changes to the document.**

6 **Print out the document.**

INSERTING GRAPHICS

Inserting a ClipArt Graphic

On the principle that a picture speaks a thousand words, you may want to insert a graphic into your document. Microsoft applications comes with its own library of ClipArt, but if you can't find an appropriate image, you can get hold of thousands more graphics from the Internet. Be aware that some graphics are available for a fee and most are protected by copyright laws.

Choose Insert, Picture, Clip Art. The Insert ClipArt dialog box is displayed:

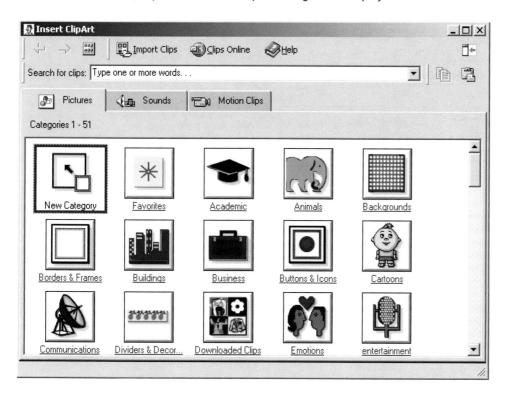

The ClipArt window contains a search facility so that you can type in what you are looking for and will attempt to find it. Alternatively, you can browse all the different categories by selecting them.

If ClipArt contains suitable graphics that match your search criteria, they will be displayed. If there is more than one, select the graphic using your mouse; a thick border will outline the chosen graphic.

To insert the graphic, select the Insert clip icon and then close the ClipArt window to return to your document.

Once the graphic has been inserted into your document, there is a possibility that it will be either too big or too small. Word allows you to resize the graphic by clicking on the small squares, called 'handles' that surround the image.

To keep the proportion, use the handles in the corner to click and drag. Note the different arrows you get when your mouse is moved over the different handles. The corner arrows are shown here. If you use the handles on either side, you will get a horizontally stretched version:

If you use the handles on the top or bottom, you will get a vertically stretched version.

To move the graphic, select the graphic and drag to the new position.

Tip

If you cannot find a suitable image, and providing you have a connection to the Internet, you can select Clips Online in the ClipArt window and try searching there.

TASK

Search for this image (or one like it) by typing in 'electricity' in the ClipArt window where it says 'Search for clips', and insert the image into your document Danger. Resize the image so that it has maximum effect. Play around with the font, font size, margins etc until you are happy – it must only use one sheet of paper.

Your document should look something like this:

Danger of Electrocution

Save the changes.

WORD PROCESSING

Inserting a Graphic from a Stored Location

In addition to ClipArt, Microsoft applications let you insert graphics from other locations – you may have been given a graphic on a floppy disk, CD, zip disk or a graphic may be stored in a folder on the C: drive.

Choose Insert, Picture, From File.

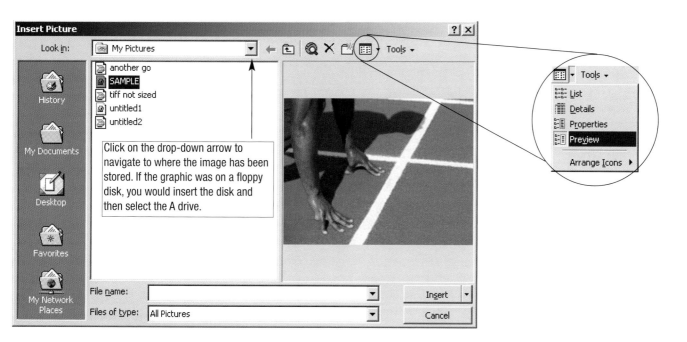

To view an image of the selected graphic, click the Views button and select Preview.

This is useful to ensure that you are inserting the correct image. Select Insert to insert the graphic into your document. As with ClipArt, these images can also be resized by clicking on the image and then clicking and dragging on the handles.

CREATING A NEW DOCUMENT

To create a new document when Word is already open, choose File, New. Alternatively, click on the New Blank Document icon.

New

41

The New dialog box will be displayed. Select Blank Document (found under the General tab), click OK to agree choice.

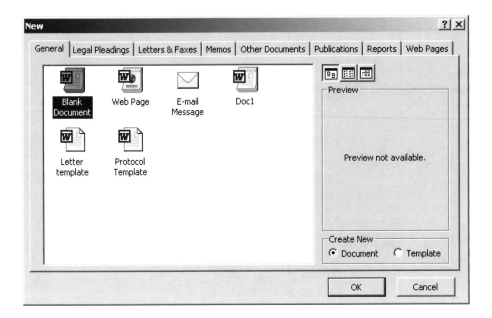

USING TABS

Tabs are used to control the vertical alignment of text in a document. This is used when you want to present text in the form of a table, without the use of a table.

Word has default tab stops set to 1.27 cm, so every time you press the Tab key on the keyboard, the cursor moves 1.27 cm (or 0.5 inches) to the right.

However, these settings may not be suitable for your requirements, to change the default settings, choose Format, Tabs.

The Tabs dialog box will be displayed.

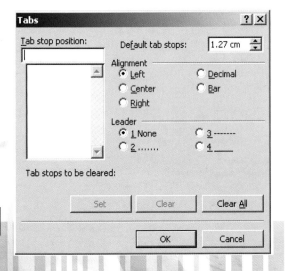

Type in the measurement of the first tab stop in the Tab stop position box, select the alignment of the tab stop, and click Set. Enter the details of the next tab stop as before. Continue until all tab stops are set. Click OK.

To remove tab stops, open the Tabs dialog box, select the tab stop that you wish to remove and click Clear. To remove all tab stops click Clear All.

Left – text is aligned evenly on the left against the tab stop
Right – text is aligned evenly on the right against the tab stop
Centre – text is centred directly under the tab stop

Decimal – data containing decimal points such as monetary values are lined up using the decimal point directly under the tab stop

Bar – places a vertical line at the tab stop

Tabs can also be positioned using the ruler. If the ruler is not visible, select View, Ruler. (This is a toggle so if the ruler is visible and you do this, the ruler is turned off).

On the extreme left of the ruler is the tab selector. The default tab stop is the left tab, which is L-shaped. You can scroll through the different options available by clicking on this button.

If you click in the ruler, you place a tab stop at that particular place. Below, a tab stop has been placed at 10.5 cm. There is no limit to the number of tabs you can place in this way in the ruler.

To utilise the tab stop, press the Tab key to jump all the way to the positioned tab stop, type in the required data, press the Tab key to jump to the next tab stop and continue as necessary.

If you need to move the tab stop, click on it and drag to its new location. A dotted vertical line is shown while the icon is selected to help you position it accurately.

To remove the tab stop completely, click on the tab icon and drag it off the ruler.

Tip

To add tabs to existing text the text must be selected before setting tab stops. If you don't, you will have to repeat the process for every line that you want to utilise the tab stop. Ensure that the text is de-selected (click anywhere on the page) before you press the Tab key and place the I-beam at the beginning of the line.

TASK

1   **Create a blank new document.**

2   **Ensure you are using portrait orientation and paper size A4.**

3   **Set the top and bottom margins of the document to 3.5 cm.**

4   **Set a left tab stop at 10 cm.**

5   **Enter your address utilising the tab stop.**

6   **Save the document as letter1. Do not close the document.**

7   **Create a new document.**

8   **Enter your address.**

9 **Right align your address.**

10 **Enter the following text (exactly as shown although your line endings may differ).**

Snowflakes Holidays
PO Box 457
Lincs.

Dear Sir
I have just returned from a 'holiday in hell' with Snowflakes Holidays and wish to complain
about it. Holidays, as I am sure you will agree, should be happy occassions, but this one was a
living nightmare. I found the following to be unacceptable:
the restaurant was dirty the food was largely inedible my accomodation was cramped and
shabby, with paint peeling off the walls the beach was further than the 200 meters stipulated
in your brochure there was a most unpleasant smell if the wind was from the north. Your
brochure made no mention of the nearby sewage works and finally, being directly under the
flight path, with the airport only tow miles away, the whole holiday was an even more
unpleasant experience. To add insult to injury, I discovered that other people had paid as
much as £270 less for the same holiday form another company. I look forward to receiving
your comments.

11 **Save the letter as holiday complaints letter.**

SWITCHING BETWEEN DOCUMENTS

Switching between documents allows you to view different documents, or copy and paste information between documents. The applications provide several ways of doing this.

At the bottom of the screen, you will see any documents that you have open, click on the document that you wish to view.

Alternatively, select Window from the menu bar, this displays open documents, then select the document you want to see.

The tick indicates the active document.

You can also display everything that you have open at the same time by selecting Arrange All, but this can sometimes get a little overwhelming!

Another way to see what you have open at the same time, but to see them one by one, is to press and hold the Alt key and press the Tab key, press the Tab key to scroll through the open documents. Release the Alt and Tab keys and you are presented with the document that you wish to view.

COPYING AND/OR CUTTING AND PASTING TEXT

Cut, copy and paste are three very useful tools. These allow you to copy or move text within a document or to other documents without having to retype the text.

Copying Text

Highlight the text to be copied, choose Edit, Copy.

Switch to another document and click where you wish to copy the highlighted text to or click on the new location within the same document where you wish to place a copy. Choose Edit, Paste. The copied text will now be displayed in the new location.

Alternatively, the Copy and Paste buttons can be used from the Standard toolbar.

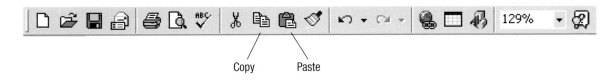

Copy   Paste

Cutting Text

Highlight the text to be copied, choose Edit, Cut (the text will disappear from the screen).

Switch to another document and click where you wish to move the highlighted text to or click on the new location within the same document where you wish to move the text to. Choose Edit, Paste. The text will now be pasted into the new location.

Alternatively, the Cut and Paste buttons can be used from the Standard toolbar.

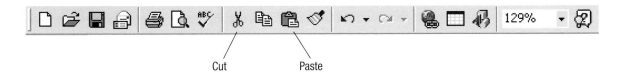

Cut   Paste

Tip

Once you've copied or cut data, that data is stored in the computer's memory – this is called a Clipboard. The Clipboard can hold up to 12 items. If you don't use this Clipboard, however every time you cut or copy something, it will replace what was in the memory.

To use the Clipboard, select View, Toolbars, Clipboard and you can see what Word is storing. Select the cut or copied information that you wish to insert into your document.

TASK

1   Highlight the text within the 'holiday complaints letter' excluding your address.

2   Copy the highlighted section.

3   Switch to the open document called 'letter1'.

4   Paste in the text below your address.

5   Left align the text excluding your address.

6   Save the file as **letter2**.

7   Close all open documents except the document called holiday complaints letter.

8   Insert blank lines to make the document more readable. (The document should appear as shown below).

Dear Sir

I have just returned from a 'holiday in hell' with Snowflakes Holidays and wish to complain about it. Holidays, as I am sure you will agree, should be happy occassions, but this one was a living nightmare.

I found the following to be unacceptable:

the restaurant was dirty

the food was largely inedible

my accomodation was cramped and shabby, with paint peeling off the walls

the beach was further than the 200 meters stipulated in your brochure

there was a most unpleasant smell if the wind was from the north. Your brochure made no mention of the nearby sewage works

and finally, being directly under the flight path, with the airport only tow miles away, the whole holiday was an even more unpleasant experience.

To add insult to injury, I discovered that other people had paid as much as £270 less for the same holiday from another company.

I look forward to receiving your comments.

Yours faithfully,

INSERTING BULLET POINTS AND NUMBERED LISTS

Bulleted and numbered lists are used to list information. This displays information clearly and makes information easier to read. When applying bullets or numbers to a list in a document, Word will insert a default bullet point design or a default number style.

46

The easiest way to add bullets or numbers is to select the Numbering or Bullets buttons on the Formatting toolbar.

Numbering   Bullets

Type the information you require and press the Enter key on the keyboard to create the next number or bullet.

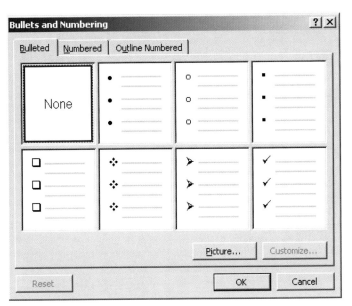

You may wish to add numbering or bullets to an existing list, the list must be highlighted first. The buttons are 'toggle' buttons, click once for on, and click again for off.

Alternatively, choose Format, Bullets and Numbering. This displays the Bullets and Numbering dialog box:

Select the type of bullet you want, or click on the Numbered tab to select a number.

Click OK to agree selection.

TASK

1 Highlight the list of complaints within the holiday complaints letter.

2 Select a bullet point for the list.

3 Replace the bullets within numbering.

4 Enter a 4th point concerning the room service 'room service never came to clean and the bathroom was filthy'. Note the change in the subsequent numbers.

5 Save the document as **Holiday letter updated**.

6 Spell check the document for errors. Manually check the document for correctness and meaning.

7 Print preview the document.

8 Make any further changes that you deem necessary.

9 Save the changes to the document.

10 Print out a hard copy of the document.

PARAGRAPHS

Indentation

Indentation can be set for individual or multiple paragraphs and lines of text. Indents refer to paragraphs that have sections of text indented, that is have a wider space between the edge of the paper and the rest of the document.

Click in the paragraph or select multiple paragraphs then choose Format, Paragraph.

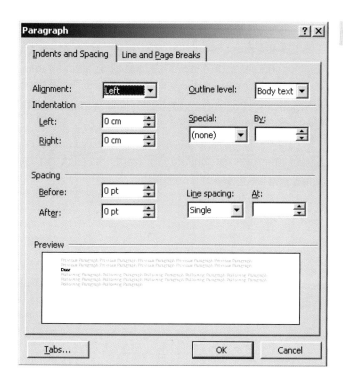

The Paragraph dialog box displaying the Indents and Spacing tab.

The left and/or right indents can be applied by selecting the spin buttons to increase or decrease the measurements

The Special box allows a selection of First line or Hanging.

Left indent – this is how a left indent of 3 centimetres is displayed within a document; notice how the text is 'indented' from the left margin.

Right indent – this is how a right indent of 3 centimetres is displayed within a document, notice how the text is 'indented' from the right margin.

First line indent – this is how a first line indent is displayed with the By measurement set at 2 centimetres within a document, notice how the first line is 'indented' from the margin by 2 cm.

Hanging indent – this is how a hanging indent is displayed with the By measurement set at 2 centimetres within a document, notice how the first line is hanging over the rest of the text by 2 cm.

Line Spacing

Line spacing refers to the measurement of vertical space between lines of text. When a new document is created, Word will automatically use single spacing. However, choosing Format, Paragraph and selecting the Indents and Spacing tab can alter this.

Single – Line spacing for each line that allows for the largest font in that line, in addition a small amount of extra space.

1.5 Lines – Line spacing for each line that is $1\frac{1}{2}$ times that of single line spacing.

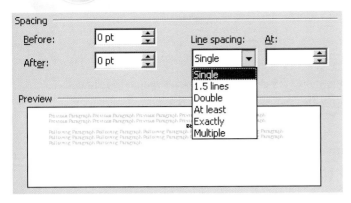

Double – Line spacing for each line that is 2 times that of single line spacing.

At Least – Minimum line spacing that Word can adjust to allow for larger font sizes or graphics that would not otherwise fit.

Exactly – Fixed line spacing that Word does not adjust. All lines are evenly spaced using this option.

Multiple – Line spacing that is increased or decreased by a percentage specified by you. For example, setting line spacing to a multiple of 1.2 will increase the space by 20%. Use the At box default amount or use the spin buttons to increase or decrease the amount.

At – The amount of line spacing selected. The option is only available when selecting either, At least, Exactly or multiple.

Select the line spacing that you require and click OK.

Tip

Remember to select the paragraphs to which you wish to apply the line spacing.

PAGE BREAKS

Soft Page Breaks

When Word reaches the end of the page (as dictated by the margins in Page Setup) it will automatically create a new page and continue as normal. These page breaks are known as 'soft' page breaks. In Normal view, where the edges of the paper are not shown, soft page breaks are indicated by a horizontal dotted line:

Tip

If your work spills over onto another page but it is imperative that it doesn't, you can try making the margins smaller and/or reducing the font size. However, there is a limit to how much you can fit on a page for the document to still have its impact.

Hard Page Breaks

Sometimes you may want to force a page break if, for example, the break occurs in an awkward place. These are known as hard page breaks. To insert a hard page break, choose Insert, Break. This displays the Break dialog box:

Select Page break and click OK.

There are a number of different types of break you can select, and you can also divide your document into different sections. This is particularly useful if some pages, for example, need to be portrait whilst others need to be landscape. Section breaks allow this kind of formatting but Page breaks do not.

In Normal view, they are shown by a dotted line and 'Page Break' is written in the middle:

Tip

Alternatively, without using the Menu bar at all, just hold down the Ctrl key and press Enter.

--- Page Break ---

PAGE NUMBERS

Page Totals

Word automatically counts the number of pages within a document and the information is displayed on the status bar at the bottom of the Word window. The information includes the section number and the current page displayed out of how many pages there are in total.

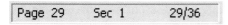

Page 29   Sec 1   29/36

This illustration indicates that page 29 is currently being viewed and there are 36 pages in total.

Inserting Page Numbers

Inserting page numbers is particularly useful if there is any chance that the pages could get out of order!

There are various options when deciding where to place page numbers on a document. Page numbers are placed in areas of the document called the Header and Footer. The header is a section at the top of the document on each page above any existing text and the footer appears at the bottom of the document on each page.

Choose Insert, Page Numbers. This will display the Page Numbers dialog box.

At Word's simplest, select OK. You can change the position and the alignment of the page number as well as choose whether to have the page number shown on the first page or not. More functionality is available if you select Format.

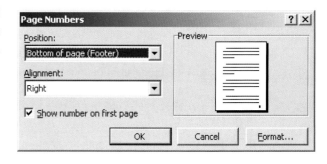

The Page Numbers dialog box has three sections:

Position – place the page number in the header or the footer.
Alignment – select from left, centre, right, inside or outside.
Preview – displays how the page numbers will look.

TASK

1   **Create a blank new document.**

2   **Set the paper size as A5, portrait orientation.**

3   **Set all the margins to 3 cm.**

4   **Enter the following text:**

Wind Farms in Scotland – A guide for tourists
There are currently four wind farms in Scotland; Beinn Ghlas, Hagshaw Hill, Nova and Windy Standard. In total they generate 63 megawatts of electricity, enough to meet the average annual electricity needs of over 39,500 homes. Windy Standard wind farm is located 5km south of Taynuilt, near Oban. The wind farm became operational in May 1999 and was officially opened in July. There is no pubic access to the site, but distant views may be gained

from the eastern shores of Loch Awe. One of the turbines is named 'Jessica' after a local schoolgirl who wrote to NWP describing the turbines as 'angels'. Hagshaw Hill wind farm lies 4 km west of Douglas, Lanarkshire. It was developed by TriGen LTD and is operated by Windfarm Management Services LTD on behalf of Scottish Power plc. The site is to the north of the A70. There is no access to the site on foot, but clear views can be gained along the minor road between Douglas and Crawfordjohn, turning right off the B740, 3km south west of the village of Crawfordjohn. The village can be reached from junction 13 of the M74. The surrounding area was extensively mined for lead from 1740 to 1850. At Wanlockhead on the B797, there is as open-air mine museum.

5   Create new paragraphs at the sentences beginning:

'Windy Standard wind farm is located 5km south of Taynuilt...'
'There is no public access to the sight, but distant views...'
'Hagshaw Hill wind farm lies 4 km west of Douglas...'
'The site is to the north of the A70...'
'The surrounding area was extensively mined for lead...'

6   Insert a page break so that information about Hagshaw Hill starts on a new page.

7   Change the title 'Wind farms in Scotland.' to Courier, size 28, bold and centred.

8   Change all other text to Arial, size 12.

9   Insert the words 'Hagshaw Hill' as a heading on page 2. Format this to size 14 and make bold.

10 Set line spacing to double for the text contained on page 2.

11 Apply a left indent of 2 cm to paragraphs 3 and 6.

12 Add page numbers to the document.

13 Insert a suitable graphic into page 1 of the document (some text may move).

14 Spell check the document, amend any errors found. Check the document for correctness and accuracy.

15 Preview the document. Make any necessary changes.

16 Save the document as **Wind Farms**.

17 Print out a copy of the document.

CREATING A TABLE

Tables are used to make information easier to take in. There are many ways to create a table, but perhaps the easiest ways are to click on the Insert Table icon on the Standard toolbar, ▥ or select Insert, Table. The former enables you to click and drag to highlight how many rows and columns you want and the latter allows you to type in these numbers in the Insert Table dialog box:

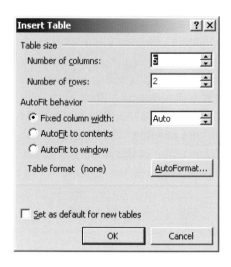

Fixed column width – columns set to a default or specified width.

AutoFit to contents – columns resize to fit the data entry.

AutoFit to window – columns equally distributed between left and right margins.

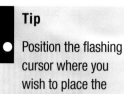

Tip

Position the flashing cursor where you wish to place the table.

Click OK to agree table settings. The table will be added to the document. To enter text into the table, click into a 'cell' and begin typing. To move between cells use the Tab key or arrow keys on the keyboard.

The inserted table can be formatted further to enhance the table displayed. Choose Table, Table Properties or click on the table and right click the mouse button, select Table Properties from the sub menu.

The Table Properties dialog box will be displayed.

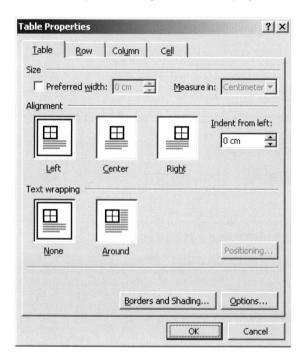

Tip

You can highlight a whole row by placing the cursor on the left next to the table and when you click the mouse button, the whole row is highlighted. This is useful for formatting all the text in that row or deleting the contents of the row if that's what you want to do.

To select more than one row, keep the mouse button pressed and drag until all the rows you require are highlighted.

You can highlight a whole column by placing the cursor just above a column. The cursor changes to a small, black, downward pointing arrow. This is useful for formatting all the text in that column or deleting the contents of the column.

To select more than one column, keep the mouse button pressed and drag until all the columns you require are highlighted.

A simple way to create an extra row at the end of a table is to place the cursor in the bottom right hand cell and press the Tab key.j59

Table tab – allows you to resize the table, select text alignment, text wrapping around the table and buttons for adjusting table borders and shading and an options buttons.

Row tab – allows you to specify the row height and further options.

Column tab – allows you to specify the column width.

Cell tab – allows you to specify cell width and text alignment.

Select the setting and click OK to agree changes.

FIND AND REPLACE

The 'Find' and the 'Find and Replace' commands are particularly useful for finding text within a large document. Find is a facility which will search a document for specified text (words, sentences and phrases). The whole document will be searched unless a specific section has been highlighted or selected.

Choose Edit, Find or Edit, Replace. Alternatively, click on the Find button on the Standard toolbar 🔍 (if available). Any of these methods will open the Find and Replace dialog box.

Select the Find tab to locate information. Type in the data that you want to find and click Find Next. The located word will be highlighted, click Find Next to find more occurrences of the word or click Cancel.

Select the Replace tab to find and replace information. Type in the data that you want to find and the new data that you wish to replace it with. Click Find Next. Click Replace to replace the data with the new data or click Replace All to replace all occurrences of the data.

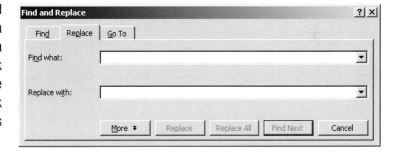

When Word has finished checking the document a dialog box will indicate that it has completed the search, click OK. Close the Find and Replace dialog box to remove from the screen, or continue with another search.

EXTRA EXERCISES

A Flyer

Create an A5 portrait flyer to go through peoples' doors giving notice of essential road works necessitating the cutting off of all mains water for 72 hours beginning Monday next week at 10:00. Keep it simple and make it as easy to read as possible, using text enhancements as you think necessary.

Use a bulleted list to inform people what they need to do, such as fill kettles, saucepans and baths, use water sparingly during this period and so on.

Check the flyer for any spelling mistakes and save it on a floppy disk. Call the document 'road works flyer'.

A Letter

Write a letter to yourself as if from Snowflakes Holidays answering the points you raised in your letter of complaint.

Copy and paste their address from your letter and insert any suitable logo above their address. This logo is in clip art (search for 'weather'):

Snowflake's address should appear centred beneath their logo (also centred) at the foot of the letter. Make sure there are no spelling mistakes.

Indent the first line of each paragraph.

Check the letter for any spelling mistakes and save your letter.

Membership Form

Design an application form for membership of a local organisation and sketch it out. Information required will be title (they could circle the one that applies – Mr, Mrs, Ms, other etc), name, address, telephone no, email address etc. Also required is a table with age ranges so they can tick which range they fall into:

16 – 26	27 – 36	37 – 46	47 – 56	57 – 66	67+

Create the form, basing it on your sketch.

Check the application form for any spelling mistakes and save it with an appropriate name.

Close any open document, saving the changes.

Close the word processing application.

e-Quals
UNIT 003
SPREADSHEETS

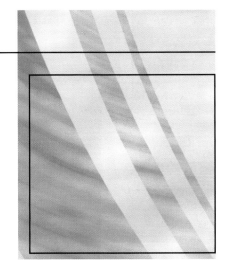

USING SPREADSHEET SOFTWARE

If you wish to create a file that consists of rows or columns of figures and perhaps some calculations, then you need to use spreadsheet software.

A spreadsheet file offers you a 'grid' (rather like a sheet of graph paper). The grid makes it easy to input labels and figures and set out the information in a table format. Spreadsheet software can also recognise calculations. You can write calculations on the sheet to work with and analyse the figures. There are also a large range of 'functions', which enable you to carry out comprehensive calculations and analysis.

Also, because a spreadsheet is made up of rows and columns, it is useful for storing lists of information. Most spreadsheet software includes features for working with lists of information, such as sorting and filtering.

You can create charts from your data if you want a graphical representation of your data – you can pick from a vast range of different chart types and you can format and edit charts.

As well as being used for accounting purposes and for storing data, most spreadsheet software also comes with a range of more advanced data analysis tools, so you can 'play' with the figures, carry out 'what-if' analysis and solve mathematical problems.

LAUNCHING YOUR SPREADSHEET SOFTWARE

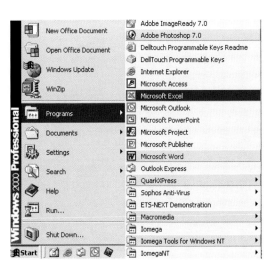

Click on the Start button at the bottom left of the screen. Choose Programs and then click on the program you wish to launch i.e. Microsoft Excel.

Alternatively, you may have a 'shortcut' to the program on your computer's desktop. If you can see an icon representing the program on the screen, double-click on it.

The spreadsheet software will have a menu bar and rows of buttons. The main area of the screen contains the worksheet itself, made up of rows and columns. Each 'square' on the spreadsheet is called a cell and each cell has a reference (rather like a map reference). For example, the first cell on the worksheet is A1 (Column A, Row 1). The cell reference appears at the left end of the Formula Bar, which runs along the top of the worksheet.

Title Bar   Menu Bar   Toolbars

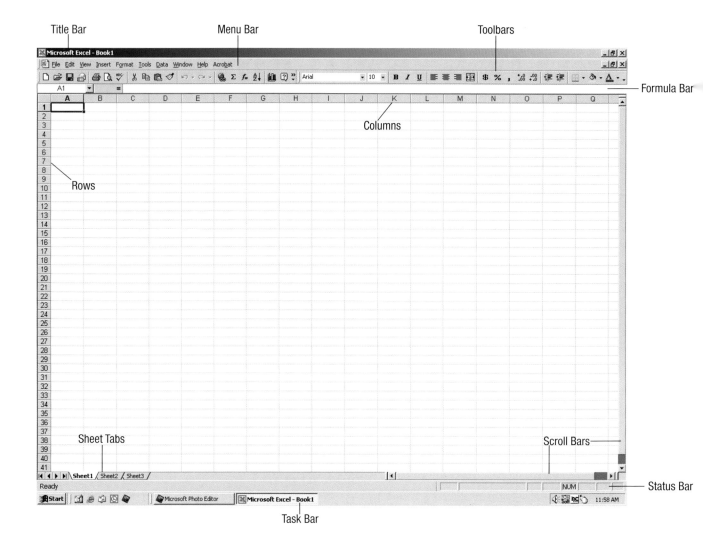

Formula Bar

Columns

Rows

Sheet Tabs   Scroll Bars

Status Bar

Task Bar

Under the worksheet are the sheet tabs. Each sheet in the file is called a worksheet, but the whole file is called a workbook. There are generally three sheets in each new workbook you start, although more can be added.

Under the sheet tabs is the Status Bar. The word Ready appears at the left end of the Status Bar. You can use the Status Bar to view calculations (see AutoCalculate).

The Windows Taskbar runs along the bottom of the screen. This contains the Start menu and other icons, enabling you to switch into another application if you wish to.

NAVIGATING AROUND SPREADSHEETS

Using the Keyboard

To move from cell to cell on your worksheet, use the arrow keys on the keyboard to indicate the direction you wish to move (up, down, left or right).

To move to the beginning of a row, press Home on the keyboard. To move to the end of a row, press End on the keyboard.

To move to the beginning of the worksheet, press Ctrl+Home at the same time. To move to the end of the worksheet, press Ctrl+End at the same time.

To move down one screen, press Page Down on the keyboard. To move up one screen, press Page Up on the keyboard.

To move right one screen, press Alt+Page Down at the same time. To move left one screen, press Alt+Page Up at the same time.

Using the Mouse

To move to another cell on the worksheet, click on the cell you wish to move to with the mouse.

| ◄ | ◄ | ► | ►| \ **Sheet1** / Sheet2 / Sheet3 /

To move to another sheet in your file, click on the sheet tab of the sheet you wish to move to.

SELECTING CELLS ON THE WORKSHEET

▌ A worksheet with a selected range.

Salesperson	Sales
Conroy	8300
Alboucq	11600
Wilson	10200
Wheeler	10500
Lugo	7400

Before you can make changes to data you have entered onto the worksheet, you will need to 'select' the cell(s) that contain the data.

When you select cells, the first selected cell remains clear, but the other selected cells become shaded. A group of cells on the worksheet is known as a range of cells.

Using the Keyboard

Hold down the Shift key on the left side of the keyboard (above Ctrl) and then use the arrow keys to indicate the direction you wish to select (up, down, left or right).

To select to the beginning of a row, hold down Shift and press Home. To select to the end of a row, hold down Shift and press End.

To select to the beginning of the worksheet, hold down Shift and then press Ctrl+Home. To select to the end of the worksheet, hold down Shift and then press Ctrl+End.

To select an entire column, press Ctrl + the space bar at the same time. To select a whole row, press Shift + the space bar at the same time.

To select the entire worksheet, press Ctrl+A.

Using the Mouse

When your mouse is on the worksheet, a white cross icon represents it. You use this icon to select a cell or a range of cells. To select one cell, click on the cell that you wish to select. This is known as the active cell and has a heavier black border around it. To select a range of cells, click and hold the left mouse button and then drag the mouse to select the cells.

To select an entire row, click on the grey number tile to the left of the row. To select an entire column, click on the grey letter tile at the top of the column.

To select the entire worksheet, click on the grey square at the top left of the worksheet. (To the left of the first column tile (A) and above the first row tile (1)).

ENTERING AND EDITING DATA

Click on the cell (or navigate to it using the keyboard) that you wish to enter data into. Type your data into the cell. If you type text into a cell, it will automatically align to the left of the cell. If you type figures into a cell, they will automatically align to the right of the cell.

If you prefer, you can enter data into the formula bar. The formula bar runs across the top of the worksheet, just below the toolbars. Click in the white space on the formula bar to activate it. Type your data. When you press Enter or click on the Green tick, the data will appear in the active cell (the cell you were sitting in before you clicked onto the formula bar).

If you wish to edit the contents of a cell, you can either click on the cell and then click on the formula bar, or double-click on the cell and the cursor will appear inside. You are now in Edit mode. You can use the cursor movement keys, back-space and delete when you are in Edit mode to amend the contents of the cell. Click outside the cell or press Enter to switch off Edit mode.

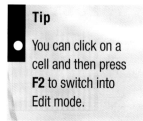

Tip

You can click on a cell and then press **F2** to switch into Edit mode.

SAVING SPREADSHEETS

Using Save

If you wish to keep the spreadsheet file, so that you can use it again, you will need to save it. The first time you save a spreadsheet, you will be prompted to give the file a name and to choose which folder you wish to save it into.

Choose File, Save. The Save As dialog box will appear (it looks very similar to the Open dialog box). Open the drop-down list by Save in and navigate to the folder that you wish to store your spreadsheet file in (folders are indicated by the yellow icon). Double-click on a folder to move into it, or use the Back or Up One Level buttons to move up out of a folder.

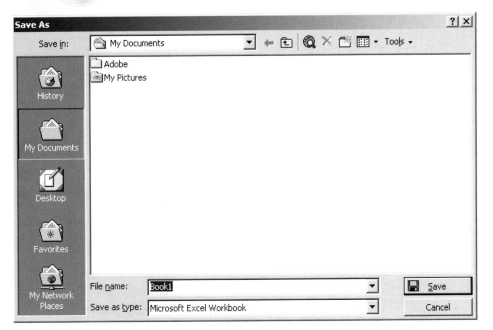

The Save Dialog Box displaying the contents of the My Documents folder.

Single click on drop-down arrow to display options.

Double-click to move into other folders.

Type a name for the spreadsheet in the File name box and check that it will be saved into the correct format (under Save as type). Your filename can be up to 250 characters long – use an obvious name for your file so that you remember what you called it in the future! You do not need to type the .xls filename extension as this will be added automatically. (The filename extension may not be visible if it has not been set in Windows Explorer). Click on the Save button at the bottom right of the dialog box.

Once you have saved a spreadsheet, the name of the file will appear in the Title Bar across the top of the screen. All Excel spreadsheets have the file extension .xls. This will help you recognise which of your files are Excel spreadsheets.

If you have previously saved a spreadsheet, choosing Save will overwrite the previous version of the spreadsheet with the updated version. (It still has the same name and is stored in the folder that you initially put it in).

The Save button also appears on the Standard Toolbar. You can click on this button instead of choosing File, Save.

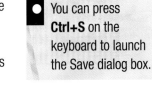

Tip

You can press **Ctrl+S** on the keyboard to launch the Save dialog box.

Save

Using Save As

If you do not wish to overwrite a previously saved spreadsheet that you have re-opened, you can use Save As and give the new version of the spreadsheet a different name, or store it in a different folder. Choose Save As from the File menu.

Saving Automatically as you work

If you want Excel to save your file automatically after set time intervals, choose Tools, AutoSave. AutoSave is an Excel Add-In – if you don't see it on the Tools menu, choose Tools, Add-Ins and check the AutoSave Add-In box). Check the Automatic save every box and specify how often you want Excel to save the file (in minutes).

Having this feature enabled protects against loss of work should your computer 'crash'. If this feature is switched on, you will only lose work that you have done since the last AutoSave.

AutoRecovery

Should your system crash while you are in the middle of creating a spreadsheet, and you haven't yet saved, Office 2000 is very good at recovering files. Once you have rebooted your computer and relaunched Excel, the spreadsheet should re-open onto the screen with the word (Recovered) up on the Title Bar.

TASK

1 **Input the following data onto a new spreadsheet.**

FIRST NAME	LAST NAME	EMP. ID	SALARY (Gross)
Adam	Smith	E63585	£18,000.00
Daniel	McDonald	E04242	£41,500.00
David	Meeks	E27002	£19,250.00
George	Wright	E00127	£53,500.00
Kim	Arkwright	E10001	£57,000.00
Richard	Piper	E43128	£15,900.00
Tim	Sturgeon	E03003	£27,000.00
Tony	Bennett	E10297	£32,000.00
Yvonne	Rampley	E39483	£29,900.00

2 **Head up Column E – Pension Contribution (2%).**

3 **Head up Column F – Salary (Net).**

4 **Save the spreadsheet with the name Employee.**

CLOSING THE SPREADSHEET

If you wish to remove the spreadsheet from the screen, you need to close it. If you wish to keep the file on your computer, you must save the spreadsheet before closing it.

Choose File, Close. If you haven't previously saved the spreadsheet, the following message will appear on the screen.

If you do wish to save changes, click Yes. If you wish to close the spreadsheet without saving, click No.

Clicking Cancel will remove the dialog box from the screen.

OPENING EXISTING SPREADSHEETS

You may need to retrieve saved spreadsheets, to view data, print or edit.

The Open Dialog Box displaying the contents of the My Documents folder. Double-click to move into other folders.

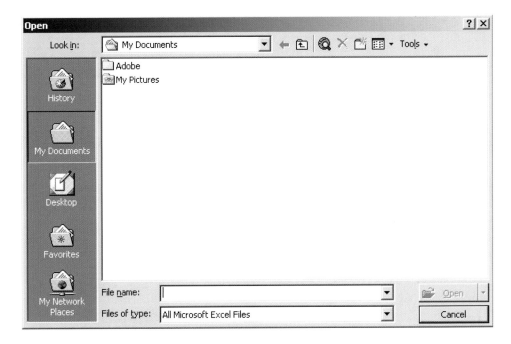

Choose File, Open. The Open dialog box will appear. (A dialog box appears when you need to have some 'dialog' with your computer). Open the drop-down list by Look in and navigate to the folder that your spreadsheet file is stored in (folders are indicated by the yellow icon). Double-click on a folder to move into it, or use the Back or Up One Level buttons to move up out of a folder.

Locate the spreadsheet you wish to open, click on it and then click on the Open button at the bottom right of the dialog box. (Alternatively, you can double-click on the file).

If you cannot see your spreadsheet files in a folder, make sure the Files of type list at the bottom of the dialog box is showing the correct file types. Excel recognises spreadsheet files because they have a .xls filename extension. This filename extension may not be visible if it has not been set in Windows Explorer.

Tip

You can press **Ctrl+O** on the keyboard to launch the Open dialog box.

The Open button also appears on the Standard Toolbar. You can click on this button instead of choosing File, Open.

Open

SPREADSHEET DESIGN

There are a few tips to bear in mind when designing a new spreadsheet.

Remember, the 'worksheet' is not the A4 paper. You do not need to layout the spreadsheet as you want it to appear on the A4 page when printed. You use Page Setup to specify how it should print onto A4.

Always start a new spreadsheet in the top left cell (A1). Do not leave empty columns or rows within the structure of your spreadsheet. Any empty cells are treated as zero, which could impact the results of formulas you create.

61

It is a good idea to format your headings (or labels) so that they appear differently to the data itself. This makes it easier to read the information.

The quickest way to navigate around the worksheet is to use the arrow keys on the keyboard. Simply indicate the direction you wish to move in.

The 'gridlines' that appear on the worksheet do not print. If you want lines to print around your data, you need to apply borders or select the option in Page Setup.

Always make use of print preview to see how the worksheet will look when printed onto A4. Once you Print Previewed a dashed line will appear down and across the worksheet. This indicates the A4 page break and makes it easy to know when you are reaching the edge of a sheet of A4.

USING DELETE AND CLEAR

If you wish to delete the contents of a cell, the quickest way is to use the Delete key on the keyboard. Select the cell or cells that you wish to remove the contents of and press Delete on the keyboard.

However, if you have added formatting to a cell or a range of cells, e.g. bold and underline and borders and shading, or you want to be able to choose what to remove from the cell, use the Clear command.

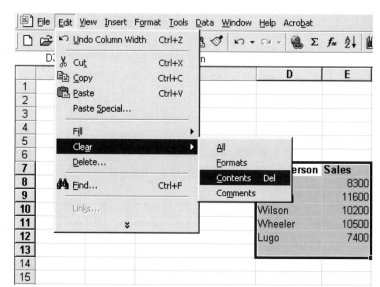

Select the cells that you wish to clear and choose Edit, Clear. You can choose whether you wish to remove everything from the cell, just the formats or just the contents.

REMOVING FORMATTING FROM A RANGE OF CELLS

If you have added a lot of formatting to cells, i.e. bold and underline and borders and shading, you can individually switch off each formatting. However, it is quicker to use the Clear command.

Select the cells that contain the formatting you wish to remove and choose Edit, Clear. Click Formats in the sub-menu. The formatting is stripped from the cells, but the contents remain.

USING UNDO AND REDO

The Undo command will 'undo' your last action. For example, if you have deleted a range of cells by mistake, you can use Undo to undo the deletion. Choose Edit, Undo or press the Undo button on the Standard toolbar.

Tip
You can press **Ctrl+Z** to undo your last command.

If you wish to undo more than one action, click on the drop-down arrow by the Undo button to open a list of your recent actions. (You can undo the last 16 actions). Click on the action you wish to undo and all actions back to that one will be undone.

The Redo command will 'redo' your last action. For example, if you have undone something by mistake, choose Edit, Repeat or press the Redo button on the Standard toolbar to carry out the action again.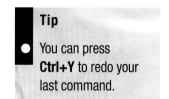

If you wish to redo more than one action, click on the drop-down arrow by the Redo button to open a list of your recent actions. (You can redo the last 16 actions). Click on the action that you wish to redo and all actions up to that one will be redone.

> **Tip**
> You can press **Ctrl+Y** to redo your last command.

MODIFYING ROW HEIGHTS AND COLUMN WIDTHS

When you start a new spreadsheet, each cell is a standard size. As you enter data, you will notice that sometimes your data does not fit into the cell.

Changing Cell Height and Width using the Mouse

Move your mouse onto the grey column tiles (lettered) or the grey row tiles (numbered).

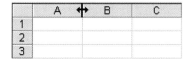

Move the mouse so that it rests on the line between two column tiles or two row tiles. The white cross icon will change to a double-headed black arrow. Click and drag to resize the column or row.

AutoFit – double-click with the resizing handle to have the row or column automatically resize to its widest entry.

Changing Cell Height and Width using the Menu

Click in the column or row that you wish to resize and choose Format, Column, Width or Format, Row, Height.

Type the measurement you require. (Column widths are measured in characters and row heights are measured in point sizes). Click OK.

AutoFit – choose Row, AutoFit or Column, AutoFit selection to have the row or column resize automatically to fit the widest entry.

Changing Standard Column Width

If you want to change the standard width for a range of columns, select the columns, choose Format, Column, Standard Width.

Specify the standard size you want the columns to be (in characters) and click OK.

To change the standard width of all columns on the worksheet, select the entire worksheet (click on the grey tile at the top left of the worksheet), choose Format, Column, Standard Width and specify the measurement for all columns. Click OK.

INSERTING ROWS AND COLUMNS

Although there are plenty of rows and columns available to you on the worksheet (256 columns × 65 536 rows), you might wish to insert a row or column within the structure of a worksheet you have already created.

Rows are inserted above the row you are sitting in and columns are inserted to the left of the column you are sitting in.

Inserting rows or columns is a simple operation, but you need to ensure that you are sitting in the right row or column on the worksheet before using the command.

Inserting Rows and Columns using the Insert Menu

Ensure you are sitting in the row below or the column to the right of where you want to insert a row or column. Choose Insert, Rows or Insert, Columns. A new row or column is inserted and the existing row or column is pushed aside to make room for the new one.

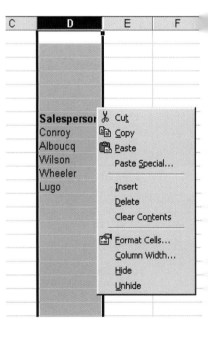

Inserting Multiple Rows or Columns

Select the number of rows below where you wish to insert the new rows, or select the number of columns to the right of where you wish to insert the new columns. (For example, if you wish to insert five new rows, select five rows below where you wish to insert the new rows). Choose Insert, Rows, or Insert, Columns.

Inserting Rows and Columns using the Shortcut Menu

Point to the row tile or column tile of the row or column you wish to select and click with the right-mouse button. A shortcut menu appears. The shortcut menu offers you a number of commands appropriate to what you are pointing to when you right-click. Click Insert with the left-mouse button.

DELETING ROWS AND COLUMNS

Although there is an Insert menu to insert rows and columns, there is no Delete menu for deleting rows and columns. Instead, you need to use the Edit menu. Select the column or row, choose Edit, Delete.

TASK

1 Input the following data onto a new worksheet:

Staff Member	Cost	Total
Bob	0.22	
Helen	0.22	
Trevor	0.40	
Anne	0.22	
Louise	0.40	
Rachel	0.40	
Chris	0.22	
Grand Total		

2 Adjust column widths and row heights as appropriate.

3 Insert a new row above row one and insert the heading 'Fuel Costs'.

4 Insert a new column to the left of the Cost column and head it up Mileage. Insert the following data:

50
40
120
256
128
15
72

5 Use the Formatting toolbar and the Format Cells dialog box to add formatting to the worksheet.

6 Save the workbook as **Fuel Costs**.

Deleting Cells using the Edit Menu

Select the cells that you wish to delete and choose Edit, Delete.

Select the option you require and click OK.

Deleting Rows and Columns using the Edit Menu

Select the row or column that you wish to delete and choose Edit, Delete. (The dialog box will not appear if you have selected the entire row or column).

Deleting Multiple Rows or Columns

Select the rows or columns that you wish to delete and choose Edit, Delete.

Deleting Rows and Columns using the Shortcut Menu

Point to the row tile or column tile of the row or column you wish to delete and click with the right-mouse button. A shortcut menu appears. The shortcut menu offers you a number of commands appropriate to what you are pointing to when you right-click. Click Delete with the left-mouse button.

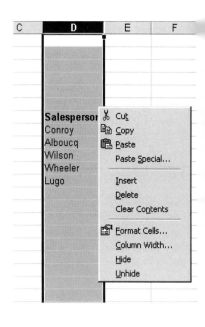

PRINTING SPREADSHEETS

Page Setup

Before you are ready to print your spreadsheet, you need to use Page Setup to layout the worksheet on the A4 piece of paper. (N.B. Everything you do in the Page Setup dialog box affects how each worksheet will look when printed, *not* how it looks on-screen).

Choose File, Page Setup. (You can also access Page Setup from the Print Preview screen).

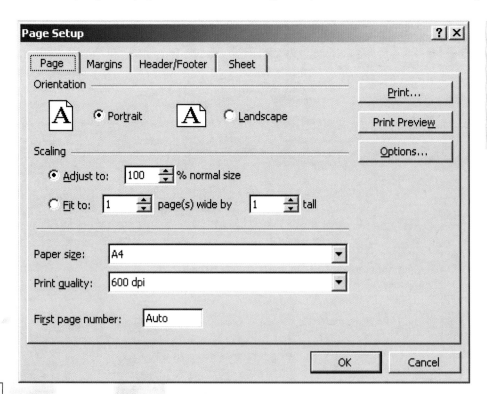

The Page Setup Dialog Box displaying the Page tab. On this tab you can change page orientation, scale the worksheet up or down, fit it to a specified number of pages and change paper size and print quality.

The Page Setup dialog box has four tabs:

Page – to change the page orientation, scale the worksheet and adjust it to fit on a set number of pages. You can also change the paper size and print quality.

Margins – to adjust the margins of the page and the header and footer margins. (By default these are always set halfway between the edge of the page and your actual work). You can also centre the worksheet horizontally and/or vertically on the printed page.

Header/Footer – to choose from a list of available Headers and Footers, or create a Custom Header and/or Custom Footer.

Sheet – to specify a print area if you do not want to print the whole worksheet. You can also specify rows and/or columns that you want to be repeated each time a new page is printed.

Changing Page Orientation and Scaling

By default, your worksheet will print onto A4 portrait. If you wish to change the page orientation to landscape, choose File, Page Setup, click on the Page tab and click the Landscape button.

If you wish to enlarge or reduce the size of your worksheet (i.e. to squeeze it onto one page), you can scale it. Choose File, Page Setup, click on the Page tab and use the spin button to scale the worksheet to smaller than 100% or larger than 100%. (It is helpful to make use of Print Preview when scaling, so you can see the results of your actions).

Changing Margins and Centering

Margins are set at 2.5 cm Top and Bottom and 1.9 cm Left and Right.

The Page Setup Dialog Box displaying the Margins tab. On this tab you can change page margins and header and footer margins and also centre the worksheet on the A4 printed page.

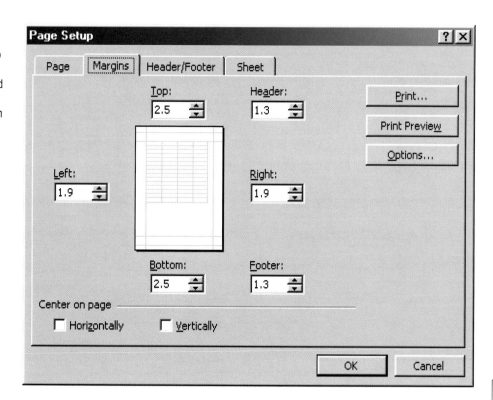

If you wish to change the margins, choose File, Page Setup, click on the Margins tab and use the spin buttons to adjust the margins. (The smaller the margin, the larger the work area and vice versa).

To centre your worksheet on the A4 page, choose File, Page Setup, click on the Margins tab and check the boxes to Center on Page horizontally (between the left and right margins) and/or vertically (between the top and bottom margins).

Creating Headers and Footers

A header is information that appears in the top margin area of every printed page and a footer is information that appears in the bottom margin area of every printed page. You can choose from a range of preset headers and footers, or you can create your own.

Choose File, Page Setup and click on the Header/Footer tab.

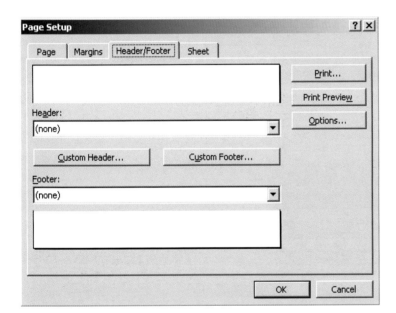

The Page Setup Dialog Box displaying the Header/Footer tab. On this tab you can apply a built-in header and/or footer or create your own custom header or custom footer.

To choose a preset Header or Footer, click on the drop-down arrow for Header or Footer and choose from the list. The information is taken from user names, file names and sheet names.

Alternatively, you can create your own Header and/or Footer. Click Custom Header or Custom Footer.

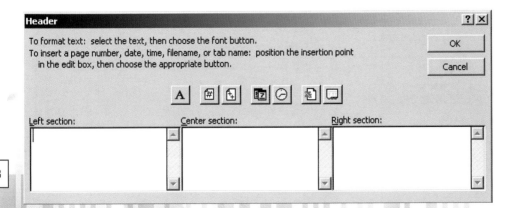

There are three sections in the Header or Footer dialog box. You can type data into any of the sections, or use the buttons to insert information.

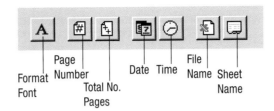

Format Font   Page Number   Total No. Pages   Date   Time   File Name   Sheet Name

Format Font – click on this button to format text you have typed. You can change the font, font style, font size and underline and add other text effects.

Page Number – inserts the current page number. It will appear as a code – &[Page] – in the Header/Footer dialog box.

Total Number of Pages – inserts the total number of A4 pages. It will appear as a code – &[Pages] – in the Header/Footer dialog box.

Date – inserts the current date. This will update each time the file is opened. The date will appear as a code – &[Date].

Time – inserts the current time. This will update each time the file is opened. The time will appear as a code – &[Time].

File Name – inserts the name of the current file. The file name will appear as a code – &[File] in the Header/Footer dialog box.

Sheet Name – inserts the name of the current sheet. The sheet name will appear as a code – &[Sheet] in the Header/Footer dialog box.

Other Page Setup Options

The sheet tab of the Page Setup dialog box offers you more options for setting up the A4 page.

The Page Setup Dialog Box displaying the Sheet tab. On this tab you can set a print area, set rows or columns to repeat when printing, set other print options and choose the page order when printing.

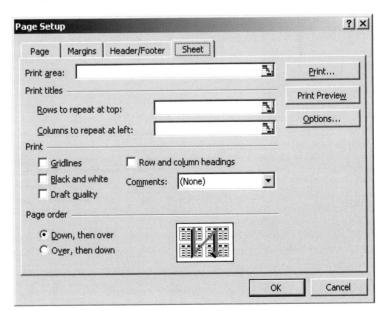

To set a print area, select the range on the worksheet that you wish to print. (The absolute cell range is inserted into the box – hence the $ signs).

You can also set a print area by choosing the Print Area option from the File menu.

(If the Page Setup dialog box is sitting on top of the worksheet, you can drag it by its Title Bar (the bar across the top). Alternatively, if you press the button with the red arrow on this will temporarily collapse the dialog box in order that you can see the worksheet behind. Press the red arrow button again to expand the dialog box.

The Page Setup dialog box when collapsed. Press the red arrow button to expand the dialog box.

If your worksheet is likely to print onto more than one page of A4, you may want the headings to repeat each time a new A4 page is started. Click in the appropriate box in the Page Setup dialog box (Rows to repeat at top, or Columns to repeat at left). If necessary, collapse the dialog box and click on the row(s) and/or column(s) that you want to repeat. (The absolute cell range is inserted into the box – hence the $ signs).

If you want to print the gridlines that appear on the worksheet, tick this box. BE CAREFUL – ASKING FOR GRID-LINES TO PRINT MAY GIVE YOU MORE GRIDLINES THAN YOU WANT. You will have far more control if you do not specify that gridlines should print and instead apply borders where you want lines to print.

If you have a colour worksheet and you print to a colour printer, but you only want a black and white print-out, tick the Black and white box.

If you don't want to see any formatting, borders or shading – just a print-out of the raw data – tick the Draft quality box.

If you wish to be able to see the row and column headings of the worksheet on the printed page, tick the Row and column headings box.

If you want the on-screen comments to print, choose the appropriate option from the Comments drop-down list.

Print Preview

Before you print your worksheet, you may wish to view it as it will look when printed onto plain A4 paper. Choose File, Print Preview or press the Print Preview button on the Standard Toolbar.

Print Preview

The Print Preview screen will open. Your worksheet displays on A4 paper and a set of buttons appears across the top of the screen.

Next – to view the next page if the worksheet goes onto more than one A4 sheet.
Previous – to view the previous page if the worksheet goes onto more than one A4 sheet.
Zoom – to zoom in on or out on the print preview. (You can also click on the sheet itself).
Print – to open the Print dialog box.
Setup – to open the Page Setup dialog box. (This can also be accessed from the File menu).

A spreadsheet shown in Print Preview.

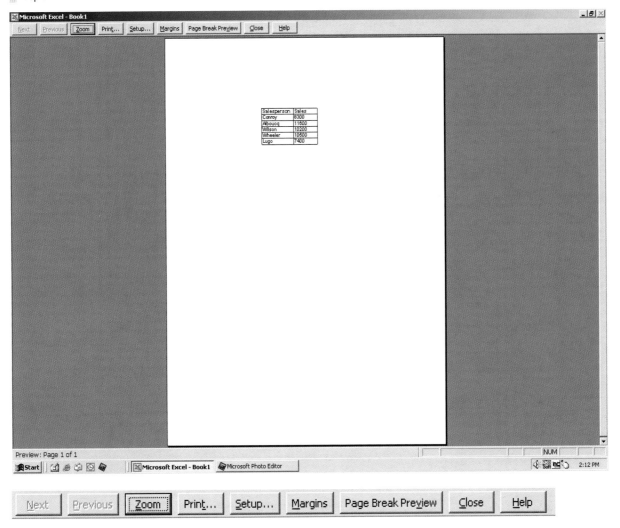

Margins – to switch on margin markers. You can move the margins by dragging the margin markers with the mouse.

Page Break Preview – to show the worksheet divided into A4 pages. You can move page breaks on the worksheet by dragging them.

Close – to close the Print Preview window and return to the worksheet.

Help – to access the online help files.

Setting a Print Area

If you do not wish to print the whole worksheet, but wish to specify an area to print, you can set a Print Area.

Select the cells that you wish to print and choose File, Set Print Area. A dashed line will appear around the selected cells and only this print area will print.

To clear a print area, choose File, Clear Print Area. The dashed line will disappear.

Printing

Choose File, Print or press the Print button on the Standard Toolbar.

Print

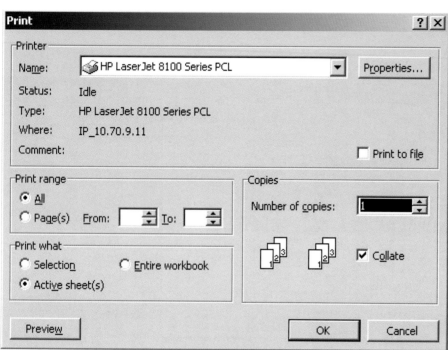

The Print Dialog box displayed here indicates that the HP LaserJet 8100 Series PCL printer has been selected, the print range has been set to print all pages, number of copies is 1 and the active sheet will be printed.

Choose the Printer that you wish to print to. (Click on the down arrow to the right of the printer name and choose from the list of available installed printers).

Choose whether you want to print all the pages or a page range.

Choose the number of copies you want to print.

Choose whether you want to print a selection on the worksheet, the active worksheet (the one you are currently sitting on), or the entire workbook (all sheets).

Click OK to send your spreadsheet to the printer.

Tip

You can press **Ctrl+P** on the keyboard to launch the Print dialog box.

MOVING AND COPYING DATA ON THE SPREADSHEET

If you wish to move or copy data from one place to another in your spreadsheet file, you can use the Windows clipboard. The clipboard is a temporary storage area that enables you to move or copy data from one place and then paste it back at another location within the same file, into another file, or into another application. The Windows clipboard can only hold one item at a time. If there is something already sitting on the Windows clipboard and you then cut something else, this will replace the original item.

If you wish to copy multiple items and then paste them into other locations, you can use the Office clipboard. The Office clipboard enables you to cut or copy data from one Office application and paste it into another Office appli-

cation. The Office clipboard can hold up to 12 items at a time. These items can then be placed at different locations throughout the file, or can be pasted in altogether.

Moving Data using the Clipboard

Select the cells that you wish to move and choose Edit, Cut. Alternatively, you can click on the Cut button on the Standard toolbar.

Cut

A moving border appears around the selected cells. Navigate to the new location and click in the cell that will be at the top left corner of the new location and choose Edit, Paste. Alternatively, you can click on the Paste button on the Standard toolbar.

Paste

When you cut data to the clipboard, it does not actually disappear from the screen. Instead, a moving border appears around the range that you have cut. When you click on the Paste button, the range will move to its new location.

Copying Data using the Clipboard

Select the cells that you wish to copy and choose Edit, Copy. Alternatively, you can click on the Copy button on the Standard toolbar.

Copy

A moving border appears around the selected cells. Navigate to the new location and click in the cell that will be at the top left corner of the new location and choose Edit, Paste. Alternatively, you can click on the Paste button on the Standard toolbar.

Paste

When you copy data to the clipboard, it does not disappear from the screen. Instead, a moving border appears around the range that you have copied. When you click on the Paste button, the range will be copied to its new location. The copied contents also remain on the clipboard, so that they can be pasted in at another location, if required.

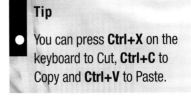

Tip

You can press **Ctrl+X** on the keyboard to Cut, **Ctrl+C** to Copy and **Ctrl+V** to Paste.

Moving or Copying Multiple Items using the Office Clipboard

Select the first range of cells that you wish to move or copy and choose Edit, Cut or Edit, Copy. (Alternatively, use the buttons on the Standard toolbar). Now select the next range of cells that you wish to move or copy. The Office Clipboard will automatically appear on the screen. (If the Office Clipboard does not appear, choose View, Toolbars

and click on Clipboard). Continue selecting ranges and choosing Cut or Copy. (You can place up to 12 items on the Office Clipboard).

Move to the new location. Paste each item in turn by clicking on the appropriate entry on the Clipboard. (When you point to the item on the Clipboard, a screen tip appears indicating what the item is). If you wish to paste all the items you have cut or copied into one place, click Paste All. If you wish to clear the Clipboard, click Clear Clipboard.

Moving Data using Drag and Drop

If you wish to move data a short distance on the worksheet, you do not need to use the clipboard. Instead, you can use a technique called 'drag and drop'.

Select the cells that you wish to move. Point to the edge of your selected area. The white cross icon changes to a mouse pointer icon. Drag and drop the selected cells to the new location on the worksheet.

Copying Data using Drag and Drop

If you wish to copy data a short distance on the worksheet, you do not need to use the clipboard. Instead, you can use a technique called 'drag and drop'.

Select the cells that you wish to copy. Point to the edge of your selected area. The white cross icon changes to a mouse pointer icon. Hold down Ctrl on the keyboard – a small + is now attached to the mouse pointer. Drag and drop the selected cells to the new location on the worksheet.

N.B. Release the mouse button before releasing Ctrl on the keyboard.

FORMATTING THE SPREADSHEET

When you add formatting to spreadsheet contents, you add the formatting to the cell rather than to its contents. For example, if you wish to make the text in cell A1 bold and centred, you make cell A1 bold and centred rather than selecting the text inside.

The lines that appear on the worksheet are called 'gridlines'. By default, these lines do not print. If you wish to have lines around your data, you need to apply borders.

Formatting Data using the Formatting Toolbar

Select the cell or cells that you wish to apply formatting to.

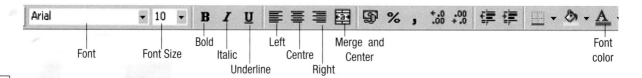

To change the font or font size – click on the drop-down arrow beside each window and choose from the list.

To add enhancements – click Bold, Italic and/or Underline. These buttons are 'toggle' buttons, which means you can switch them on and off. When they are on they appear pressed down. To switch off, click on the same button again and it will come back up.

To change alignment – click Left, Centred or Right.

To centre a heading across the worksheet – select across the entire width of the worksheet and click Merge and Center.

To change data colour – click on the drop-down arrow beside the Font Colour button and choose a colour from the palette.

Formatting Data using the Format Cells Dialog Box

Select the cell or cells that you wish to apply formatting to and choose Format, Cells.

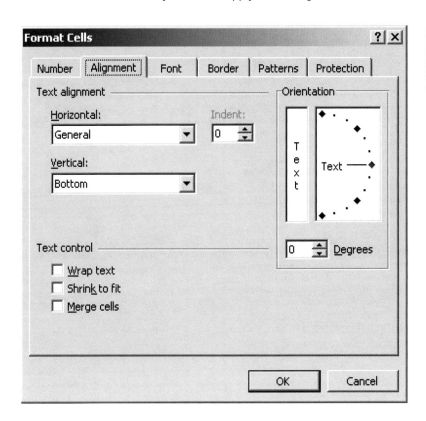

The Format Cells Dialog Box displaying the Alignment tab. On this tab you can change horizontal and vertical alignment, wrap text and merge cells, and change text orientation.

Alignment

Horizontal – choose from Left, Centre, Right, Fill, Justify, and Centre Across Selection.

Vertical – choose from Top, Centre, Bottom, and Justify.

Orientation – drag the red diamond on the scale, or use the spin buttons to choose the degrees. You can also choose vertical text.

Wrap text – force text to wrap within a cell so that you can adjust column widths.

Shrink to fit – shrink cell contents to fit into the current size of the cell.

Merge cells – merge multiple cells into one cell.

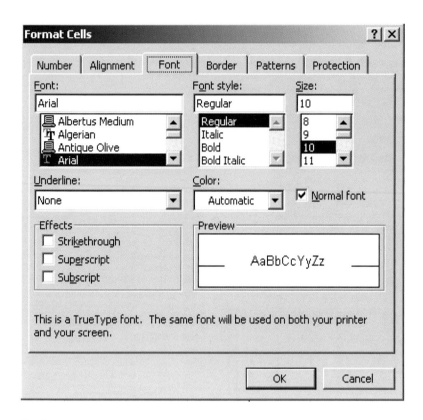

The Format Cells Dialog Box displaying the Font tab. On this tab you can change the font, font style and font size, choose different underline options, change font colour and add other text effects. (The Preview area allows you to see the results of your changes).

Font

Font – choose from a range of different typefaces.

Font style – choose from a range of different font styles.

Font size – choose from a range of different font sizes.

Underline – click on the drop-down arrow to open a list of underline options. (Includes Single, Double, Single Accounting and Double Accounting).

Color – click on the drop-down arrow to open the colour palette.

Strikethrough – puts a single line through the data.

Superscript – lifts the data above the baseline. (For example, 36°C).

Subscript – drops the data below the baseline. (For example, H_2O).

NUMBER FORMATTING

There is a large range of different number formats that you can apply to your figures on the spreadsheet.

Formatting Numbers using the Formatting Toolbar

Select the cell or cells that you wish to apply formatting to.

Currency

Percent

Comma

Increase Decimal

Decrease Decimal

76

Currency – apply currency formatting – pound sign, comma and two decimal places.

Percent – apply Percent formatting – multiply the figure by 100 and add a % sign.

Comma – apply comma formatting – comma as a thousand separator and two decimal places.

Increase Decimal – increase the number of decimal places being displayed.

Decrease Decimal – decrease the number of decimal places being displayed.

Formatting Numbers using the Format Cells Dialog Box

Select the cell or cells that you wish to apply formatting to and choose Format, Cells.

The Format Cells Dialog Box displaying the Number tab. On this tab you can choose from a large range of different number formats and customise them to suit your requirements.

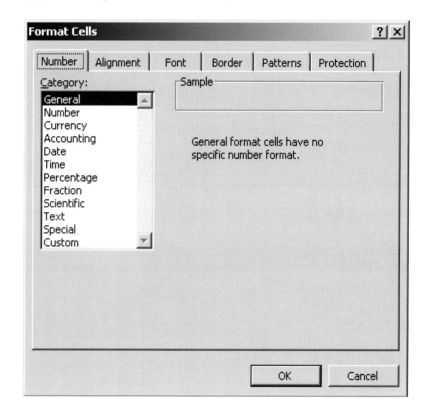

Number

Number – choose how many decimal places to display, whether to use the thousand separator and how you want negative numbers to be displayed.

Currency – choose how many decimal places to display, the currency symbol you wish to use and how you want negative numbers to be displayed.

Accounting – choose how many decimal places to display and the currency symbol you wish to use.

Date – choose how you want a date to be displayed.

Time – choose how you want a time to be displayed.

Percentage – choose how many decimal places to display.

Fraction – choose how you want a fraction to be displayed.

Scientific – choose how many decimal places to display.

Text – choose this option if you want a number to be treated as text (i.e. not included in calculations).

Special – special formats for databases.

Custom – create your own number format.

77

CELL FORMATTING

You can apply borders and shading to your cells, so that lines and shading appear on the printed A4 page.

Formatting Cells using the Formatting Toolbar

Select the cell or cells that you wish to apply formatting to.

Borders   Fill Color

Borders – click on the drop-down arrow to display the border palette. You can choose from a range of black borders.
Fill Color – click on the drop-down arrow to display the colour palette. Click on the colour you wish to apply.

N.B. Dark colours will appear black when printed on a black and white printer. If you do wish to apply cell colour, use the shaded colours at the bottom of the colour palette.

Formatting Cells using the Format Cells Dialog Box

Select the cell or cells that you wish to apply formatting to and choose Format, Cells.

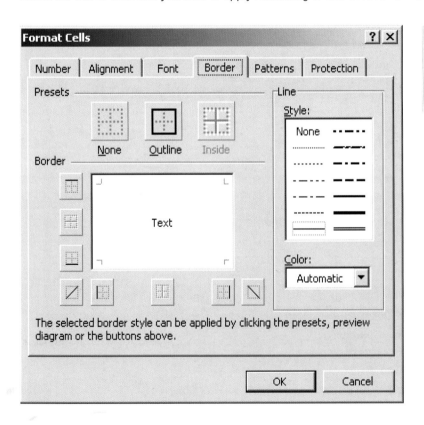

The Format Cells Dialog Box displaying the Border tab. On this tab you can apply borders to the cells. You can also choose the line style and colour for the border. The Text area allows you to see the results of your changes.

Border

Presets – choose None, Outline or Inside. (Inside will only be available if you have selected a range of cells on the worksheet).

Border – choose which border you want to apply – Top, Middle, Bottom, Diagonal Up, Left, Centre, Right, Diagonal Down.

Style – choose the line style for the border.

Color – choose the colour for the border (click on the drop-down arrow).

The Format Cells Dialog Box displaying the Patterns tab. On this tab you can apply cell colour and patterns. You can also choose a pattern colour from the second palette. The Sample area allows you to see the results of your changes.

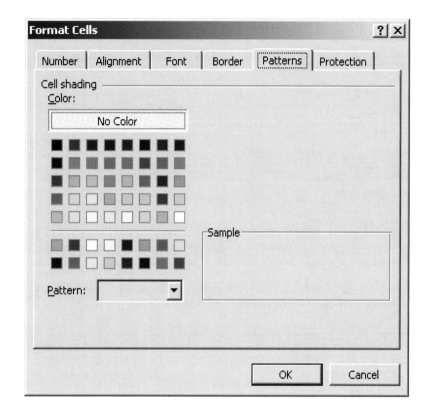

Patterns

Color – choose a cell colour from the palette.

Patterns – click on the drop-down arrow to open the patterns list. Choose a cell pattern and a colour for the pattern. (You will need to open this list twice – once to choose the pattern and again to choose the pattern colour).

WRITING CALCULATIONS

The reason many people choose to use spreadsheet software is its ability to calculate. A calculation is called a formula.

A formula is made up of cell references (for example A1, D7, etc.), and mathematical operators. The four most common mathematical operators are:

add	+
subtract	–
multiply	*
divide	/

These four mathematical operators appear on the number keypad of a desktop computer's keyboard, together with the numbers and Enter. (It is rather like a calculator). You may find it useful to use this keypad when creating formulae.

If you wish to create a formula in a cell, the formula must begin with an = sign. This informs the software that you are not typing text or a figure, but are about to create a formula.

For example, if you wanted to multiply the value in cell D2 with the value in cell E5, the formula would look like this:

=D2*E5

It might help to write the calculation on a piece of paper, or perhaps do it on a calculator so that you are clear what calculation you wish to do. Then you simply replace the values with the cell references of the cells that the values appear in.

The reason you use cell references rather than the actual values in a formula is that, should the values in the cells change, the formula will automatically recalculate without the need to re-write the calculation.

Formulae are laid out in the same way that you would write a calculation on paper, except that the values are replaced with their cell references.

Brackets (parentheses) change the order of the mathematical calculation. For example, if you wanted to add the value in cell D2 to the value in cell E5 and then multiply by cell F6, the formula would look like this:

=(D2+E5)*F6

The addition part of the calculation is placed inside the brackets to ensure the result of that calculation is multiplied by the cell reference outside the bracket.

Percentage Calculations

Your computer keyboard has a % button, rather like a calculator. Thus, when carrying out percentage calculations, you can use this % button at the end of the calculation. For example, £40.00*17.5%.

Typing Formulae into a Cell

If you wish to calculate the Fee Due for F Bloggs, click in the cell D2. (The result of your formula will appear in the active cell).

Type = to start your formula.

Type the first cell reference **B2**, type the mathematical operator * and then type the second cell reference **C2**.

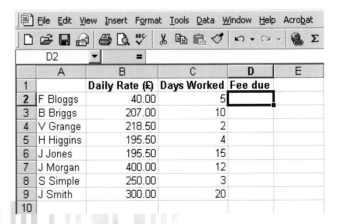

	A	B	C	D	E
1		Daily Rate (£)	Days Worked	Fee due	
2	F Bloggs	40.00	5		
3	B Briggs	207.00	10		
4	V Grange	218.50	2		
5	H Higgins	195.50	4		
6	J Jones	195.50	15		
7	J Morgan	400.00	12		
8	S Simple	250.00	3		
9	J Smith	300.00	20		
10					

Thus, the formula would look like this:

    =B2*C2

Press Enter when you have finished writing a formula. The result of the calculation will appear in the active cell, but the calculation itself appears in the formula bar.

Building a Formula

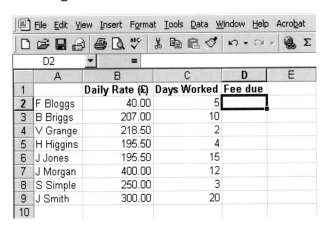

Alternatively, you may wish to build a formula using the mouse rather than simply typing it. (There is always a risk when typing a formula that you might make a typing error, which will affect the result of your formula).

If you wish to calculate the Fee Due for F Bloggs, click in the cell D2. (The result of your formula will appear in the active cell).

Type = to start your formula.

Click on the first cell reference with the mouse **B2**. The cell reference appears in the formula. Type the mathematical operator * and then click on the second cell reference with the mouse **C2**. The cell reference appears in the formula.

Thus, the formula would look like this:

    =B2*C2

Always press Enter when you have finished writing a formula. The result of the calculation will appear in the active cell, but the calculation itself appears in the formula bar.

Creating a Formula using the Formula Bar

Click on the cell that you wish the answer to appear in, to make it the active cell. Click up on the formula bar. Create the formula by typing it or using the mouse to indicate cell references. When you have finished writing the formula, click on the green tick or press Enter.

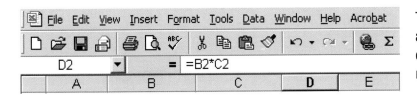

The result of the calculation will appear in the active cell, but the calculation itself appears in the formula bar.

COPYING FORMULAE

Once you have written a formula, you do not need to write it again and again for each row or column it needs to refer to. There are various ways to copy the formula.

Copying Formulae using Copy and Paste

Click on the cell that contains the formula you have just written, choose Edit, Copy (or click on the Copy button on the Standard toolbar). Select the cells that you wish to copy the formula into and choose Edit, Paste (or click on the Paste button on the Standard toolbar).

Copying Formulae using the Fill Handle

Click on the cell that contains the formula you wish to copy. Move to the bottom right corner of the cell over the small black square – the fill handle will appear. Drag the fill handle over the cells that you wish to copy the formula to.

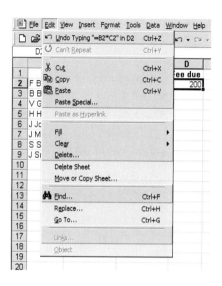

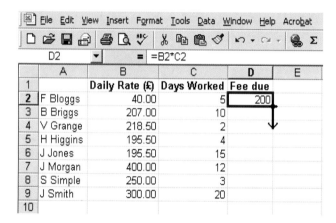

AUTOSUM

If you wish to add up a row or column of values on the worksheet, you can use the AutoSum button on the Standard toolbar.

Autosum

Using AutoSum for Rows and Columns

Click in the cell at the end of the row or at the bottom of the column where you want the result to appear and press the AutoSum button. A moving border indicates the row or column that will be added. If this is the right range, press Enter on the keyboard. If this is not the right range, drag the mouse to indicate the correct range.

Using AutoSum for Selected Ranges

Select the range that you wish to add up. (It is a good idea to also include the empty cell where you want the result to appear). Press the AutoSum button. The result is inserted into the empty cell that you selected.

Tip

You can press **Alt+=** on the keyboard to carry out AutoSum.

TASK

1 Enter the following data onto a new worksheet:

STAFF HOLIDAYS

	Jan	Feb	Mar	Total
Bob	5	4	12	
Helen	3	10	5	
Trevor	12	2	8	
Anne	8	9	16	
Total				

2 Use AutoSum to calculate the Totals row and Totals column.

3 Save and close the workbook with a suitable name.

AUTOCALCULATE

To see what a range of cells will add up to, select the range on the worksheet and the total will appear on the Status Bar at the bottom of the screen.

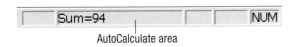

AutoCalculate area

To carry out other functions, such as Average, Min, Max, etc, click the AutoCalculate area on the status bar with the right-mouse button to open the shortcut menu and choose the appropriate function you wish to use.

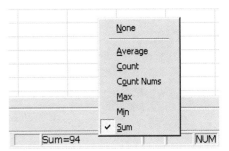

VIEWING FORMULAE IN CELLS

If you wish to see the actual formula rather than its result in the cell, choose Tools, Options and click on the View tab. Check the Formulae box under Window options. Click OK. To remove Formula view, repeat the process removing the tick.

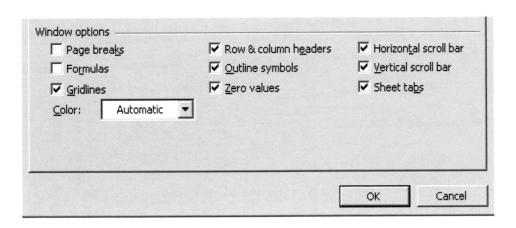

USING FUNCTIONS

If you wish to add up rows or columns on the worksheet, you can use AutoSum. Alternatively, you can write formulas (calculations) yourself. There are also a large number of built-in 'functions' that you can use to carry out mathematical calculations. To access these functions, choose Insert, Functions or press the Paste Function button on the Standard toolbar.

Paste Function

A function is a special pre-written formula that takes a value or values, performs an operation, and returns a value or values. The simplest function is the SUM function. For example, instead of typing =A1+A2+A3+A4, you can use the SUM function to build the formula =SUM(A1:A4).

When you choose Insert, Function or press the Paste Function button, you are taken into a list of available functions.

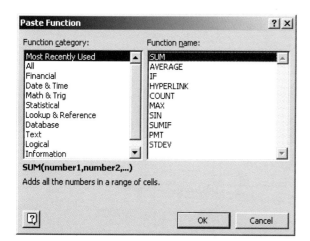

This list is divided into categories. You will always go into the Most Recently Used category. This means if you use the same functions regularly, they will be available in this list. To see a complete alphabetical list of all the functions that are available, click All in the list on the left.

On the right side of the dialog box you will now see a list of all the functions that are available. When you click on a Function name, a description of that function appears at the bottom of the dialog box. Click on the Function you wish to use and then click OK.

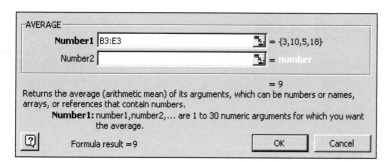

The second stage of the Paste Function is to indicate the cells that contain the values you wish to use in the function. Sometimes this might just be one cell (Number1), or it may be a range of cells.

When you have indicated all the relevant values, click OK.

If the dialog box is sitting on top of your worksheet, collapse it by pressing the red arrow button. Press the red arrow button again to expand the dialog box.

TASK

1 Open or switch to the **Employee** spreadsheet.

2 Add up the Salary (Gross) column, calculate the Pension Contribution column and the Salary (Net) column.

3 Starting in Cell C18, calculate the minimum salary paid, the maximum salary paid, the number of salaries paid (Count function) and the average salary paid.

4 Change column widths and row heights as you feel appropriate.

5 Format the worksheet. Make any final adjustments (e.g. margins, headers & footers, etc).

6 Print the worksheet.

7 Save and close the spreadsheet.

8 Open the **Fuel Costs** spreadsheet.

9 Calculate the Totals and the Grand Total.

10 Save the changes and close the spreadsheet.

TASK

1 Input the following data onto a new worksheet and calculate the Totals and Profit.

Six Month Report							
	Jan	Feb	Mar	Apr	May	June	Total
Income							
Training	2000	3500	8400	2500	3600	3800	
Hardware	3000	2100	2100	3500	1200	1800	
Software	4000	5100	3200	4200	1500	4200	
Total							
Expenses							
Stock	1200	2500	2000	2000	2500	2000	
Admin	2500	1100	3000	1000	2500	1200	
Supplies	1000	1900	1500	1200	1600	1000	
Total							
PROFIT							

2 Use suitable cell formatting to enhance the appearance of the spreadsheet.

3 Save the workbook as **Profit**. Close the spreadsheet.

4 Input the following data onto a new worksheet and use the built-in functions to calculate Maximum, Minimum and Average prices. Calculate the totals.

Supermarket Price Comparison							
ITEM	Food Max	Better Buys	Canned Goodies	Fresher Better	Max	Min	Av
White Wine	1.29	1.72	1.89	1.45			
Sugar	0.55	0.62	0.61	0.59			
Baked Beans	0.27	0.25	0.26	0.24			
Lemonade	0.89	0.99	1.02	0.97			
Tomato Soup	0.25	0.27	0.31	0.32			
Salad Cream	0.76	0.88	0.74	0.76			
TOTAL							

5 Use Print Preview and Page Setup to prepare the workbook for printing.

6 Insert a Header and Footer. Scale the worksheet to fill more of the page. Centre the worksheet vertically and horizontally. Set a print area.

7 Use suitable formatting to enhance the appearance of the spreadsheet.

8 Save the workbook as **Supermarket Prices**.

TASK

Name	Gross	Pension	Taxable	Tax	Net
T Smith	20000				
A Jones	18500				
L Peters	25000				
J Clarke	17000				
P Allan	16500				
E Davis	14000				

1 Enter the above data into a new spreadsheet.

2 Pension is 3% of the gross salary. Calculate pension.

3 Taxable income is Gross less Pension.

4 Tax rate is 30%. Calculate tax.

5 Net income is Taxable less Tax.

6 Save the workbook as **SALARY**. Close the spreadsheet.

7 Enter the data below into a new spreadsheet.

8 Use cell formatting to enhance the appearance of the spreadsheet.

HOUSEKEEPING												
	Jan	Feb	Mar	Apr	May	Jun	Jul	Aug	Sep	Oct	Nov	Dec
Income												
Expenditure												
Mortgage	320	320	320	320	320	320	320	320	320	320	320	320
Poll Tax	0	0	0	25	25	25	25	25	25	25	25	25
Gas	0	0	50	0	0	50	0	0	50	0	0	50
Elec	10	10	10	10	10	10	10	10	10	10	10	10
Food	280	320	400	310	370	230	200	320	400	340	395	420
Petrol	80	85	60	22	76	88	90	78	67	59	51	62
Loan	35	35	35	35	35	35	35	35	0	0	0	0
Total												
Savings												

9 Calculate the total amount of expenditure.

10 Make up your own monthly income (!) and work out your annual savings.

11 Save the worksheet with a suitable name.

12 Close any open spreadsheets.

13 Close the application software.

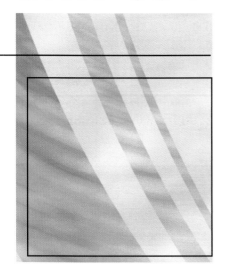

e-Quals
UNIT 004 DATABASES

INTRODUCING MICROSOFT ACCESS

What Exactly is a Database?

The term **database** means different things to different people. For many years, in the world of xBase (dBASE, FoxPro, CA-Clipper), **database** was used to describe a collection of fields and records. In Access terms, a database is a collection of objects that make up a complete system. The main objects include tables, queries, forms, reports, macros, and modules and each has its own special function. The Access environment also consists of several additional features, which include relationships, toolbars, menus, database properties and import/export specifications. Together, all these objects enable you to create powerful, user-friendly, integrated applications.

An Access application contains all the queries, forms, reports and macros necessary to display the data in a meaningful way and update it as necessary. A self-contained, single-user Access application also includes tables in the application database. A multi-user Access application usually consists of two database files, one housing the tables and the other containing the objects (detailed above) that access the data.

The Structure of an Access Database

Access databases can include any the following objects:

Tables act as the main data repositories, storing data items in a row-column format similar to that of a spreadsheet, with each column consisting of one field, each row containing an individual record and the first row displaying the field names. Tables are the starting point for your application. All objects in your database are based either directly or indirectly on your tables.

Queries enable you to select specific records that fulfill certain criteria and either display them with all or with some of the fields they contain, in any sort order you define or perform certain actions on them. Queries in Access are powerful and multifaceted. *Select* queries enable you to view, summarise, and perform calculations on the data in your tables. *Action* queries enable you to add to, update, and delete table data. Because

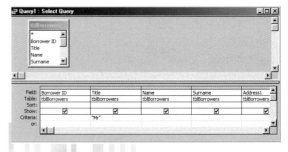

the result of a query is actually a dynamic set of records, called a *dynaset*, based on your table's current data, data in a query result can be updated.

Forms customise the way data contained in tables or queries is viewed and displayed on the screen; also used for entering new data and modifying existing data. Can contain pictures, graphs and even sound. Forms are a user-friendly interface for data entry.

Reports present data contained within the database in a presentable format either for printing or on-screen display. Reports allow you to show all or some of the data fields as well as any graphics of your choice.

Macros store sequences of actions that can be repeated at any time and which provide a simple and flexible way to automate tasks and procedures.

Modules are procedures written in code to perform more sophisticated database operations or complex tasks.

LAUNCHING YOUR DATABASE SOFTWARE

Click on the Start button at the bottom left of the screen. Choose Programs and then click on the program you wish to launch i.e. Microsoft Access.

Alternatively, you may have a 'shortcut' to the program on your computer's desktop. If you can see an icon representing the program on the screen, double-click on it.

The Microsoft Access dialog box will be displayed. Access provides two methods to create a database. You can create a blank database and then add the tables, forms, reports, and other objects later – this is the most flexible method, but it requires you to define each database element separately. The other method is to use the Database Wizard to create in one operation the required tables, forms, and reports for the type of database you choose.

Alternatively, you can open a previously created database.

Make your selection and click OK to proceed.

Creating a New Database

To create a new blank database, select the Blank Access Database option from the Startup dialog box and click OK.

The File New Database dialog box will be displayed.

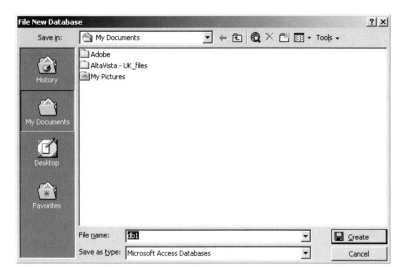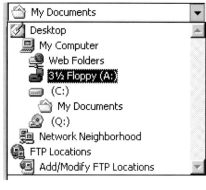

Open the drop-down list by Save in and navigate to the folder that you wish to store your database in (folders are indicated by the yellow icon). Double-click on a folder to move into it, or use the Back or Up One Level buttons to move up out of a folder.

Type a name for the database in the File name box or accept the default name **DB1.MDB** supplied by Access and click Create. If a database file has been previously saved with the name you proposed a dialog box will appear to overwrite the old database with the new one or choose a new name.

Access displays a blank Database window shown below, selects by default the Tables tab and enables all the buttons on the Database toolbar. The Database window acts as your 'home base' for all operations within the database and stores all database objects you create. Almost any action you perform in Access begins with a choice you make in the Database window.

IMPORTANCE OF DESIGN

Designing Databases

Before you use Microsoft Access to actually build the tables, forms, and other objects that will make up your database, it is important to take time to *design* your database. Good database design is the keystone to creating a database that does what you want it to do effectively, accurately, and efficiently.

Determine the purpose of your database

The first step in designing a database is to determine its purpose and how it's to be used. You need to know what information you want from the database. From that, you can determine what subjects you need to store facts about (the tables) and what facts you need to store about each subject (the fields in the tables).

Talk to people who will use the database. Brainstorm about the questions you and they would like the database to answer. Sketch out the reports you'd like it to produce. Gather the forms you currently use to record your data. Examine well-designed databases similar to the one you are designing.

Determine the tables you need

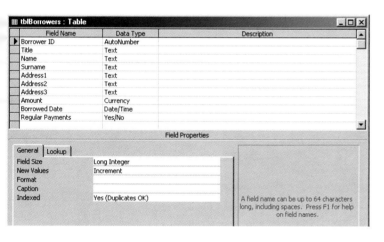

Determining the tables can be the trickiest step in the database design process. That's because the results you want from your database – the reports you want to print, the forms you want to use and the questions you want answered – don't necessarily provide clues about the structure of the tables that produce them.

You don't need to design your tables using Microsoft Access. In fact, it may be better to sketch out and rework your design on paper first. When you design your tables, divide up pieces of information by keeping these fundamental design principles in mind:

- A table should not contain duplicate information and information should not be duplicated between tables. In this respect, a table in a relational database differs from a table in an application such as a spreadsheet. When each piece of information is stored in only one table, you update it in one place. This is more efficient, and it also eliminates the possibility of duplicate entries that contain different information. For example, you would want to store each customer address and phone number only once, in one table.

- Each table should contain information about one subject. When each table contains facts about only one subject, you can maintain information about each subject independently from other subjects. For example, you would store customer addresses in a different table from the customers' orders, so that you could delete one order and still maintain the customer information.

Determine the fields you need

Each table contains information about the same subject, and each **field** in a table contains individual facts about the table's subject. For example, a customer table may include company name, address, city, and phone number fields. When sketching out the fields for each table, keep these tips in mind:

- Relate each field directly to the subject of the table.

- Include all the information you need.

- Store information in its smallest logical parts (for example, First Name and Last Name, rather than Name).

Borrower ID	Title	Name	Surname	Address1	Address2	
1	Mr	John	White	10 Acacia Aven	London	
2	Mr	John	Holt	34 Dorset Squa	London	
3	Miss	Myra	Arendt	98 Wall Street	London	

Refine your design

After you have designed the tables and fields you need, it's time to study the design and detect any flaws that might remain. It is easier to change your database design now than it will be after you have filled the tables with data.

- Use Microsoft Access to create your tables and enter enough sample data in your tables so you can test your design. Create rough drafts of your forms and reports and see if they show the data you expect. Look for unnecessary duplications of data and if you find problems, refine the design.

- Enter data and create other database objects

When you are satisfied that the table structure meets the design principles described here, then it's time to go ahead and add all the data to the tables.

WORKING WITH TABLES

There are several ways to add a new table to an Access database. These include using a wizard to assist you with the design process, designing the table from scratch, building the table from a spreadsheet-like datasheet, importing the table from another source, and linking to an external table.

Select the New button in the database window.

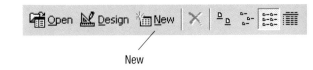

New

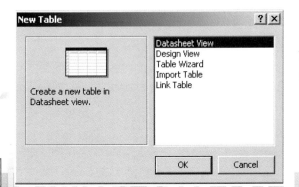

The New Table dialog box enables you to select the method you wish to employ to create your new table.

Datasheet View creates a blank datasheet view ready for data insertion, the table contains no formatting at this stage, however, by clicking Design view field headings and sizes etc can be added.

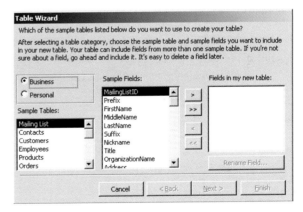

Field1	Field2	Field3	Field4	Field5	Field6

Design View allows you to format the table from the specified database design before data entry takes place.

Table Wizard displays a series of dialog boxes, which create tables depending upon your selection. On completion of the process the tables will be created.

Import Table this wizard imports tables and objects from an external file into the current database.

Link Table this wizard creates tables in the current database that are linked to tables in an external file.

Designing a Table from Scratch

Designing tables from scratch is a method of creating a table that offers flexibility while encouraging good design principles. Select the Design View option from the New Table dialog box. The Table Design view window will appear.

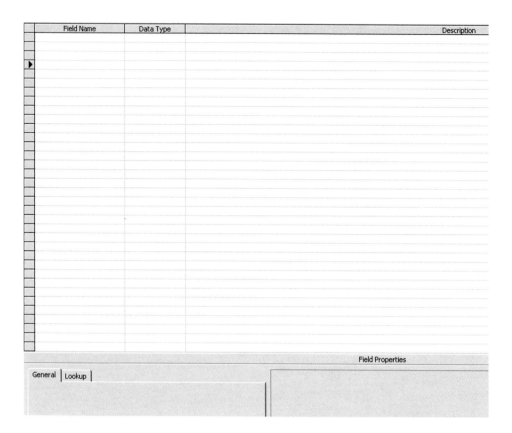

Field Name	Data Type	Description

Field Properties

General | Lookup |

Define each field in the table by typing the name of the field in the Field Name column.

- Field names must be unique and can be up to 64 characters long. For practical reasons, you should try to limit them to 10 – 15 characters, enough to describe the field without making the name difficult to type.

- Field names can include any combination of letters, numbers, spaces, and other certain punctuation marks, but they must exclude full stops, exclamation marks, accents, and square brackets. Spaces in field names cause inconvenience when you are building queries, modules, and other database objects and should therefore, if possible, be avoided.

- Field names cannot begin with a leading space.

- Try not to duplicate property names or the names of other Access objects when naming your fields. In some circumstances, you may get unpredictable results.

Tab to the Data Type column. Select the default field type, text, or use the drop-down box to select another field type. You can find details on which field type is appropriate for your data in the section 'Selecting Appropriate Field Types for Your Data.' (See page 95)

Tab to the Description column. What you type in this column appears on the status bar Mr, Miss, Mrs, Dr when the user is entering data into the field. This column is also useful for documenting what data is actually stored in the field. Entries in the Description column are optional.

You can change a field name by placing the insertion point over an existing field name and entering a new name for that field.

Selecting Appropriate Field Types for Your Data

The data type you select for each field can greatly affect the performance and functionality of your database. Several factors should influence your choice of data type for each field in your table:

- The type of data that is stored in the field
  The type of data you need to store in a field has the biggest influence on the data type you select. For example, if you need to store numbers that begin with leading zeros, you cannot select a Number field because leading zeros entered into a Number field are ignored. This factor is a consideration for data such as phone numbers and department codes.

- Whether the contents of the field need to be included in calculations
  If the contents of a field need to be included in calculations, you must select a Number or Currency data type. You cannot perform calculations on the contents of fields defined with the other data types. The exception to this rule are date fields, which can be included in date/time calculations.

- Whether you need to sort the data within the field and the way you want to sort it
  It is important to consider whether you need to sort or index the data within a field. Memo and OLE fields cannot be sorted; do not select these field types if the data within the field must be sorted or indexed. Furthermore, you must consider the way you want the data to be sorted. For example, within a Text field a set of numbers would be sorted in the order in which they appear (i.e., 1, 10, 100, 2, 20, 200). On the other hand, within a Number or Currency field the numbers would be sorted naturally (i.e., 1, 2, 10, 20, 100, 200).

The field types available in Access are summarised in the table below, including information on the proper uses for each field type and the amount of storage space occupied by each type.

FIELD TYPE	APPROPRIATE USES	STORAGE SPACE
Text	Data containing text, combination of text and numbers, or numbers that do not need to be included in calculations; examples are names, addresses, department codes and phone numbers.	Based on what is actually stored in the field; ranges from 0 to 255 bytes
Memo	Text and numeric strings up to 32,000 (64K) long; examples are notes, synopses and descriptions.	Ranges from 0 to 64,000 bytes
Number	Any numeric data (other than currency) on which you are likely to perform calculations. You can include whole numbers or fractional values (using decimals) and negative values can be preceded with a minus sign or placed in brackets; examples are ages, quantities, exam results or payment methods.	1, 2, 4, or 8 bytes, depending on the field size selected
Date/Time	Includes automatic validation of entries (you cannot enter invalid dates or times like, for example, **31/02/94** or **17:30AM**), allows you to perform calculations (for example, subtracting one date field from another gives the number of days between them); examples are date ordered, birth date.	8 bytes
Currency	Any numeric data that represents monetary values, includes by default 2 digits after the decimal point and displays the currency symbol as set in the Windows Control Panel; examples are amount due, price.	8 bytes

FIELD TYPE	APPROPRIATE USES	STORAGE SPACE
AutoNumber	Automatically inserted unique sequential values for each record, which can be used as a *Primary Key* because of their uniqueness. If a record is deleted, the remaining records are not renumbered; examples are invoice numbers, project numbers, Customer ID.	4 bytes (16 bytes for replication ID)
Yes/No	Logical fields containing either of two conditions that are mutually exclusive (yes/no, true/false, on/off or a Boolean entry such as -1 for yes and 0 for no); examples are paid, tenured, passed, available.	1 bit
OLE Object	Any objects created in other Windows applications (pictures, graphics, documents, spreadsheets, sound and video) can be *linked* to or *embedded* in an Access database using this data type field. In Datasheet View Access displays only information about the *type* of the OLE object; viewed through a Form, you can see either the actual linked or embedded object itself, or its representation; examples are employee reviews or employee photos.	0 bytes to 1 gigabyte depending on what is stored within the field
Hyperlink	Text or combinations of text and numbers stored as text and used as a hyperlink address. A hyperlink address can have up to three parts: *display text*: the text that appears in a field or control, *address*: the path to a file or page (URL), sub address: a location within the file or page. The easiest way to insert a hyperlink address in a field or control is to click Hyperlink on the Insert menu. A hyperlink address may also contain more specific address information (for example, a database object, Word bookmark, or Microsoft Excel cell range that the address points to). When you click a hyperlink, your Web browser or Microsoft Access uses the hyperlink address to go to the specified destination.	
Lookup Wizard	Creates a field that allows you to choose a value from another table or from a list of values by using a list box or combo box. Clicking this option starts the Lookup Wizard, which creates a Lookup field. After you complete the wizard, Microsoft Access sets the data type and storage space based on the values selected in the wizard.	

TASK

You are required to set up a database to keep a record of students' progress in their assignments. Students' progress is recorded as **Yes** for assignment passed, **Refer** for assignment failed and **No** for assignment not attempted.

Sketch a database plan that will hold the following data:

Candidate Number; Surname; Forename; Gender; Group; Word Processing; Spreadsheet; Database

Indicate on the sketch suitable field types for the new database.

Create a new database and save with the name **Assignments**. Create a new table using Design view following your planned database sketch.

SETTING FIELD PROPERTIES

Each field type contains a set of properties you can use to specify how you want data stored, handled, and displayed. You set the properties in the bottom part of the Table window's Design view. The data type you select for the field determines the properties you can set for each field.

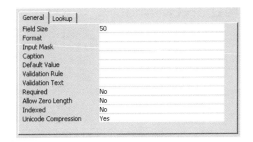

1   In the table's Design view, select the field whose properties you want to set.

2   Click the property you want to set in the bottom part of the window.

3   Set the property, as explained below.

Size Property

The first property is Size. It is available for Text and Number fields only, setting the maximum length of a Text field and limiting the allowable values in a Number field. For Text fields, a small size improves performance; for Number fields, a small size means lower storage requirements and faster performance. If you reduce the size of this property at a later time, data could be lost: text data may become truncated and numeric data may lose precision or, in extreme cases, can be converted to empty fields.

DATA TYPE	SIZE OPTION	DESCRIPTION
Text	0 – 255	Any number from 0 to 255 can be specified for the length of the field. The default is 50
Number	Byte	Stores integer numbers (no fractions) from 0 to 255. Occupies 1 byte
	Integer	Stores integer numbers (no fractions) from –32,768 to 32,767. Occupies 2 bytes
	Long Integer	Stores numbers (no fractions) from -2,147,483,648 to 2,147,483,647. Occupies 4 bytes
	Single	Stores numbers with 6 digits of precision from -3.402823E38 to 3.402823E38. Occupies 6 bytes
	Double	The default. Stores numbers with 10 digits of precision from -1.79769313486232E308 to 1.79769313486232E308. Occupies 8 bytes.
	Replication ID	A unique number for the purposes of identifying a record when a database is replicated. Occupies 16 bytes

Format Property

The Format property is available for all but OLE Object fields and it allows you to specify how Access displays your data. You can select from predefined formats or create your own custom formats. The formats available differ depending on the data type of the field.

Text and Memo

There are no pre-set formats to choose from but you may type your own. The following table shows an example of possible format settings:

FORMAT	EXPLANATION	EXAMPLE
@	Text character (character or space) required	
&	Text character not required	
>	Forces all characters to be upper case	➢ smith displays as SMITH
<	Forces all characters to be lower case	➢ Smith or SMITH displays as smith
@>	First character must be a text character or a space and the entire field will display in upper case	➢ smith displays as SMITH ➢ *jones would be disallowed as the asterisk is not a text character ➢ sMITH displays as SMITH ➢ 293a displays as 293A
@;;'N/A'	Text entries must begin with a text character, zero length entries display blank. N/A is displayed if the field is left completely empty	➢ a skipped entry would display N/A
@@/@-@	If four characters are entered, the other two literals are automatically placed in the field	➢ 12GX displays as 12/G-X

Number and Currency

The following table shows some of the pre-set format options available:

FORMAT	EXPLANATION	EXAMPLE
General Number	The default. The number is displayed as entered	➢ 28765.386 displays as 28765.386
Currency	Follows the pre-set Windows default: inserts a currency symbol, a thousands separator and a decimal point and rounds the number to two decimal places	➢ 28765.386 displays as £28,765.39
Fixed	Fixed number of digits with no currency symbols or comma separators (default is two decimal places)	➢ 28765.386 displays as 28765.39
Standard	Fixed number of digits with no currency symbols but *with* comma separators (default is two decimal places)	➢ 28765.386 displays as 28,765.39
Percent	Multiplies the value by 100 and appends the % symbol. (Default is 2 decimal places)	➢ 0.5672 displays as 56.72%
Scientific	Forces exponential scientific notation with one digit displayed to the left of the decimal point	➢ 28765.386 displays as 2.88E+04

Tip

Decimal precision can be governed using the Decimal Places property

98

Date and Time

Clicking on the drop-down box in the Format property cell displays the available pre-set formats; they all correspond to the relevant settings in the International section of the Windows Control Panel.

FORMAT	EXPLANATION	EXAMPLE
General Date	The default. If the value is date only, no time is displayed; if the value is time only, no date is displayed	6/10/94 9:30:00 AM 6/10/94 9:30:00 AM
Long Date	Same as the Long Date setting in the International section of the Windows Control Panel	Thursday, October 6, 1994
Medium Date		06-Oct-94
Short Date	Same as the Short Date setting in the International section of the Windows Control Panel.	06/10/94
Long Time	Same as the Long Time setting in the International section of the Windows Control Panel	09:30:00 AM
Medium Time		09:30 AM
Short Time	Same as the Short Time setting in the International section of the Windows Control Panel	9:30 ('Military Time')

Tip

The Short Date setting assumes that dates between 1/1/00 and 31/12/29 are 21st century dates (that is, the years are between 2000 and 2029). Dates between 1/1/30 and 31/12/99 are assumed to be 20th century dates (that is, the years are between 1930 and 1999).

Yes/No

Clicking on the list box in the Format property cell displays three available pre-set formats: Yes/No, True/False and On/Off. (Data entered in this field is actually stored by Access with a Boolean value of 0 for No and -1 for Yes, but it is displayed according to the formatting you choose.)

Decimal Places Property

Specifies the number of digits that appear to the right of the decimal point in the display of numbers. This setting overrides the Format property setting, but if no entry is made here, Access sets the number of decimal places in the Format property setting. Note that this property has no effect if the Format property is set to General Number.

Input Mask Property

Sets controls as to how data elements entered in Text and Number fields appear and restricts entries to exact, user-defined formats, by employing various combinations of generic placeholders and literal characters (such as ? & / #) to arrive at specific display formats. When you employ an input mask, the user is always in overtype mode. This behaviour is a feature of the product and cannot be altered.

Input Mask Wizard

If you need to create a commonly-used input mask, such as a telephone number, driving licence, postcode or social security number, it is probably easiest to use the Input Mask Wizard (this works only with Text and Date/Time fields. Select the Input Mask you require from a pre-defined list and answer the remaining questions regarding how you wish the data to be stored.

Caption Property

Displayed in datasheets, forms and reports based on the table, the Caption property overrides the field name. If you don't enter any value in the Caption property, Access uses the name of the field as a label. Captions are typically used to provide more thorough explanations of fields to users in database applications and can include up to 255 characters.

It is important to set the Caption property for fields *before* you build any forms or reports that utilise the fields. When a form or report is produced, Access looks at the current caption. If the caption is added or modified at a later time, captions for that field on existing forms and reports are not modified.

Default Value Property

Specifies a default value for a field, which will be automatically placed in that field when a new record is added. For example, in a database of addresses you could specify *London* as the default value for the *City* field; this will appear automatically whenever a new record is added. You can leave this value unchanged or enter the name of another city. Default values can be set for all field types except OLE Object and AutoNumber fields. In Yes/No fields Access sets automatically the default value to *No*; you can change this to *Yes* if most of your records are likely to have a Yes value stored in this field.

Validation Rule and Validation Text Properties

The Validation Rule property defines an expression that is evaluated when existing data in the field is changed or new data is added. The new data is compared to the Validation Rule and if it conforms, Access allows you to include it in the field, but if for some reason it breaks the Validation Rule and does not satisfy the specified conditions, the Validation Text property, which specifies the text of the message that appears to warn and inform you that a violation occurred, comes into effect. A validation rule cannot be violated; the database engine strictly enforces it and unless it is satisfied, the record cannot be saved. Both these properties help to ensure that the data you enter is valid and maintains the integrity of your tables. If you create a validation rule for a field, Access does not allow null values to be entered in the field. This means that the field cannot be left blank.

If you set the Validation Rule property but not the Validation Text property, Access automatically displays a standard error message whenever the validation rule is violated. To display a custom message, you must enter something appropriate in the Validation Text property.

Required Property

Specifies whether data entry in a field is required with Yes or No options. If you choose the Yes setting for this property and try to add a record without making an entry in this field, Access will display a message box saying 'Field (FieldName) cannot be null' and if you set the Required Property to Yes in a table with data, Access will ask you whether you wish to ensure that the existing data meets the new condition. This property is useful for foreign key fields, where you want to ensure that data is entered into the field. It is also useful for any field that contains information that is required for business reasons (company name, for example).

Allow Zero Length Property

The Allow Zero Length property determines if a zero-length data entry is considered valid by Access, with *Yes* and *No* options and the latter as the default. By setting this property to *Yes* you can differentiate between unknown values (null value) and non-existent values (zero length values). During the data entry process zero-length settings are entered in fields by typing a set of double quotation marks (""). For example, you can enter two double quotation marks "" in a Mobile Phone Number field, to indicate that a contact does not have a mobile phone number, or leave it blank to indicate that a contact may have a mobile phone number but it is unknown.

Indexed Property

The Indexed property enables you to find and sort records using a single table field, which can hold either unique value ('*No Duplicates*') or non-unique value ('*Duplicates OK*') records. If the primary key is a single field, Access automatically sets this field to '*No Duplicates*'. You can create as many indexes as you wish. The indexes are created when you save the table design and are automatically updated when you change existing or add new records. You can add or delete indexes whenever you wish in Design View, but you cannot index Memo or OLE type fields.

You may want to index the fields you use repeatedly to search for data. However, be aware that indexes slow record updating and take up disk space.

You can create indexes based on a single field or on multiple fields. For example, you can index just on a Last Name field or on both the *Last Name* and the *First Name* fields. Multiple-field indexes enable you to distinguish records in which the first field may have the same value. Thus, instead of finding five records for *Smith*, you can find only one record for *Diane Smith*.

SETTING A PRIMARY KEY

Assigning a primary key to a field and thereby setting the main index for the table on that field gives you a unique way to identify every record in the table. Primary keys usually consist of a single field, but you can designate more than one field as a primary key or specify that a primary key be based on several fields. By default, records appear in ascending order based on the contents of the field assigned as the primary key (you can always change the order by sorting the table on any other field). Any unique identifier field can serve as primary key: ID numbers, sequential numbers, unique names, unique dates, etc. Although you do not need to use primary keys in Access, there are several advantages to doing so:

- The index created by Access on the primary key speeds up sorting and querying of the database and any other internal operations related to it.

- The existence of primary key enables you to establish relationships between tables in a relational database.

- Primary key reduces the possibility of accidental duplication of records: Access will prevent you from entering two records with the same primary key value.

To set a primary key for a field in Design View, select the field by highlighting its row and choose Edit, Primary Key or select the Primary Key button 🔑 on the toolbar. A primary key icon is added next to the selected field in the Row Selector column. To re-designate a primary key to another field, repeat this process selecting another

field. If you do not set a primary key during the table design stage, Access encourages you to do so when you save the table, displaying a dialog box asking if you wish to create a primary key. Choosing Yes automatically adds a sequentially numbered field called *ID* with the *AutoNumber* data type in your table and when you later add records to the table, Access automatically inserts sequential numbers as values in this field.

If you create a table without a primary key and later decide to add one in, you can do so easily by switching to Design view and going through the process outlined above. If the field you are trying to designate as a primary key contains duplicate values, Access will warn you of this fact by displaying an appropriate message on your screen. If this occurs, you must either designate a different field as the primary key or delete (or edit) the duplicate records before you can save the changes to the table's design.

SAVING A TABLE

To save the table, choose File, Save or click on the Save button 💾 on the toolbar. In all cases Access displays the Save As dialog box with the temporary name Table 1 or Table 2 or Table 3, etc. for your table. Enter a name for the table: table names can be up to 64 characters long and can include numbers and spaces but not square brackets or full stops, which are routinely used as parts of various other Access expressions.

It is advisable to devote some thought to the names you select for your tables. They should not be too long for convenience sake but should be sufficiently descriptive to define the tables and distinguish them from other tables in the database. Naturally, they should be unique from any other table names in your database but you should also bear in mind that they should be distinct from any query names which your database may already contain or which might be added to it in the future: a single database must not contain two tables or queries bearing identical names.

SWITCHING BETWEEN DESIGN AND DATASHEET VIEW

You may wish to switch between views to enable further changes to be made and viewed. Structural changes to the table need to be saved. Choose View, Design View or Datasheet View. Alternatively select the Datasheet button 🔲 or Design button 📐 on the toolbar.

> **TASK**
>
> **Using the table created from the sketch previously produced, enter suitable field properties. The sketch may need further amendment.**
>
> **Save the table with the name Assignment Log.**

WORKING WITH DATASHEETS

With the table design complete, you can now proceed with the task of adding data to the table. To open a table, click on the Table object in the Database window to display a list of all the available tables in the database and double-click on the name of the required table or select it and click the Open button. In Datasheet view Access displays multiple records in the familiar row and column format shown below (as opposed to displaying single records one at a time in a Form view), and you can use it to add new and edit existing records.

	Borrower ID	Title	Name	Surname	Address1	Address2	Address3
	1	Mr	John	White	10 Acacia Avenue	London	NW3 8GF
	2	Mr	John	Holt	34 Dorset Square	London	NW1 6SE
	3	Miss	Myra	Arendt	98 Wall Street	London	NW10 7FD
	4	Mr	Robert	Park	25 Eaton Rise	London	W8 7HF
	5	Mrs	Penny	Abbot	13 Baron Court	London	NW8 6HG
	6	Mr	Andrew	Green	56 Cherry Lane	Harrow	HA8 6CJ
	7	Mrs	Shirley	Jones	7 Grange Road	London	NW6 7DS
	8	Miss	Linda	Raven	234 Park Road	London	NW8 5HK
▶	9	Miss	Lisa	Mount	20 Blake Avenue	London	NW2 6DS
	10	Dr	Harvey	Wilde	28 Berry Close	London	N5 8JG
	11	Mr	Alan	Brown	12 Bentley Drive	London	NW10 8FG
	12	Mrs	Irene	Haber	132 Brook Green Road	London	NW2 5RJ
✳	(AutoNumber)						

tblBorrowers : Table

Record: 9 of 12

When a database has been fully designed, data will rarely be edited directly in the table; tables provided the least controlled environment for issues such as entry control or record viewing.

More likely the table's data will be edited via forms. During the design of a database, however, sample data might be entered and edited for testing purposes.

ADDING AND EDITING DATA

The following indicators show the current status in record entry: when you place the insertion point in a field of a *Blank Record*, its asterisk symbol changes to indicate that it is now the *Selected Record* and when you start entering data in it, the triangle symbol changes to indicate that it is now being *Edited* and the asterisk symbol moves to the next row. To enter new records choose Insert, New Record. Alternatively, select the New Record button on the toolbar. ▶✳

Currently Selected Record

Currently Edited Record

Blank (New) Record

Pressing the Tab key after data entry into a field moves the cursor to the next available field. As you reach the end of a row (record) pressing the Tab key will create a new blank record.

Once you have entered the details for a record, Access automatically saves the new record to the database. You do not have to save when you add, edit or delete records, Access handles this automatically.

Tip

If you type the new record over an existing record, the existing record details will be lost. You must always create a new blank record before entering the new record details

TASK

Open the Assignment Log table within the Assignment database.

Enter the data displayed in the tables below using the following code letters:

MON   for candidates in the Monday Group
FRI   for candidates in the Friday Group
F   for female candidates
M   for male candidates

Your table design may need further amending to ensure all data can be entered.

MONDAY GROUP

Candidate Number	Surname	Forename	Word Processing	Spreadsheet	Database
FEMALES					
176	MAPLES	FRANCES	YES	YES	YES
122	MARTIN	PAULINE	YES	YES	YES
155	TOWNSEND	MARLENE	REFER	YES	YES
169	KABOLE	MAUREEN	YES	NO	YES
197	MASTERS	CHRISTINE	YES	YES	NO
MALES					
142	SMITHSON	TERRY	NO	REFER	YES
82	WALKER	BRIAN	NO	NO	REFER
128	COTTON	ANTHONY	YES	YES	YES
162	BOLA	RAJINDER	NO	REFER	YES

FRIDAY GROUP

Candidate Number	Surname	Forename	Word Processing	Spreadsheet	Database
FEMALES					
103	JEFFREY	ANITA	YES	YES	NO
191	MYERS	ANNEKE	Refer	YES	YES
89	CAVE	LIZZIE	YES	YES	NO
MALES					
135	BROWN	CHARLES	YES	YES	NO
96	BRYANT	DAVID	YES	Refer	YES
184	BIERHOFF	FRANK	NO	YES	NO
148	CLIFTON	DAVID	YES	NO	YES
115	GERBER	DANIEL	YES	Refer	Refer

Data Editing Techniques

Access not only lets you make any changes you wish to specific cells, but it also enables you to use general Windows cut-and-paste techniques and keyboard shortcuts to move large amounts of data within the same table or between different tables.

If you are working with a field containing a large amount of text (like a Memo field), you can view and edit the text more conveniently by opening the Zoom box: whilst the insertion point is in the field you wish to edit select the Zoom command from the shortcut menu by clicking on the right mouse button.

To minimise repetitive data entry use the keyboard shortcut: Ctrl+ " (the ditto key). Remember the general Windows rule that typing always replaces selection: if a word or an entire field is highlighted, typing will automatically delete and replace the selection.

Record: |◄| |◄| | 1 |►| |►I| |►*| of 1

You can navigate in a table with your mouse by clicking on the vertical and horizontal scroll bars, boxes and arrows. The navigation buttons in the lower left hand corner of the table window will enable you to move quickly to the First, Last, Next, Previous and New records.

Undoing Data Entries

As long as you have not moved the insertion point from the Currently Edited record, you can undo any changes you made to it by choosing Edit, Undo Current Record. After you have moved the insertion point to another record, you cannot undo the changes by using the above option, but you can use the general Undo option by clicking on the Undo button. ↺

This option reverses the last action you have performed, whether it is editing records, cut and paste operation or deletion.

Deleting Records

To delete a record, position the cursor on the record you want to delete and choose Edit, Delete Record. You can also select several sequential records by dragging your mouse pointer over their record selector buttons. If you wish to select ALL the records in the datasheet choose Edit, Select All. Access prompts you to confirm the deletion with the following dialog box:

TASK

Save the structural changes to the Assignment Log table.

CLOSING THE DATABASE

If you wish to remove the database from the screen, you need to close it. If you wish to keep the file on your computer, you must save any structural changes made to the database.

Choose File, Close.

CLOSING THE DATABASE SOFTWARE

If you wish to close down the application, you need to exit out of it. Choose File, Exit. Alternatively, click on the cross in the top right-hand corner. ✖

OPENING AN EXISTING DATABASE

Click Start, Programs, Microsoft Access or select the shortcut on the desktop (if available).

Select Open an existing file and click OK.

Navigate to the folder or drive where the file is saved, select the file and click Open or double-click the file to open the database.

If you have the database application open and wish to open the database, choose File, Open or select the Open button on the toolbar.

Navigate to the folder or drive where the file is saved, select the required file and click Open or double-click the file to open the database.

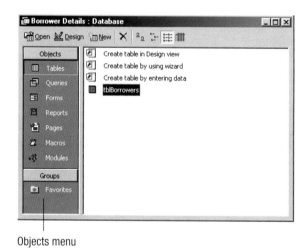

Objects menu

Access displays the Database; lists all the objects contained in it under the relevant categories (objects), selects by default the Tables objects and enables all the buttons on the toolbar. The Database window acts as the 'home base' for all operations within the database and stores all database objects you create. Almost any action you perform in Access begins with a choice you make in the Database window.

TASK

Close the Assignment Log table and the Assignment database. Open the Assignment database.

CUSTOMISING THE DATA DISPLAY

As you work with your data in a datasheet, you may wish to alter the default layout of the table to facilitate the type of work you do or the task you want to perform. Access allows you to make many such changes: you can rearrange the order of the fields by moving the locations of the columns, increase or decrease column widths and row heights, change the fonts and the point sizes used for data display and much more.

Any changes you make to a table's layout will apply only to the current session. However, when you close the table, Access asks you whether you wish to make these changes permanent by saving the new table's layout. If you answer Yes, the next time you open the table the changes you have made will be in effect.

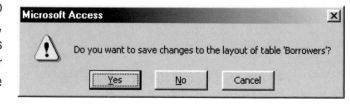

Rearranging the Fields Order

The original display of fields in a datasheet matches the order in which they were saved in the table design stage. You may wish to rearrange this order to match specific data entry requirements. To rearrange a table's fields:

- Select the field(s) you wish to move by clicking on the field selector(s) (you can select several fields that are adjacent to each other by dragging the mouse pointer over their selectors).

- Place the pointer over the field selector, click and hold the left mouse button. As you do this, the pointer assumes the rectangular base of the drag-and-drop symbol and a heavy vertical bar appears to the left of the selected column(s).

- Drag the pointer to the desired new location (as you drag it, the vertical bar moves along with it) and release the mouse button. The column(s) will drop into the new location.

Changing the Column Widths

You can change the column width with the mouse:

Position the mouse pointer over the right edge of the field selector for the desired field, where it assumes the shape of a horizontal double-headed arrow with a thick vertical bar down the centre, hold down the left mouse button, drag the column edge to the desired location and release the mouse button. The width of the column will change accordingly.

Or you can change the width of a single column or several columns using menu commands:

- Select the column whose width you wish to change by clicking on its field selector (you can select several columns that are adjacent to each other by dragging the mouse pointer over their field selectors).

- Choose Format, Column Width and enter the desired value in the dialog box that appears. Alternatively, you can also select the Standard Width option or the Best Fit option, which will set the column width to accommodate the longest text entry within that column in the entire table.

Address1
10 Acacia Avenue
34 Dorset Square
98 Wall Street
25 Eaton Rise
13 Baron Court
56 Cherry Lane
7 Grange Road
234 Park Road
20 Blake Avenue
28 Berry Close
12 Bentley Drive
132 Brook Green Road

Changing the Row Heights

You can change the row height with the mouse:

Position the mouse pointer in the record selector area over any line separating two records, where it assumes the shape of a vertical double-headed arrow with a thick horizontal bar down the centre, hold down the left mouse button, drag the pointer to the desired location and release the mouse button. This changes the height of all the rows in the table. It is not possible to alter the height of an individual row.

You can also change the row height using menu commands:

Choose Format, Row Height and enter the desired value in the dialog box that appears. Alternatively, you can also select the Standard Height option.

Changing the Fonts

You can change the font, its appearance and the point size Access uses for data display by choosing Format, Font. Click in the dialog box that appears on your screen on the desired font in the Font list box to select it, choose a style in the Font Style box (the default is Regular; other options include Bold, Italic and Bold Italic) and select the desired size in the Size list box. Changes in fonts and point sizes can make major differences in legibility, usually at the expense of how many records will be viewed in the database window.

Hiding and Showing Columns

You can hide one or more columns in datasheet view:

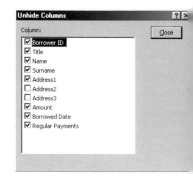

- Select the column you wish to hide by clicking on its field selector (you can select several columns that are adjacent to each other by dragging the mouse pointer over their field selectors).

- Choose Format, Hide Columns.

- To reveal columns you have hidden previously, choose Format, Unhide Columns and click on the columns you wish to reveal.

The ability of Access to hide required columns can be of value if you wish to generate a quick Report which will include the precise data you want, without the necessity of originating custom reports or queries. Bear in mind, however, that by using this method there is a danger of perpetuating certain changes to a table's layout, which you may not remember to undo in the future and which, in turn, can cause confusion and loss of data, especially if you are sharing the database with other users. A much better long-term solution is to design and save a specific query, which will provide you with the required fields and records and then design a report based on this query.

Freezing Columns

If you wish to keep certain fields in constant display whilst scrolling the table window left and right, hiding certain columns can be a partial answer. A much better solution to avoid losing the view of the extreme left columns (which often contain the most critical data, such as names or record numbers) when scrolling to the right of the window, is to freeze columns, so that they remain in place. To freeze a column or columns:

- Select the column you wish to freeze by clicking on its field selector (you can select several columns that are adjacent to each other by dragging the mouse pointer over their field selectors).

- Choose Format, Freeze Columns and the selected column(s) will become frozen. Whilst columns are frozen, a thicker dividing line appears between the last frozen column and the rest of the table. Also, if the column you freeze is not the first column in the table, Access will automatically re-locate it to appear at the extreme left.

- To unfreeze columns you have previously frozen, choose Format, Unfreeze All Columns. If the column you have frozen was not the first in the table and Access has automatically relocated it to appear at the extreme left, you will need to reposition it manually to its previous location.

TASK

Ensure that all the data within the Assignment Log table is clearly visible. Save the changes.

SORTING DATA

Access sorts data contained in different types of fields in different ways:

Text fields – can be sorted alphabetically in *Ascending Order* (from A to Z) or in *Descending Order* (from Z to A).
Number fields – can be sorted numerically in *Ascending Order* (from lowest to highest) or in *Descending Order* (from highest to lowest).
Date/Time fields can be sorted chronologically in *Ascending Order* (from earliest to latest) or in *Descending Order* (from latest to earliest).

To conduct a sort based on a single field, place the insertion point anywhere in the field you wish to use as the basis for your sort (you can also select the field by clicking with your mouse pointer over the field selector) and, depending on the sort direction you wish to effect, choose Records, Sort/Ascending or Records, Sort/Descending. Alternatively click on the Sort Ascending or Sort Descending buttons on the toolbar.

Sort Ascending   Sort Descending

Sorted data is not saved. When you close the table, the records are returned to their original order.

FINDING AND REPLACING DATA

Part of the editing process is finding the data you need to edit. Choose Edit, Find or click on the Find button on the toolbar to display the Find and Replace dialog box.

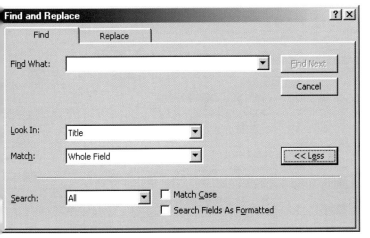

Here you can specify any text you wish to find and your search can be further refined by the following options:

Find What	Here you enter the string of text you wish Access to find. You can use wild-card characters to make the search more general: entering *Wil** will find all occurrences of William, Wilkins, Williams, Williamson, Willis, etc.
Match	Clicking on the drop-down arrow displays a list of all possible search locations, with the following options: Any Part of Field – searches for any occurrence of the text string: searching for col will find Coleman, Malcolm and protocol. The Whole Field option – recognises a match only if the searched-for string matches the entire contents of the field and the Start of the Field option – will search for the text string at the beginning of the field only (e.g., searching for *col* will find Coleman but not Malcolm or protocol).

Look In	Selecting this option will cause the search to be conducted only in the current field. Deselecting it will conduct the search in the entire datasheet.
Match Case	Select this option only if you wish Access to search for the text string exactly as you typed it in the Find What section. For example, searching for *Road* will find all occurrences of *Road* but not *ROAD* or *road*.
Search Fields As Formatted	Select this option if you wish to find data based on its display format. For **As Formatted** example, although dates in a database are stored as date/time values, they may be displayed in a particular format, such as *19 Jan 45*. To search for records in September of the year 1963, you could turn on this option and specify **Sep 63*.

Access also enables you to search for specific text strings and replace them with other strings. The strings can include a phrase, a word or part of a word and as with the Find command, you can include wildcard characters to make the search more general. Clicking on the Find Next button finds the first and any subsequent occurrences of the searched-for text. Clicking on the Replace button replaces the found text with the text in the Replace With box, clicking again on the Find Next button finds the next occurrence of the search text without replacing the previously found occurrence and clicking on the Replace All button replaces all the occurrences of the searched for text without confirmation.

FILTERING DATA

The Find option allows you to look in turn at each record that meets your find criteria. This does not, however, isolate the records. To do this you need to create a *filter*, which includes only the records you wish to isolate. This can be performed using three different options: Filter by Selection, Filter Excluding Selection and Filter by Form.

Filter by Selection

This allows you to group together all records which match the value of the currently selected field.

- Click inside the field you wish to filter by or in a record containing the value you wish to filter by.

- Choose Records, Filter by Selection or click the Filter by Selection button .

- Only those records matching the value of the field or the record under the cursor will be displayed.

- To view all the records again, choose Records, Remove Filter/Sort or click the Remove Filter button .

Filter Excluding Selection

Sometimes you need to find all records *except* those that match your current selection.

- Click inside the field you do not wish to filter by or in a record containing the value you do not wish to filter by.

- Choose Records, Filter, Filter Excluding Selection.

- To view all the records again, choose Records, Remove Filter/Sort or click the Remove Filter button .

Filter by Form

When you wish to filter your data with several find criteria.

- Choose Records, Filter, Filter by Form or click on the ⊞ Filter by Form button.

- Access displays the Filter by Form window:

- Select the filter criteria in the combo boxes that appear in each field and click the Apply Filter button ▽ .

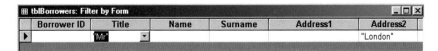

PRINTING RECORDS

It is possible to print all of the records in a table (not often required) and a query or to print a subset (selected) records in a table.

Select one or more sequential records, choose File, Print, Selected Records and click OK. To print all records, choose File, Print, All and click OK.

CREATING A BASIC FORM FOR DATA ENTRY

Forms often resemble paper-based documents. You can use a form to edit or view information within your database, or input information with relative ease. Forms can be used to enter, change or view data. Forms are considered to be a more user-friendly method of entering data into a database, thereby improving the way in which data is displayed on the screen.

Type of forms available are:

Design View – Design a form from scratch.
Form Wizard – Automatically creates a form based on the fields selected.
AutoForm: Columnar – Creates a columnar form with all the field labels appearing in the first column and the data in the second. The form displays one record at a time.
AutoForm: Tabular – Tabulates a screen full of records in tabular form with the field labels appearing at the head of each column.
AutoForm: Datasheet – Similar to tabular form, but displayed in datasheet display format.
Chart Wizard – Displays data graphically.
PivotTable Wizard – Creates a form with an Excel PivotTable – an interactive table that can summarise a large amount of data using the format and calculation methods specified by the user.

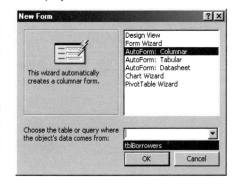

Click Forms from the objects menu in the database window and click New. The New Form dialog box will be displayed, select AutoForm: Columnar or Tabular, select the desired table from where the objects data is to be used from the drop-down box. Click OK to confirm.

Adding Records with a Form

Use the New Record button at the bottom of the form to create a new record and then type in the details for the record, using Tab or Enter to move to the next field. When adding records into a form Access automatically adds them to the table from which the form was created.

TASK

Using the Assignment Log table:

Sort the data into alphabetical order of surname and print all the information. Brian Walker has moved out of the district. Delete his record.

Create a basic form using AutoForm: Columnar. A female student has accidentally been missed off the original information for the Friday Group, add the students' details: Janet Green, candidate number 11 and she has passed all of the assignments. Mistakes were made when entering the information for Anneke Myers and Anthony Cotton. Anneke has not attempted the Database assignment but has completed the Word Processing assignment. Anthony's surname has been spelt incorrectly – it should be Colton.

Save the changes and print all the records in the table.

CREATING A BASIC QUERY

A query is a question asked of the database, for example, who lives in a particular town or which people were born before a certain date? The resulting information from the querying database can be sorted, specific fields can be selected and the query can be saved.

There are two types of query: Select and Action queries. Many different variations of these queries can be created. In this book we only cover select queries.

Select queries are those in which the data resulting from the query is viewed. The select query is the most common.
Action queries are different from select queries in that they perform an operation, which will make permanent changes to the database.

Wildcards

You use wildcard characters when you are specifying a value that you want to find:

● where you know only part of the value

● which contains a specific character or matches a certain pattern

Character	Example	Resulting in records with
*	Wil*	Willis, Williams, William, Wilkins
Any group of characters in the specified position	L*ng	Lang, Long, Living, Lending, Leasing
	col*r	color, colour, collar
?	Sm?th	Smith, Smyth
Any single character in the specified position		
[ ]	Rom[ea]	Rome, Roma **but not** Romo, Romp, etc.
Exact matches to any single characters in brackets	Pa[sr]t	Past, Part **but not** Pant, Palt, Pact, etc.
!	Rom[!ea]	Romo, Romp, etc. *but not* Rome or Roma
Exact matches to all characters apart from any of those specified in brackets	Pa[!sr]t	Pant, Palt, Pact, etc. *but not* Past or Part
#	#1	11, 21, 31, 41, 51, 61, 71, 81, 91
Any single digit in the specified position	#th	4th, 5th, 6th, 7th, 8th, 9th, 10th, etc.
	3#	3D, 31 (*in a date*)

Selection Criteria (expressions)

Criteria is entered in the criteria box in query design view for the required field. See table for details:

OPERATOR	EXAMPLE	RESULTING IN RECORDS WITH
= or " "	Smith	Smith in the field
Equal to (exact match)	"Smith"	
	=Smith	
	="Smith"	
<	<20,000	Any value lower than 19,999
Less than a numeric value,	<1/1/94	Any date prior to 01/01/1994
a date or a character	<"M"	Text with first letter between A and L
<=	<=15	Any value lower than or equal to 15
Less than or equal to	<=1/1/94	Any date prior to or including 01/01/1994
	<="M"	Text with first letter between A and M
>	>0	Any value greater than 0
Greater than a numeric value,	>#1/1/94#	Any date after 1/1/1994
a date or a character	>"M"	Text with first letter between N and Z
>=	>25	Any value greater than or equal to 25
Greater than or equal to	>#1/1/94#	Any date after or including 01/01/1994
	>"M"	Text with first letter between M and Z
<>or not	<>1994	Any year apart from 1994
Not equal to	not London	Any city other than London
between... and...	between 10 and 20	Any value between and including 10 and 20
A range between two values	between #1/1/94#	Any date between and including 1/1/1994 and
	and #30/6/94#	30/6/1994
Null	is Null	No values listed
No characters in the field		
Not Null	is not Null	Any values listed
Any characters in the field		
Like " "	Like "A*"	Any text starting with the letter A
Exact matches according to	Like "Joh*"	John, Johnson, Johanson, Johanssen, Johns
the specification	Like "[A-M]*"	Any text starting with any letter between A and M

Creating a Query

Select the Queries button from the objects menu in the database window, double-click Create Query in Design View. The Show Table dialog box will be displayed, click on the table you wish to use, click Add and then Close.

To enter field names individually: click on the field name of the required field and drag down into the first field box available or double-click on the field name required and it will automatically be placed in the first available field box. Continue this procedure until all the desired fields are placed into the query.

To enter all the fields from a table: double-click on the table name to select all fields. Drag the highlighted names to the Field row in the grid.

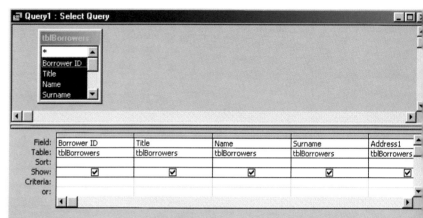

Adding Criteria (expressions) and Wildcards

Search requests need to be placed in the Criteria row. Use the information contained within the tables to specify the criteria.

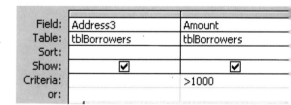

Switching between Design and Datasheet view

You may wish to switch between views to enable further changes to be made and viewed. Choose View, Design View or Datasheet View. Alternatively select the Datasheet button 🔲 or Design button 🖊 on the toolbar.

Saving a Query

To save the query, choose File, Save or click on the Save button 💾 on the toolbar. In all cases Access displays the Save As dialog box with the temporary name, this can be accepted or an alternative used.

TASK

Search the database for all of the male candidates who have not yet attempted the Word Processing assignment. Print the results.

Save the file with any changes made and exit the application.

BACKING UP A DATABASE

Just like with any other files that you work with on your computer, it is always a good idea to create and maintain backup copies of your databases. This way, if the original files are lost or damaged, you can restore them from the backup copy. At its simplest, backing up a database file might mean copying it to another location on your system (a tape drive, a different folder on your hard disk, or another computer on your network). You can also back up files to floppy disks, Zip disks or CD-ROMs. The frequency of your backup procedures will depend largely on the amount of work you perform on your database. If you work with your database frequently, changing and updating records or adding new records, a daily backup would certainly be advisable. Otherwise, a weekly backup might suffice.

To backup the database a copy of it can be created using Windows Explorer and then renamed to display the file name, date and time and an indication that it is a backup.

For example, **Borrowers 14-06-02 10-29am backup.mdb**

ADDITIONAL EXERCISE QUESTIONS

MUSIC RECORDS

1   Start a database application and create a new database file, which will contain information about a stock of musical records. Use the following field names (which can be abbreviated, if you wish) and code letters (where appropriate):

ARTIST
TITLE
STYLE: *PO*   POP
                    EL   EASY LISTENING
                    CL   CLASSICAL
                    RO   ROCK
RECORDING COMPANY
TYPE: *LP*   LONG-PLAYING RECORD
                    CD   COMPACT DISC
NUMBER IN STOCK

2   Enter the following data:

ARTIST	TITLE	RECORDING COMPANY	TYPE	NUMBER IN STOCK
POP				
John Dalton	Heaven	Delta	Long Play	4
Karen Green	Bournemouth	Golding	Compact disc	2
Harder	Better than planned	Rowlands	Long Play	5
Dylan	Imagination	DIP	Compact disc	10
Precious Stones	Meadows of the mind	Capps	Compact disc	3
Katie Denning	Love lasts	DIP	Long Play	4

115

ARTIST	TITLE	RECORDING COMPANY	TYPE	NUMBER IN STOCK
EASY LISTENING				
Donna Kingston	In Concert Vol. 2	Preston	Long Play	5
John Dowl	Bridges	Fellows	Long Play	6
Kevin Denton	Awakening	Arizon	Compact disc	8
CLASSICAL				
Elpov	Violin Concerto	CBH	Long Play	6
Rachanock	Piano Concerto	Benna	Long Play	4
Haven	Symphony No. 42	Benna	Long Play	3
ROCK				
Iron Girder	Traces	DIP	Long Play	5
Dark Trails	Rock around	Verity	Compact disc	4
Hard Rock	The Best Of	Harvey	Compact disc	8
Dan Vandenburg	Vandenburgs Lot	Atlantas	Long Play	7

Make sure the correct CODE LETTERS are used for the TYPE and STYLE.

3 Save the database and print all the information in table format.

4 The title Bournemouth by Karen Green has been withdrawn; delete this record from the database.

5 One copy of Rock around by Dark Trails has been sold; amend this number in stock accordingly.

6 A new POP record is now being stocked; add it to the list: The Ham – Snip – Preston – Compact disc – 8.

7 Sort the database into alphabetical order by TITLE and print a copy showing all the fields.

8 Find all the records with 4 or fewer copies in stock and print them out showing all the fields.

9 Find all the LONG PLAYING records published by DIP and print them out showing the ARTIST, TITLE and STYLE fields only.

10 Save the file and exit the application in the correct sequence with the data secure.

DATABASES
e-Quals

ADDITIONAL EXERCISE QUESTIONS

PERSONNEL

You work in the Personnel Office of Parfitt Designs. The company has decided to computerise its personnel records and you have been requested to set up and maintain a database and provide information to the Personnel Manager.

1 Create two new folders called DATABASE and BACKUP.

2 Start a database application software.

3 Create a new database called COMPANY and save it in the folder called DATABASE.

4 Create a table structure for employees as shown below.

Field Name	Data Type	Field Length
CODE	Numeric/integer	
SURNAME	Text	20
FIRSTNAME	Text	20
POSITION	Text	30
DEPARTMENT	Text	25
STARTDATE	Date	

5 Enter the following records.

CODE	SURNAME	FIRSTNAME	POSITION	DEPARTMENT	STARTDATE
178	Wilson	Sally	Manager	Sales	01/11/96
234	Thomas	Judith	Supervisor	Computing	01/01/92
105	Crosby	Chris	Programmer	Computing	21/10/88
76	Stevens	Brian	Clerk	Sales	05/05/92
69	Johnson	Martin	Clerk	Sales	23/10/97
26	Michaloski	James	Manager	Finance	18/03/88
182	Godwin	Jane	Programmer	Computing	10/10/81
156	Cordwaller	Roger	Clerk	Finance	06/07/88
129	Martyns	George	Manager	Sales	01/04/93
130	Baldwin	James	Programmer	Computing	10/11/94
166	Gotar	Shrewti	Clerk	Sales	25/09/95
45	Walters	Robin	Clerk	Finance	13/02/00
29	Atkinson	Natalie	Programmer	Computing	20/04/98

6 Print out all the records in the database.

7 Search for all employees who work in the SALES department and print out all the records that meet this condition.

8 Add a field named SALARY to the record structure. This field should be currency, 2 decimal places.

9 Enter the data from the table on the next page in the SALARY field.

CODE	SALARY
178	£20000.50
234	£18500.75
105	£19000.00
76	£10000.00
69	£9000.80
26	£23000.10
182	£12000.25
156	£8000.45
129	£21000.75
130	£17000.30
166	£11000.60
45	£9500.90
29	£15950.65

10 Sort the records in ascending order of the SURNAME field and print out all the records in the sorted order.

11 James Baldwin has left the company. Delete his record.

12 Search for employees whose SALARY is less than or equal to £19000 and print out all the records that meet this condition.

13 Jane Godwin has married, change her surname to Williams.

14 Print out all the records including only the fields CODE, SURNAME, FIRSTNAME, DEPARTMENT and STARTDATE.

15 Search for employees who started after January 1st 1992 and print out all the records that meet this condition, including only the fields SURNAME, FIRSTNAME and STARTDATE.

16 Save and exit the database.

17 Copy all the files for the database into the BACKUP folder.

18 Rename the files in the BACKUP folder to identify them clearly as backup.

19 Close any open databases.

20 Close the Access application.

e-Quals
UNIT 005
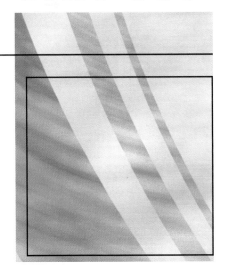

USING THE INTERNET

WHAT IS THE INTERNET ALL ABOUT?

Is:
The Internet the font of all knowledge and human experience?
Or is:
The Internet the biggest reference library in the world?

The Internet contains much honest factual knowledge, but this is not always the case. Books are subject to rigorous checking for factual accuracy before publication and because of the permanent nature of the media, authors and publishers are much more accountable for errors and inaccuracies whereas, much of the content of the Internet is unregulated by anyone other than the authors.

The other statement above says that the Internet is the biggest source of knowledge in the world; again whilst the ease of publication of information on websites means that a huge amount of information is available, you must also consider that there is no coherent filing structure for this information. Imagine if you will, all the books in the biggest library were piled up outside its doors and the head librarian then put the books back into the building...*using a bulldozer.* All the information would be in there but finding it would be like looking for a needle in a haystack, and when you found it, how would you decide whether the story that you had just read was true or not?

These days, computers of all kinds and sizes are very often wired together across telegraphic communications networks. In particular, millions of computers are linked across the international telephone network into a grand data-swapping system called the Internet. This has become practicable because ways have been found to organise coded electrical pulse messages into 'switched packets' which are marshalled from one computer to another like trains being shunted between stations.

This networking has led to the emergence of the client/server concept. Broadly, a server is a large, fast, powerful computer that physically may occupy floors of a factory building or just the top of someone's dressing table. The important point is that its job is to store and dispense requested information; at least *most of the time*. On the other hand a client, which is typically a small PC, but could be a big mainframe, spends most of its life passively accepting programs and data which it uses. But when appropriate even the smallest computer can be organised to be a temporary or permanent server. Indeed, most of the big corporations and research laboratories entrusted with Internet servers use massive supercomputers to handle Net traffic, yet some large companies use 'farms' of thousands of linked PCs to service their enormous Internet client base.

GETTING CONNECTED

In order to access the Internet there are a few things that you will need:

- A computer

- A modem

- A telephone line

- An Internet access account

- A suitable browser application.

Computer

The minimum PC specifications that would recommended would be:

CPU (Central Processing Unit)	For general home working, typing letters, using the Internet/ email etc a 200 Mhz processor would be adequate
RAM (Random Access Memory)	32 Mb would be acceptable. (More would be better)
Hard Disk drive	The size is not really relevant for browsing the Internet, but again the more space you have the better
Monitor (VDU)	14" but again, the bigger the better.
Graphics card	A good quality graphics card would be an advantage
Keyboard and Mouse	Look for quality: Consider a scroll-wheel mouse

Any computer manufactured in the last two or three years would probably be more than capable of accessing the Internet.

Modem

The word Modem is an abbreviation of the words **Mo**dulator/ **Dem**odulator. Its task is to translate the digital instructions from your computer to an analogue (wave) signal for transmission down normal telephone cables and to decode the incoming analogue signal into a (digital=pulse) form that your computer can understand.

There are three main types of modem nowadays: external, internal and broadband cable modems.

Most modems today will run at a speed of 56Kbs (Kilobytes per second). This refers to the speed that information can be sent and decoded by the modem and is often talked about as bandwidth.

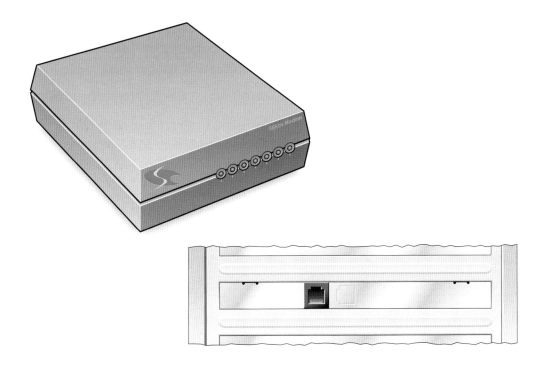

External modems are situated outside your system box and are connected to your computer through a serial port and need their own power supply, the advantage of these types of modem is that you can move them from one machine to another.

Internal modems are situated inside your system case and plugged directly into your computers motherboard, there is no need for an external power supply as they take their power directly from the computer. Internal modems are by far the most common types of modem around as they tend to be included when a new system is manufactured.

Broadband cable modems are usually external to your PC's case but have one distinct advantage – speed. Cable modems can run at speeds of up to 512Kbs (*almost 10 times faster than a normal modem*). They require a special connection to the web (usually fibre-optic), rather than a normal phone line and so are not available in all areas. They are also usually much more expensive to run but this cost will probably decrease over time.

Ordinary modems, whether internal or external, require one more thing to enable them to work – a phone line. Many people run their modem over the same telephone line that they use for their normal voice calls. This has one disadvantage in that you can only use the phone line for one thing at a time, so if you are busy on the Internet

then you are unable to take incoming calls. Many people opt to have more than one phone line into their house, keeping one exclusively for the Internet. Depending on how often you use the internet this can be a cost effective solution as a nominal charge is usually made for the second line by your phone company.

Selecting an Internet Service Provider (ISP)

After selecting your computer the next step is to choose an ISP. Internet Service Providers (ISPs) are forwarding agents who manage your contact with the Net. They act in collaboration with and pay fees to, but are not usually part of, the actual telephone companies who own the physical infrastructure. To establish contact with the Internet through your computer you will need to take out a subscription with one or more ISPs, who will charge according to the speed of your link and the times when you use the Net. There are a few things that you need to consider.

- **Local Phone number**: Ensure that the ISP that you choose has a local connection number. Some ISP's even have a free phone number for you to connect to, you would usually pay a flat monthly charge.

- **Web space**: Most ISP's provide their customers with some space for them to create their own personal web sites.

- **Customer services**: Most people will have problems with their Internet connection at some point. More often than not you will have problems at weekend or in the evening so you really want an ISP who's customer support desk is open 24 hrs. Be aware, too, that some ISP's help lines are premium rate numbers and could prove very expensive if they keep you on hold for a long time.

- **Reliability**: Difficult to gauge. The best way is to talk to friends and acquaintances. The most frustrating thing when you are trying to log-on to the net is to keep getting a busy tone.

- **Price**: The bottom line for many people will be price. Investigate different pricing options from different providers. It can often be a good idea to find out from your telephone service provider if they offer an Internet service. Computer magazines may also be a good source for up-to-date ISP comparison tables.

It is relatively easy to obtain a 'free' ISP CD-ROM, either from a shop or by ringing the ISP to order one. The installation of the ISPs mediation software is then a matter of following the onscreen instructions and registering your serial code and particulars, either online or by post.

Browser Software

Now that you are connected to the Internet you need to find some way of viewing the wealth of information available. The other essential part of a computer system is called software. This is coded information (data) including programs (applications). In its most basic form a browser is merely a reader for HTML files on the web. (HTML is the usual computer language for web site text and graphics compositing). Like any program a browser waits on your hard disk until you invoke it. Then its job is to

Tip	
CPU (Central Processing Unit)	The Brains of our computer. The higher the number the faster it will go.
Bandwidth technology	The capacity of the data stream coming into our PC
ISP	Internet Service provider
Monitor (VDU)	Visual display unit. This is the screen.
A Modem	The device which makes it possible for our computer to talk to others on the Internet. Short for Modulator/Demodulator.
Broadband technology	Ultra fast Internet connection, usually using fibre-optic cables
Gb	Gigabyte (Approx 1000 megabytes)
Mb	Megabyte
Kb	Kilobyte(approx 1000 Bytes)

fetch data in the form of web pages from distant servers and to help you view, record or even alter this Web data according to your orders.

A web page is basically a list of text instructions that tell the browser what to put on screen. The browser interprets these instructions and displays the page.

LAUNCHING YOUR BROWSER SOFTWARE

Click on the Start button at the bottom left of the screen. Choose Programs and then click on the program you wish to launch i.e. Internet Explorer.

Alternatively, you may have a 'shortcut' to the program on your computer's desktop. If you can see an icon representing the program on the screen, double-click on it.

The Internet Explorer software will appear on your screen. Your page will look a little different from this one, as it will show your homepage.

123

The Internet explorer toolbar

This is the Internet explorer toolbar. The top line is called the title bar, and contains the name of the web page that you are viewing. In this case the page is called Internet explorer.

This line of the browser contains the most common functions that we will be using when we browse the Internet

Back: navigates back to the last page you were looking at.
Forward: navigates to the next page (only available after using the back button).
Stop: will halt the loading process.
Refresh: reloads the page you are looking at, shows any updates made to the page.
Home: navigates back to the designated home page.
Search: opens a search facility at the side of the browser window.
Favorites: storage of web page addresses that you would like to revisit.
History: facilitates a look back at the pages you have been to today, yesterday, last week etc.
Mail: opens up your designated e-mail program
Print: prints the web page as a paper hardcopy (may be several physical sheets).

THE ANATOMY OF A URL (Uniform Resource Locator)

A URL is the technical term for a web address. The Internet is split conceptually into compartments of grouped Web pages. The compartments are called websites. Physically, the component pages of site data could be scattered across servers all over the World, but they are linked to these compartments which each have a unique numerical address called an Internet Protocol Address (IP-address).

For example, a site about statistical mining history. As far as humans are concerned its title maybe 'Some Studies of the Historical Time Series of British and European Lead Mine Production', but this is not nearly snappy enough for computers and worse still someone else might decide to use exactly the same title.

So the Internet registration authorities may award the site an IP-address such as 217.199.174.188, which is lovely for computers, being short and singular. Using the http (hypertext transfer protocol) you could enter this address in the browser address bar as http://217.199.174.188 and summon-up the site.

But IP-addresses are very unmnemonic (unmemorable for humans). It would be nicer for them to have a more literary and suggestive code such as miningstatistics.com that at least says something about the site's content. miningstatistics.com is called the domain name. miningstatistics.com is still unique, tolerably brief and hopefully memorable. To find a website the web address (URL) is typed into the Address bar.

The general anatomy of a Web Address is:

protocol://Resource.SecondLevelDomain.TopLevelDomain

Protocol

A protocol is a structured coding convention for electronic data transfer and it 'introduces' data packages sent to a client after the client and server have established that they are 'speaking the same language' after exchanging a coded handshake (yes, it really is called a 'handshake').

We are interested in the Hypertext Transfer Protocol for almost all our Net traffic and it is this we will canvass on our Web requests.

Other protocols include FTP (File Transfer Protocol) but you will tend to steer clear of that unless you want to upload Web pages to hosting servers.

Resource

A resource is a particular application-targeted software assemblage. For our purposes this is The World Wide Web (www) and you can often afford to miss it out (as it may be entered automatically for you).

Second Level Domain (SLD)

This is the interesting, unique identifier that the Web site author asks for, and if it is not already spoken-for gets. The SLD is 'miningstatistics' for the above example.

Top Level Domain (TLD)

This is often in two parts:

(a) Generic Top Level Domain (gTLD)
   This specifies the general nature of the *entity* presenting the site (this is not an exhaustive list):
   .com   A private company or individual
   .net   A specialist computer firm
   .org   A non-profit organisation

(b) Country Code Top Level Domain (ccTLD)
   This specifies the *nation* where the site is 'based' (this is not an exhaustive list), e.g.:
   .us   United States
   .uk   United Kingdom
   .de   Germany
   (When used with a ccTLD .com is modified to .co)

For example:

   http://www.adlerkrankenhaus.org.de

defines the site of a German (deutschland) charitable or governmental (i.e. non-profit) agency which sounds like it is a hospital for eagles, *though such literal readings might not be correct*.

Taken together, the Web address forms a Universal Resource Locator (URL). The URL of the mining website is:

   http://www.miningstatistics.com

 TASK

Load the browser software and visit the *http://www.miningstatistics.com* website.

HOW TO LOCATE AND SELECT SEARCH ENGINES

You can of course consult friends, teachers and magazines to find and compare search engines (which can be summoned from the Net using their URLs) but you can also use convenient Net meta searches like that provided by *www.locate.com*.

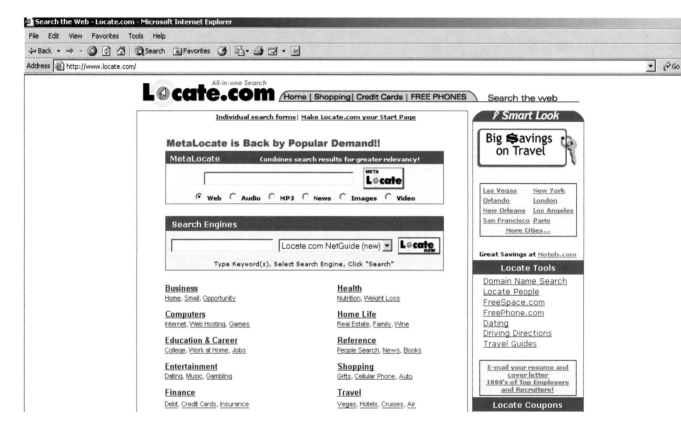

A Search Engine section will be available, select a suitable search engine from the ever-growing list. There is no guarantee that the particular search engine will be able to find the particular website you wish to view.

HYPERTEXT LINKS (HOTSPOTS)

Text that is underlined and normally coloured blue indicates that it is hypertext.

Hypertext links connect to another part of the same page, web page or site. When the mouse is moved over an image that is a hotspot or linked image on a web page, your mouse pointer will change to a pointing finger. Mouse click to activate the link.

TASK

Using the links available navigate the mining document to view other pages or areas of the website.

e-Quals

USING SEARCH ENGINES TO LOCATE INFORMATION

If you don't know the URL of the information you are trying to gather, the best way to find it is to use a search engine. A search engine is like a program that does all the legwork for you and dips in and out of websites ferreting for references to the words that you have entered.

There are many search engines and web directories on the Internet. Search engines differ slightly from directories in that people edit web directories (they do more or less the same job though). Specialist subject search sites are more frequently web directories.

Here are a few of the leading website look-up programs:

Google   www.google.co.uk
HotBot   www.hotbot.co.uk
AltaVista   www.altavista.co.uk
Lycos   www.lycos.co.uk
Yahoo   www.yahoo.co.uk

Search engines use special bits of information called Metatags, which are put on sites by web authors. These metatags contain keywords that relate to the page or site, for example if you were to write a site about 'training' the words to include in the metatag would be 'training', 'teacher', 'tutor', 'learning'. Another of these metatags contains a description of the page or its content. This is what the search engine returns with a link to the appropriate page.

You may need to try several search engines to find the website or information you are looking for.

Each search engine has its own features and layout, although they all basically have the same facilities.

The search engines mentioned above are displayed below (not in their entirety):

Simple Searches

If you wish to gather information for a friend who is a Kevin Keegan fan, you can simply search for 'Kevin Keegan'. To do this enter the words Kevin Keegan into the search box then click 'Go', 'Search' or press the **enter** key on your keyboard.

This search may return thousands of matching documents, far too many for any one person to search through. The search can be narrowed to avoid long hours looking through unwanted search results.

Advanced Searches

Depending upon the search engine you choose you will get a slightly different result. An advanced search via the search engine gives you prompts to complete to narrow the search.

Click on the Advanced Search link or button to define your search. A page displaying the advanced search criteria will be displayed (Lycos advanced search page displayed here).

Placing words within quotes such as "Kevin Keegan" will force the search engine to look for both words in the specified order.

Complete as much of the advanced criteria as possible to narrow the search as much as possible.

For example, enter the words 'football', 'liverpool'.

Specify the language and any other requirements that may be relevant.

Click Go, Search or press the Enter key on the keyboard.

TASK

Navigate to your choice of search engines. Search for websites containing information about Toads. Keep a note of how many websites this search results in.

Navigate back to the search engine and define your search to search for Natterjack and Toad. Keep a note of how many websites this search results in.

Repeat the following using a different search engine.

WEB PAGES ON A WEB SITE

As stated, a Web site can group one or more files called Web pages, which are designed for display and usually linked via clickable hotspots which may be hypertext lines or graphical links.

Such pages are editorially composited using a high-level programming language called a markup language. The traditional markup language is Hypertext Markup Language (HTML).

Most hosts (firms which support your uploaded Web site on a 24-hour base server) will insist that you designate some particular page on your site the 'home page'. The rationale is that this simplifies access for surfers and search engines.

The home page is therefore what normally confronts the surfer when you first address your site by URL. However, if you happen to know the name of a secondary page and you want to dive straight into it you can specify a full URL file path, e.g. *http://www.miningstatistics.com/minepix.htm*. (Note that subordinate pages have the extension .htm; not .html). This will save him some time and some hotlink clicking.

INTERROGATIVE ENGINES

Interrogative search engines are designed for you to actually pose a question in (more or less) grammatical English to search for relevant sites. A good example is 'Ask Jeeves', a site that comes in both American and British forms.

The 'Ask Jeeves' URL is *www.ask.co.uk*

The search turns up a selection of useful and irrelevant leads. In this case it seems to be a good idea to open the list of Web Directory names:

TASK

Find the Ask Jeeves website and ask the following question: How do I use Internet directories to search for information.

Navigate to view some suitable websites.

CREATING BOOKMARKS (FAVORITES) OF INTERESTING VISITED WEBSITES

When you are looking for information quite often you may see a web page or site that you would like to refer back to. The Favorites function of Internet explorer allows you to keep a list of sites that you regularly visit so that you can visit them easily. The list can be categorised into folders, for example, you might have one folder for work related sites and another for games or music or children's sites.

Choose Favorites, Add to Favorites on the menu bar.

The Add Favorite dialog box will be displayed.

The name of the page that is currently being viewed will be displayed in the Name box, however you can type an alternative name.

After putting in a name you can click on the OK button or you can click the Create in >> button to specify where you wish to put the bookmark, what category or create a new folder.

A bookmark is a name and associated URL recorded locally on your computer after you have chosen to make the your computer 'remember' it for convenient future call-up.

To access a previously stored bookmark (favorite) click on the Favorites button on the toolbar. This will display the Favorites section of the Internet Explorer window.

Click on the correct link or open the folder and select the correct link. The software will locate the web page for your viewing, click on the Favorites button to hide the favorites section.

USING FORWARD, BACK AND PAST SITE HISTORY TO LOCATE SITES

When you wish to review pages you have seen in the last few minutes you can usually use the Forward or Back buttons on the ISP browser toolbar to leaf back to the material of interest.

Pages which you saw maybe several hours or days ago and which it is impossible or inconvenient to leaf back or forward to may be accessible by using a drop-down menu of URLs (or their title aliases).

Click on the History button on the toolbar.

This will display the available timeslots, click on the day that you last accessed the desired web page. This will expand the selection, showing the pages accessed that day or week, locate the web page and click on it to view it.

Click on the History button to remove the History section from the screen.

TASK

Create a bookmark (favorite) for the website you are currently viewing, save it with your name. Navigate back to the search engine, then select the bookmark (favorite) with your name.

Use the History button to view the previously viewed websites on your machine.

BOOLEAN SEARCHES

Boolean takes its name from George Boole (mathematician 1815–1864), who wrote about a system of logic designed to produce better search results. We have derived Boolean logic and its operators: AND, OR and NOT which we use to link words and phrases for precise queries. Different search engines handle Boolean operators differently, some require the operators to be typed in capital letters while others do not. The following is a guide.

Using AND will provide links to sites which have all of the words present, for example:

New AND York AND Shopping

Will return all sites that have all those keywords present. Could return the following result:

New Shopping complex in York.

Using OR will provide links to sites which have any of the words present:

New OR York OR Shopping

Will return all sites that have any of those keywords present. Could return the following results:

New Hampshire
Guides around York
Online shopping

Using NOT will provide links to sites by returning the search on the first word and not the second, for example:

New NOT Orleans

Will return all sites that have the keyword 'New' and not the keyword 'Orleans'. Could return the following results:

New York
New Hampshire
New Haven

Tip

Use the plus (+) and minus (-) symbols in place of the operators AND and NOT. Use the quotation marks " " around two or more words will force them to be searched as a phrase in that order.

TASK

Navigate to a search engine of your choice (different to that you have already used). Search for Queen NOT Music. View a couple of the resulting websites.

ADVANTAGES AND DISADVANTAGES OF THE INTERNET

Serious use of the Internet tends to be in one of two contexts where more traditional resources were used in the past and still are:

- **Library** – Search, Research and Reference
- **Telephonic** – Enquiries and Purchases

First we will compare the Internet to a traditional bricks-and-mortar library in its reference function:

With billions of long pages worldwide the Internet is an even bigger information base than the great national libraries of reference. But Internet search, classification and categorisation features are relatively primitive. No one independently and authoritatively checks the accuracy or decency of 'shelved' materials. However, on the positive side, the Net is accessible almost everywhere and to almost everyone, needing no expensive memberships, travel, accommodation or dead time.

Secondly, let us have a brief look at the telephonic business function:

Electronic money transactions can be made swift, certain and relatively secure using Internet e-commerce tools. Again, expensive travel and dead time is not needed for 'shopping'. Catalogue and schedule data is more detailed, authoritative and printable than product details given over the telephone. Actual goods and original documents need to be delivered, as with traditional telephone orders.

INTERNET SERVICES

We can list some key Internet services as:

Reference	pages of text and pictures about almost everything.
Trade	avenues of contact and product descriptions, as well as purchasing facilities, for almost every established firm.
Schedules	time-lists of almost all public events from detailed railway and air timetables to TV listings. Also many private schedules such as university course syllabi.
Search	Computerised 'engines' usable to find relevant pages by keyword (i.e. topics) or by URL.

The most drastic change the Internet has made so far (2002) is in the internationalisation of trade and scholarly contact. Since 1914 the ability of individuals to trade across frontiers (both legitimately and otherwise) has been severely curtailed. But since 1995 the Net has to some extent restored the Victorian tradition of international small commerce and the Net has also partially restored the tradition of peripatetic scholarship lost in the Napoleonic Wars over two hundred years ago.

THE VIRUS

A computer virus is not of course a living germ. It is a computer program, which shares with living creatures the ability to reproduce itself in some sense. Like real viruses, most computer viruses are relatively harmless (just replicating themselves), but some can be made to do major damage to the honest data, which they 'infest'.

Also like real viruses, computer viruses do not just arise where they are found but are transmitted by 'vectors' or carriers. Computer viruses can be transferred on infected floppy disks taken from one machine to another or as a hidden part of Internet downloads, especially file attachments to email letters.

To defend yourself against computer viruses be reluctant to accept unwrapped disks or Internet files, even from respectable people; and install and maintain a good anti-virus software package.

DOWNLOADING INFORMATION FROM A SITE

Before you download information from a site it is wise to set up a specific directory (folder) on your computer or floppy disk to receive the information. Apart from organisational efficiency, there are good operational and security reasons for this. Firstly, and especially if you save the information as a 'Web Page Complete', there are likely to be a lot of unexpected attached files and directories transferred with the expected HTML web page, and these can cause clutter or even be mislaid unless planned-for. Secondly, if any virus or other nasty seems to come with the download it is a good idea to ring-fence it if practicable, and you may even wish to download to a floppy rather than your hard disk.

To Download Web Pages

Please note that there may be legal implications to downloading information from websites, especially when forwarding-on modified or unmodified downloaded copy, especially if you send it for profit.

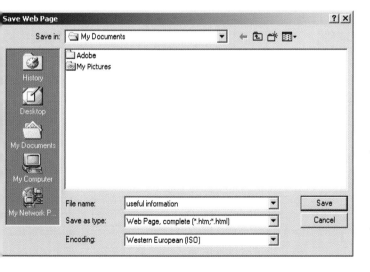

Navigate to the website that interests you. Choose File, Save As on the menu bar. This will display the Save As dialog box.

Navigate to the drive and folder into which you wish to save the downloaded information.

Type in a suitable file name in the File name box. Click Save.

However, many sites cannot be saved, the authors of the sites will have specifically created it that way to minimise loss or misuse of their data.

To Download Graphics

Right-click on the graphic that you wish to download, the sub menu shown here will be displayed. Click Save Picture As to save the picture to a specific location. Follow the above instructions to save the picture.

VIEWING DOWNLOADED PAGES OFFLINE

You do not need to be connected to the Internet to view downloaded pages.

Open Windows Explorer and type the file path of the required web page, for example:

C:\SITES\MINES\MINES-P\index.html

If the site exists on your local disk, either because you are the original author *or* because you saved it there from the Web, then this is a quick and easy way of viewing the material.

This is called offline working, because you are doing Web work without actually being on the telephonic Internet at the time. However, this file will not be updated when changes are made to the original website.

PRINTING THE WEB PAGE

Choose File, Print and the Print dialog box will be displayed.

Select the printer to which you wish to print to from the Name drop-down box, select the print range and the number of copies.

Click OK.

Alternatively, click on the Print icon on the toolbar.

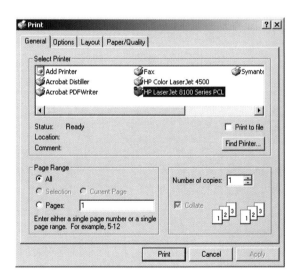

TASK

Using the Internet find information on the following:

Cast list for 'Saving Private Ryan'
Winners of the 1974 football World Cup
A plumber in the Bristol area
The first three men on the moon
Picture of a duck-billed platypus

Download some of the interesting information and print a couple of sample pages.

EXITING THE BROWSER

To exit the browser choose File, Close. Depending upon your access and browser software you may be asked to Disconnect from the Internet, click Yes.

Your actual exit may typically be interrupted by two conditions:

1 **Remaining Open Files**

Sometimes, if the computer is not sure whether you wish to record a modified file it will invite you to select a name and destination disk directory for the file before closing and exiting. In normal circumstances, you should assign an updated name and select a suitable recording directory (folder) for the queried file in an organised, orderly way.

2 **Error Conditions**

On rare occasions, the computer will generate an error condition if it gets confused about whether to play certain files, e.g. background audio files, or encounters a programming defect in the original website code.

There is no cause for alarm and no permanent danger to the machine or its data. A succession of special windows will talk you through an orderly exit, and if you are still connected to the Net, you may even be invited to send an automatic technical report to Microsoft, who may try to fix the problem.

SECURITY ON THE INTERNET

The opportunities for learning, recreation and communication provided by the Internet are limitless. However, it is also true that there are many sites which would raise the eyebrows of even the most broad-minded of adults. There are methods that parents can use to help to guard against this 'menace' affecting their children:

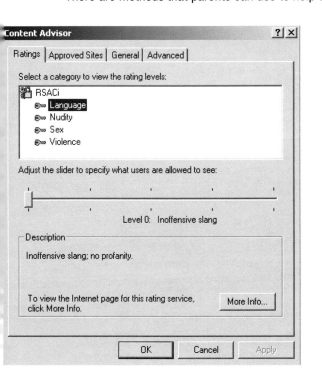

- Setting Internet Explorer's content advisor to a level that you are comfortable with.*

- Proprietary Internet filtering software, such as Cyber sitter, Net Nanny, Cyber Patrol or Surfwatch.*

- Adjust your Security settings accordingly.*

- Move your computer to a family room, and angle the screen so that it can be seen from the whole room.

*Adjusting these settings can go a long way to filtering out undesirable material, but this is a very 'broad brush' approach.

There is no substitute for common sense when considering this problem.

To change the default settings of the computer, choose Start from the task bar (bottom left of the screen), select Settings, Control Panel. Double-click the Internet options icon, select the

Contents tab and select the Enable button for the content advisor. Use the slide to change the existing settings for each category. Click Apply and OK to agree new settings.

INTERNET SPEED

Many factors influence the actual speed of Internet operation at the 'user end', but these are usually the key issues:

(a) Line Speed

This is the rated design speed (measured in KiloBaud: Thousands of bits per second) of the telephonic connection. It depends upon the details of the electronic control standard implemented, the character of the transmission medium (e.g. copper wire or fibre optic cable) and even the direction of transmission.

(b) Traffic Intensity

As with a motorway system message transmission soon slows and congeals into 'jams' when a crowd of users tries to transit the system all at once. It is sometimes called 'system degeneracy'.

(c) Software Engineering

The quality of program control structure design, and the design of file links, as well as disk management, is often an influence on the outcome speed of *any* computer system

(d) Clock Speed

This is a famous but over-rated influence upon system speed. It is the internal pulse frequency of the computers involved. The sorts of programs used on the Net, which are often geared to frequent human interventions, are only marginally influenced by clock speed.

In practical terms, your enjoyed speed will chiefly be influenced by whether you have a narrowband or broadband contract, and by the time of day.

INTERNET AND EMAIL SECURITY

Where the privacy of Internet communications is paramount, for example in transmitting credit card number or other authenticating identifications for financial instruments, you may be willing to pay the capital and time costs of scrambling transmitted data. In technical language, scrambling is called encryption, and is matched at the receiving end by unscrambling back to plain language, which is decryption.

Because of its costs and inconvenience you will want to restrict scrambling to only the most sensitive bits of the message.

Virus protection software, mounted 'between' our computer and the public Net, can be used to police the incoming data and notify us of any suspicious material likely to damage our system. The virus protection system will block this material until we decide what to do with it, or can be set up automatically to 'disinfect' or destroy infected communications.

Allied to these methods are security alerts that communicate suspicious submissions or actual violations to the human user; locks which apply or release encrypted online data checks; and passwords, a weak but convenient method of impeding unauthorised access.

Copyright

Copyright is a legal guarantee, which restricts the propagation of intellectual property (i.e. original writings) to the author. It is intended to safeguard commercial exploitation of immaterial products. In England, copyright is free of charge, requires no registration (except for trade marks) and is assumed to continue until such time as the author might contractually alienate his copyright to a specific work.

Traditional copyright covers poems, articles, books, technical reports, learned papers and other literary art of potential commercial value. Copyright also extends to other productions such as computer programs, filmed or videographed material, sheet or recorded music (including Internet music), photographs, drawings and diagrams.

Assume that everything on the Net is copyright. It does not have to display the word 'Copyright' or the © symbol to be copyright; nor does it need to have an obvious financial value or be UK-sourced.

You may make brief, unpermitted quotations of copyright material for critical, scientific or other scholarly purposes or as parts of newspaper reviews and the like. This is loosely called 'fair dealing'. To make extended quotations, or use graphical or audio resources, always obtain prior permission of the copyright holder. They may of course make a charge.

Violation of copyright is not a crime in England, but an aggrieved party may sue in the civil courts for his estimated financial loses due to the copying, plus his legal costs. This may cost the copier many thousands of pounds.

TASK

Locate information about Copyright and Internet Security from the World Wide Web.

Print out some interesting information and close the Internet Browser and ensure you are disconnected from the Internet.

e-Quals
UNIT 006
PRESENTATION GRAPHICS

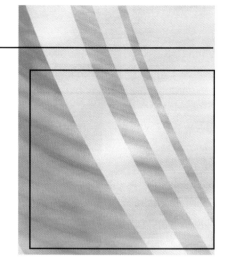

INTRODUCING MICROSOFT POWERPOINT

Microsoft PowerPoint is a flexible and powerful presentation software package with which you can create professional looking presentations in various formats and for different purposes. Its ease of use and intuitive interface, similar to Microsoft Excel and Microsoft Word, make it attractive to millions of users. With PowerPoint you can create:

- On-screen presentations
- Web pages for web use
- Colour and Black and White overheads
- Colour and Black and White paper printouts
- 35 mm slides
- Audience handouts
- Speaker notes

SYSTEM REQUIREMENTS

To use Microsoft PowerPoint 2000 you will need hardware and software that is compatible. The monitor (Visual Display Unit) you have needs to be a colour monitor, not monochrome (black and white). This is so that you can see your presentation file in full colour and create eye-catching designs.

A mouse and keyboard are necessary to operate the software and help present the presentation. Any PC-compatible mouse will be sufficient.

A floppy disk may be necessary if you need to transport your presentation to another computer, or if you need to have your file printed at an outside commercial printers. A floppy disk holds 1.44 mb of data, so you may need more than one if your presentation is larger than 1.44 mb in size.

You will also need to check the RAM (Random Access Memory) of your PC. RAM is your computer's workspace. The larger the workspace, the more work can be achieved at one time. You will need more RAM to work efficiently with photo files and high-resolution graphics. 32 mb is the minimum and 64 mb or more is recommended for best results.

To check your system's RAM, right click on the My Computer icon on your desktop, select Properties. Your system's RAM will be displayed under the General tab.

LAUNCHING YOUR PRESENTATION SOFTWARE

Click on the Start button at the bottom left of the screen. Choose Programs and then click on the program you wish to launch i.e. Microsoft PowerPoint.

Alternatively, you may have a 'shortcut' to the program on your computer's desktop. If you can see an icon representing the program on the screen, double-click on it.

The PowerPoint Startup dialog box, which prompts you as to the action you wish to take. PowerPoint provides three methods to create a new presentation:

1 Create a Blank presentation, populate it with the required contents and then apply to it one of the forty four pre-set Design Templates available;

2 Start with a similarly blank presentation but base it straight away on an existing Design Template;

3 Use the AutoContent Wizard to create in one swoop a presentation loosely based on one of twenty-four standard subjects like *Recommending a Strategy*, which will include an existing design scheme. Following this route, you can specify the type of presentation you wish to create (on-screen or Web presentation, colour or B&W overheads or 35mm slides). You can also specify a presentation title, a common Footer for all the slides in the presentation and whether the Footer should include slide numbering and the current date. You will be prompted with a series of dialog boxes. The style of the presentation will depend on the choices you make.

Whichever way you choose, you can modify and extend your presentation at any time after it has been created.

The rather sparse window with which PowerPoint starts now is the program's working surface, or its *desktop*. Apart from obtaining help, there are only two courses of action, which are open to you at this stage: you can either create a new presentation from scratch or open an existing one.

CREATING A NEW PRESENTATION

You can create a new presentation in several ways. You can start by working with the AutoContent wizard, in which you begin with a presentation that contains suggested content and design. You can also start with an existing presentation and change it to suit your needs. Another way to start a presentation is by selecting a design template that determines the presentation's design but doesn't include content. You can also begin with an outline you import from another application or with a blank presentation that has neither suggested content nor design.

139

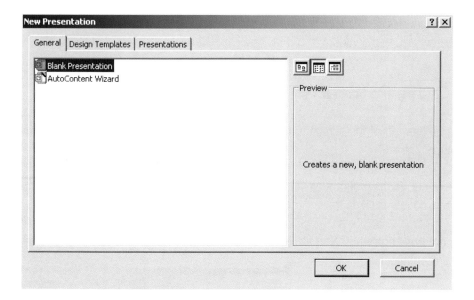

Alternatively, a new presentation can be created bypassing the PowerPoint Startup dialog altogether: choose File, New. PowerPoint displays the New Presentation dialog box. The General tab contains two options: Blank Presentation or AutoContent Wizard, the Design Templates tab lists all the forty-four templates that PowerPoint comes pre-equipped with and the Presentations tab lists all the twenty-four pre-set presentations that can also be accessed via the AutoContent Wizard. Clicking on any one of those will display the template in a thumbnail view in the Preview pane on the right of the dialog box. Select your preferred option and click OK.

PowerPoint displays the presentation window, selects by default the Normal View and enables all the buttons on the toolbars. The presentation window acts as the viewer for all operations within the presentation.

POWERPOINT VIEWS

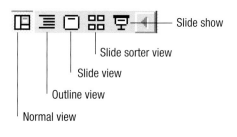

Microsoft PowerPoint comes with five different views to help you while you are creating a presentation. To switch between the views, click the buttons at the lower left of the PowerPoint window (shown here on the right). The two main views you will use in PowerPoint are Normal View and Slide Sorter View.

Normal View

Normal view contains three panes: the Outline Pane, the Slide Pane and the Notes Pane. These panes let you work on all aspects of your presentation in one place. You can adjust the size of the different panes by dragging the pane borders.

Outline Pane – Use the outline pane to organise and develop the content of your presentation. You can type all of the text of your presentation and rearrange bullet points, paragraphs and slides.

Slide Pane – In the slide pane, you can see each slide individually and this is the best view when working with slides. Here you can see how your text looks on each slide, create hyperlinks and add graphics, movies, animations effects and sounds to individual slides. The size at which you view the slides can be varied by changing the percentage zoom on the toolbar. It is usually most convenient to choose the Fit option, which allows for viewing slides in the largest possible size whilst still displaying the entire slide.

Notes Pane – The notes pane lets you add your speaker notes or information you want to share with the audience. If you want to have graphics in your notes, you must add the notes in Notes Page View.

These three panes are also displayed when you save your presentation as a Web page. The only difference is that the outline pane displays a table of contents so that you can navigate through your presentation.

Slide Sorter View

In slide sorter view, you can see all the slides in your presentation on screen at the same time, displayed in miniature. This makes it easy to add, delete and move slides, add timings and select animated transitions for moving from slide to slide. You can also preview animations on multiple slides by selecting the slides you want to preview and then clicking Animation Preview on the Slide Show menu. At any time while you are creating your presentation, you can start your slide show and preview your presentation by clicking the Slide Show button on the Views toolbar.

Slide Show View

Slide Show View displays an on-screen presentation of your slides and can be set to run automatically according to pre-set times or manually on the click of the mouse. To view your presentation in Slide Show View:

- Ensure that you are on the first slide in your presentation.

- Click the Slide Show View button or choose Slide Show, View Show.

- Whilst in Slide Show View, click the left mouse button to move forward through the presentation

- Press the Esc key on the keyboard to end the slide show at any time and return to the presentation window

Below you can see examples of the four main views of a presentation.

Normal View 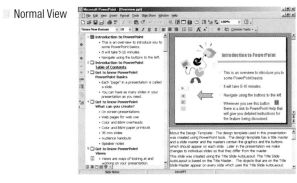 Outline View

Slide View 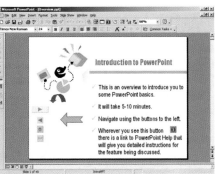 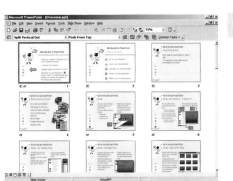 Slide Sorter View

DESIGNING PRESENTATIONS

Delivering your presentation effectively involves using a proven four-step process: Plan, Prepare, Practise and Present. Follow the guidelines and you and your message will have a high impact on your audience.

Plan

- Know your audience – what do they want, what do they need and what are their expectations.

- Decide what it is that the presentation is required to do – teach, advise, inform and motivate.

- Prepare the presentation according to the level of understanding of your audience.

Prepare

- Determine the key ideas of your message and back them up with evidence such as statistics, testimonials, demonstrations and analogies.

- Prepare an ending that relates back to your opening, this is an effective ending.

- Structure your presentation around the message that you want to convey.

Practise

Practise your presentation in front of a small audience or a colleague and ask for feedback on the content and style of your presentation. Things to consider:

- Is the message clear?

- Are your graphics and illustrations clear, appealing and relevant to the topic?

- Is the presentation effective?

- Is your ending memorable?

- Did you achieve your intended objectives?

- If possible, rehearse multiple times, trying out new ideas and new techniques for delivering the material.

Present

- Make a positive first impression. If possible, establish eye contact with your audience. Be yourself and relax.

- When speaking, be natural. Speak in a heightened conversational tone. Slow down and emphasise important points and pause before and after key points to set them apart.

- Involve the audience in the presentation. Ask your audience questions to be sure that they're following you. If appropriate, get feedback from them after the presentation and use this feedback to make your next presentation even better.

WORKING WITH SLIDES

Adding New Slides

New slides can be inserted in a newly created presentation or in an existing one. There are several ways to add a new slide to a presentation:

Choose Insert, New Slide or press the New Slide button on the toolbar.

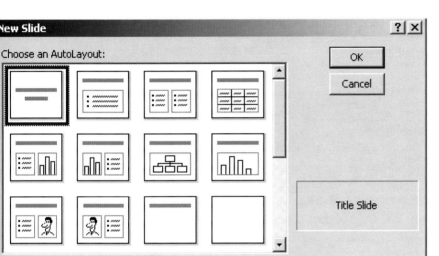

If no slide is displayed in the Slide Pane (usually, in a newly-created presentation), click the pane itself.

Whichever method is used, PowerPoint displays the New Slide dialog box. It consists of twenty-four different default slide layouts, with pre-set and pre-formatted placeholders for text and most other graphic objects that can be included in a presentation.

Select a suitable slide, a thick border should indicate the chosen slide then click OK.

WORKING WITH TEXT

To enter text in Slide View, you can either use the automatic placeholders that are pre-set and pre-formatted by the Master Slides, or you can delete those and enter text in any position on the slide. Bear in mind that the placeholders are designed to maintain continuity and uniformity in a presentation and if they are deleted, the slide is no longer following the template layout.

Adding a Title

To enter text in a title placeholder:

Click inside the placeholder.

Type the required text.

Click outside the title placeholder.

If you have a few extra lines of text that do not fit in the placeholder, PowerPoint automatically tries to fit the text within the text placeholder. To turn off this feature, choose Tools, Option and select the Edit tab and then clear the

Auto-fit text-to-text placeholder check box.

Adding Bulleted Text

Any text placeholder other than the title placeholder defaults to five levels of bulleted paragraphs. The appearance of the bullets depends on the template being used. Each level of bulleted paragraph appears in a slightly smaller font size.

Click inside the bullet placeholder. Type the required text. Press Enter for a new line.

Press the Demote button on the toolbar to indent a line.

Press Promote to outdent demoted levels.

- Level 1
  - Level 2
    - Level 3

Adding Text Outside Text Placeholders

Text can be added outside, or separately from, a bulleted text placeholder. Text that is added outside the standard text placeholders is not linked to the Master Slide layout and does not follow the template.

To enter text outside a text placeholder:

Click on the Text Box button on the Drawing toolbar.

Click on the slide to add text, the text box will automatically resize to fit the contents. Or click and drag on the slide to create a text box of a suitable size, the text will wrap in the box.

Editing Text Attributes

Once text has been entered on a slide, its appearance and overall style can be changed, either within each placeholder on an individual slide, or for all slides in the presentation. PowerPoint offers several ways to change such font attributes as the font name, size, style, colour, special effects and case or paragraph attributes, such as text alignment, line spacing and changing fonts.

To change font attributes:

Select the text you wish to change (either by dragging over it, or by selecting its placeholder.

Choose Font, Format on the menu bar.

The options available for change are: Font, Font Style, Size, Special Effects and Colour.

Click OK to agree selection.

Adding Bullets or Numbering to Text

All pre-set text placeholders are already pre-formatted with five bullet points at varying levels. If you wish to add bullets or numbering to other text:

Select the text or the placeholder you want to add bullets or numbering to.

To add bullets, click the Bullets icon on the toolbar.

To add numbers, click the Numbering icon on the toolbar.

Changing the Appearance of Bullets or Numbering

You can change the appearance, colour and size of bullets or numbers, select different bullets from the default and even make a picture into a bullet.

Select the text or placeholder whose bullet character you want to change. Choose Format, Bullets and Numbering. And do one of the following:

- To use one of the default bullet characters, click the character you want on the Bulleted tab.
- To choose a different bullet character, click Character and then choose the font and character you want.
- To use a picture instead of a bullet, click Picture and locate and select the picture you want.
  If you have the Clip Gallery installed, it appears when you click Picture. From the Clip Gallery, you can choose from a set of built-in images for bullets. If you don't have the Clip Gallery installed, the Insert Picture dialog box appears when you click Picture. From there, you can specify any picture file for use as a bullet.
- To change the size of the bullets or numbers, enter a percentage in the Size box.

To change the colour of the bullets or numbers, click the arrow next to Colour and then do one of the following:

- To change to the default colour, click Automatic.
- To change to a colour in the colour scheme, click one of the eight colours below Automatic.
- To change to a colour that isn't in the colour scheme, click More Colours. On the Standard tab, click the colour you want, or click the Custom tab to mix your own colour and then click OK.
- Changing the Text Case (Capitalisation)

To change case of text from UPPER to lower to Title:

- Select the text you want to change.
- Choose Format, Change Case.
- select the option that you wish to apply.
- Click OK to agree selection

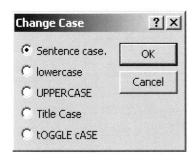

TASK

Use the wizard to create a **Presentation** on a subject that you find interesting, navigating around the screen to familiarise yourself with the various views.

Plan and design the following presentations ideas:

- Double glazing sales – a presentation is required for a local double glazing company that has flagging sales. The presentation is planned to be run in the window for passers by (general public), so keep in mind that it needs to be eye-catching, informative and something that creates interest where their wasn't any before.

- Fun day out – you have recently been out to a theme park with most of your family, but unfortunately your aunt was unwell and not able to attend. Your aunt is keen to know about what you all did and how much fun you had.

Prepare the above two presentations on paper, giving details about the layouts to be used, what if any graphics you want to include and text to be included on the slides.

Changing Paragraph Alignment

To change the alignment of text:

- Select the text you want to change.

- Choose Format, Alignment.

- Select the option that you wish to apply.

Left align   Centre   Right align

Alternatively, you can click the appropriate buttons on the Formatting toolbar.

Changing Line Spacing

To change the spacing (distance) between lines of text:

- In the Slide Pane, click anywhere in the paragraph for the spacing that you want to change.

- Choose Format, Line Spacing.

- Using the spin buttons change the number for the amount of spacing you want. Select the drop-down arrow to select the unit of measurement: Lines or Points.

- You can also set additional space both before and after paragraphs.

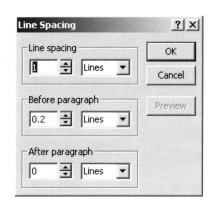

Adding Date, Time, Page Numbers and Footer Text

The time, date, page/slide numbers and footer text can be added to slides, notes and handouts:

Choose View, Header and Footer.

- To add the information to your slides, click the Slide tab.

- To add the information to Notes Pages and Handouts, click the Notes and Handouts tab.

Select the options you want.

- To add the information to only the current slide, click Apply.

- To add the information to all slides in the presentation, click Apply to All.

To add the slide number, date or time anywhere on an individual slide, use the Date and Time or Slide Number commands on the Insert menu.

SAVING PRESENTATIONS

Using Save

If you wish to keep the presentation, so that you can use it again, you will need to save it. Saving your presentations is important if you ever want to retrieve them later.

The first time you save a presentation you will be prompted to give the file a name and to choose which folder you wish to save it into.

Choose File, Save. The Save As dialog box will appear:

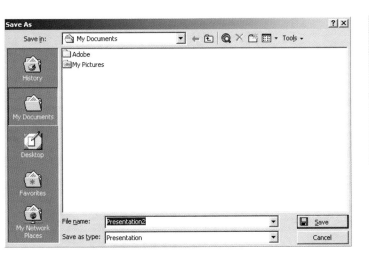

The Save As dialog box displaying the contents of the My Documents Folder. Double-click to move into other folders.

Open the drop-down list by Save in and navigate to the folder that you wish to store your presentation in (folders are indicated by the yellow icon). Double-click on a folder to move into it or use the Back or Up One Level buttons to move up out of a folder.

Type a name for the presentation in the File name box and check that it will be saved into the correct format (under Save as type). Your filename can be up to 250 characters long – use an obvious name for your file so that you remember what you called it in the future! You do not need to type the .ppt filename extension, as this will be added automatically. (The filename extension may not be visible if it has not been set in Windows Explorer). Click on the Save button at the bottom right of the dialog box.

Once you have saved the presentation, the name of the file will appear in the Title Bar across the top of the screen.

If you have previously saved a presentation, choosing Save will overwrite the previous version of the spreadsheet with the updated version. (It still has the same name and is stored in the folder that you initially put it in).

The Save button also appears on the Standard toolbar. You can click on this instead of choosing File, Save.

Using Save As

If you do not wish to overwrite a previously saved presentation, you can use Save As and give the new version a different name, or store it in a different folder. Choose Save As from the File menu.

CLOSING THE PRESENTATION

If you wish to remove the presentation from the screen, you need to close it. If you wish to keep the file on your computer, you must save the presentation before closing it.

Choose File, Close. If you haven't previously saved the presentation, the following message will appear on the screen.

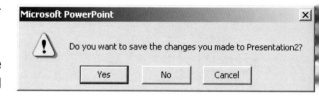

If you do wish to save the changes, click Yes. If you wish to close the presentation without saving, click No. Clicking Cancel will remove the dialog box from the screen.

If you already saved the presentation it will close leaving a blank screen.

CLOSING THE APPLICATION

If you wish to close down the application, you need to exit out of it. Choose File, Exit. Alternatively, click on the cross in the top right hand corner. ⊠

TASK

Close any open presentations.

OPENING A PRESENTATION

You may need to retrieve saved presentations, to view data, print or edit. To open an existing presentation, choose File, Open on the menu bar or click on the Open button ![open button] on the toolbar.

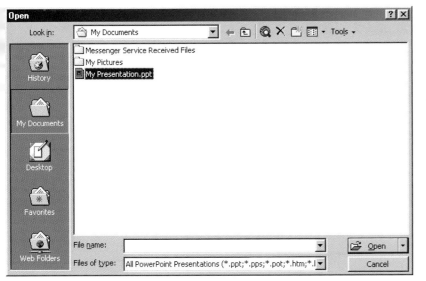

Open the drop-down list by Look in and navigate to the folder that your presentation is stored in (folders are indicated by the yellow icon). Double-click on a folder to move into it, or use the Back or Up One Level buttons to move up out of a folder.

Locate the presentation you wish to open, click on it and then click on the Open button at the bottom right of the dialog box. (Alternatively, you can double-click on the file).

If you cannot see your document files in a folder, make sure the Files of type list at the bottom of the dialog box is showing the correct file types. PowerPoint recognizes presentation files because they have .ppt or .pps filename extensions. This filename extension may not be visible if it has not been set in Windows Explorer.

The Open button also appears on the Standard toolbar. You can click on the button instead of choosing File, Open.

CHANGING THE PRESENTATION SETUP

Page Setup is used to set up and size a presentation to suit specific requirements depending on how it will be communicated to the audience. PowerPoint is set up to create and print slides that are 24cm wide by 18cm tall in landscape orientation. You can change these and other settings by choosing File, Page Setup. In the Page Setup dialog box you can set the following options:

Select from the Slides sized for drop-down arrow to display the options available such as A4 paper, On-screen show, custom size. The width and height measurements will automatically change when the slides have been sized. If you change the width or height measurement the slide is sized for Custom.

Select the orientation for slides and handouts.

Click OK to agree selection.

MOVING BETWEEN SLIDES

To display the next slide in the presentation (as long as you have multiple slides in the presentation):

Click on the Next Slide button in the lower-right corner of the slide pane. ▼

Or, press the Page Down key on the keyboard.

Or, in the Outline Pane, click the next slide number

To display the previous slide in the presentation:

Click on the Previous Slide button in the lower-right corner of the slide pane. ▲

Or, press the Page Up key on the keyboard key.

Or, in the Outline Pane, click the previous slide number.

DELETING SLIDES

To delete a single slide from the presentation:

Select the slide you want to delete.

Choose Edit, Delete Slide.

Or, click on the slide in the Outline pane and press the Delete key on the keyboard.

To delete multiple slides from the presentation:

Switch to Slide Sorter View.

Select the first slide that you wish to delete (for example, slide 2). Hold down the shift key and select the last slide that you wish to delete (for example, slide 6). All of the slides in between and including the first and last will be selected (for example, slides 2, 3, 4, 5 and 6). Press the Delete key or choose Edit, Delete Slide.

Or, select the first slide that you wish to delete (for example, slide 2). Hold down the Ctrl key and select the next slide that you wish to delete (fro example, slide 4). Continue until all the slides that you wish to delete are selected. This allows the selection of individual (non-sequential) slides (for example, 2 & 4).

DUPLICATING SLIDES WITHIN A PRESENTATION

Duplicating a slide is to make a copy of an existing slide. The advantage of duplicating slides is that any format-ting on the slide will be copied over to the new slide automatically, reducing the need to format a new slide again. Any existing text can be replaced (typed over) with the new text and any images or objects can be replaced with new ones.

To duplicate a slide within the current presentation:

Select the slide or slides you want to duplicate.

Choose Insert, Duplicate Slide.

REORDERING SLIDES

Once a presentation has been created, it may be necessary to amend the slide order. This task is carried out using Slider Sorter view, where all slides in the presentation can be viewed at once.

To reorder slides, choose View, Slide Sorter from the menu bar or click on the Slide Sorter view button.

Select a slide, the slide will be surrounded by a thick border to indicate selection. Click and drag the slide into the new position. Release the mouse once in position.

WORKING WITH GRAPHICS

There are two basic types of graphics that you can use to enhance your Microsoft PowerPoint presentations: *drawing objects* and *pictures*. Drawing objects include AutoShapes, curves, lines, freeforms and WordArt. Use the Drawing toolbar to insert these objects and further enhance them with colours, patterns, borders and other effects.

Pictures are graphic objects that were created by other programs and they can be *imported* into your PowerPoint presentation. They include bitmaps, scanned pictures, photographs and clip art. You can change and enhance pictures by using the options on the Picture toolbar and a limited number of options on the Drawing toolbar. In some cases, you must ungroup and convert a picture to a drawing object before you can use the Drawing toolbar options.

Working with Drawing Objects – The Drawing Toolbar

The PowerPoint Drawing toolbar contains various tools for entering text and for drawing and editing graphic objects. The list below shows each tool and describes its use.

＼	Line Tool	↻	Free Rotate Tool
⇄	Arrowheads Tool	▣	Shadow Effect Tool
≡	Line Thickness Tool	▨	3-D Effect Tool
⣿	Line Style Tool	◢	WordArt Tool
✎	Line Colour Tool	🖼	Clipart Tool
○	Oval/Circle Tool	🖹	Text Box Tool
▢	Rectangle/Square Tool	⌗	Crop Picture
🪣	Colour Fill Tool	🖌	Format Painter Tool

Lines

Click on the Line icon on the Drawing toolbar. Alternatively, choose AutoShapes, Lines from the Drawing toolbar and select the most suitable line from the sub menu available.

Drag anywhere on the slide to draw a line.

To manipulate the line, select it and this will display the object handles. Move the mouse pointer to one of the handles and click, move in any direction to change the angle. To lengthen the line click and drag in an outwards motion (this will stretch the line to the left or right depending upon the handle chosen). Or, press and hold the Shift and Ctrl keys whilst dragging in an outwards motion, this will lengthen at either end of the line.

Adding and Removing Arrowheads

Select the line you want to change. Click on the Arrow Style icon on the Drawing toolbar. To add an arrowhead, click the style you want; or click More Arrows and then click a style.

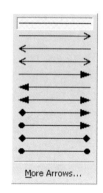

To remove an arrowhead, click the line without arrowheads at the top of the menu.

Rectangles, Squares, Circles and Ovals

When you draw an object, it automatically appears with a border around it – a thin line that defines its shape. You can also add borders to text boxes, pictures and imported art. You can change or format a border in the same way you change or format a line.

To draw a circle or a square, click Oval or Rectangle on the Drawing toolbar and then click and drag the shape on to the presentation. Alternatively, click AutoShapes on the Drawing toolbar, point to a category and then click the shape you want. Drag anywhere on the slide to draw an oval or a rectangle. To constrain the shape (i.e. draw a circle instead of an oval or a square instead of a rectangle), hold down the Shift key as you drag.

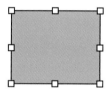

Changing the Line or Border Colour

Select the line or object that you wish to change or add a border to.

Click on the drop-down arrow for Line Colour icon on the Drawing toolbar. To change to the default colour, click Automatic. To change to a colour in the colour scheme, click one of the eight colours below Automatic.

To change to a colour that isn't in the colour scheme, click More Line Colours. Click the colour you want on the Standard tab, or click the Custom tab to mix your own colour and then click OK.

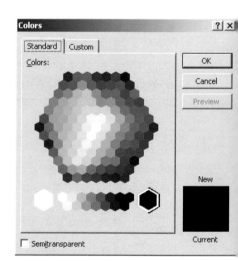

Changing the Fill Colour

Select the object you want to change. Click on the drop-down arrow for the Fill Color icon on the Drawing toolbar. To change the fill colour back to its default, click Automatic. To change to a colour in the colour scheme, click one of the eight colours below Automatic. To change to a colour that isn't in the colour scheme, click More Fill Colours. On the Standard tab, click the colour you want, or click the Custom tab to mix your own colour and then click OK.

AutoShapes

The AutoShapes menu on the Drawing toolbar includes several categories of tools. In the Lines category, you can use Curve, Freeform and Scribble to draw lines and curves, as well as shapes that combine both lines and curves. When you want to draw curves with greater control and accuracy, use Curve. Use Freeform when you want a more refined shape – one without jagged lines or drastic changes in direction. When you want a drawing object to look like it was drawn with a pen, use Scribble. The resulting shape closely matches what you draw on the screen. All AutoShapes can be resized, rotated, flipped, coloured and combined with other shapes, such as circles and squares to make more complex shapes.

You can add callouts, labels and other text to your graphics by using text boxes or inserting text directly into the shape. Text boxes can be enhanced like any other drawing object.

Changing Shapes of Objects

If an object has been drawn with the AutoShapes, Oval or Rectangle tools, the shape can be changed while still maintaining any specified attributes (such as colour or border style). To change the shape of an object:

Select the AutoShape you want to change. Click Draw, Change AutoShape on the Drawing toolbar, click on the shape that you wish to change it to.

Resize the shape with the object handles.

Moving Objects

Select the object, placeholder, multiple selection, or group you want to move.

Drag the object to its new location.

To constrain an object so that it moves only horizontally or vertically, press the Shift key as you drag the object. You can also move an object short distances by selecting it and pressing the arrow keys.

Duplicating Objects

You can quickly duplicate an object while you're working on a slide. Or you can make lots of duplicates and use them to create a *series* of evenly spaced objects (arrays) and overlapping evenly spaced objects (sweeps). You can also copy an object to another slide or to every slide in a presentation.

Making a Duplicate of an Object

Select the object you want to duplicate. Choose Edit, Duplicate from the menu bar. To make additional duplicates, repeat the process.

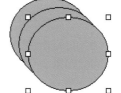

Making Multiple, Evenly-Spaced Duplicate of an Object

Select the object you want to duplicate. Choose Edit, Duplicate from the menu bar. Drag the duplicate to the position you want. Select Duplicate again. Repeat the previous step for each duplicate you want positioned equally from the others.

Adding Text to an Object

Select the object, right click the mouse button and select Add Text from the pop-up menu.

Alternatively, click on the Text Box icon on the Drawing Toolbar. Click and drag on the presentation and add in the text. Move the text box so that it floats over the object. The objects may need layering (see page 156).

Rotating and Flipping Objects

You can *rotate* an object 90 degrees to the left or right or to any other angle. You can also *flip* an object horizontally or vertically. You can flip or rotate one object, a set of objects, or a group of objects. If you rotate or flip an AutoShape that has attached text, the text rotates or flips with the shape.

Some pictures, graphs and organisational charts that you import cannot be rotated or flipped because they weren't created in PowerPoint. If you can ungroup an imported object and then regroup its components, you might be able to flip or rotate it. You won't be able to flip or rotate bitmaps, however.

Rotating an Object to Any Angle

Select the object you want to rotate. Click on the Free Rotate icon on the Drawing toolbar. Drag a corner of the object in the direction you want to rotate it. Click outside the object to set the rotation.

To constrain the rotation of the object to 15-degree angles, hold down the Shift key while you use the Free Rotate tool.

Rotating an Object 90 Degrees to the Left or Right

Select the object you want to rotate. Click Draw on the Drawing toolbar, Rotate or Flip and then click Rotate Right or Rotate Left.

Flipping an Object Horizontally or Vertically

Object rotated right

Select the object you want to flip. On the Drawing toolbar, click Draw, point to Rotate or Flip and then click Flip Horizontal or Flip Vertical. Be aware that text will not Flip Horizontally.

Adding Shadows and 3-D Effects

You can apply these enhancements to drawing objects and you can apply a limited number of shadow effects to pictures. With 3-D options, you can change the depth of the drawing object and its colour, angle, direction of lighting and surface reflection. You can add either a shadow or a 3-D effect to drawing objects, but not both. For example, if you apply a 3-D effect to a drawing object that has a shadow, the shadow disappears.

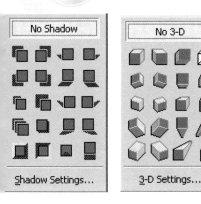

To add a shadow or a 3-D effect to a drawing object:

Select the object you want to add a shadow or a 3-D effect to.

On the Drawing toolbar, click Shadow or 3-D and then click the option you want. To change the colour or offset a shadow, click Shadow, click Shadow Settings and then click the most suitable option.

To change a 3-D effect – for example, its colour, rotation, depth, lighting, or surface texture – click 3-D again, click 3-D Settings and then click the most suitable option.

TASK

Using the plan and designs for the two presentations, prepare the presentations. Save the presentations with suitable names

Open a blank new presentation, practise inserting various objects such as lines, rectangles, squares, circles etc.

Add text to the objects and practise resizing, rotating and flipping.

Save the presentation with the name Objects practise.

Grouping Objects

Grouping several objects together can be useful especially when moving or copying several objects that make up a larger object and when combining text and graphics into a single object. It is also possible to group two grouped objects together to create a nested group. *Ungrouping* will split a grouped object into its component parts. *Regrouping* enables to group again several objects that were ungrouped. Only one of the objects needs to be selected to regroup. If regrouping is applied with no object selected, the most recently ungrouped objects will be regrouped.

To group objects together:

Select the objects you want to group. Click Draw, Group on the Drawing toolbar.

To ungroup objects:

Select any one of the objects that was previously grouped. Click Draw, Ungroup on the Drawing toolbar.

To regroup objects:

Select the group you want to ungroup. Click Draw, Regroup on the Drawing toolbar.

Stacking Objects

Objects automatically stack in individual layers as you add them to a slide. You see the stacking order when objects overlap: the top object covers a portion of objects beneath it.

You can move individual objects or groups of objects in a stack. For example, you can move objects up or down within a stack one layer at a time, or you can move them to the top or bottom of a stack in one move. You can overlap objects when you draw to create different effects. You don't have to draw the bottom object first; you can always move it later.

Bringing an Object to the Front

Select the object you want to move. On the Drawing toolbar, click Draw, Order and then click Bring to Front.

Sending an Object to the Back

Select the object you want to move. On the Drawing toolbar, click Draw, Order and then click Send to Back.

Bringing an Object One Step Closer to the Front

Select the object you want to move. On the Drawing toolbar, click Draw, Order and then click Bring Forward.

Sending an Object One Step Further to the Back

Select the object you want to move. On the Drawing toolbar, click Draw, Order and then click Send Backward.

Aligning Objects

There are several ways to *align* objects. You can align them with other objects, for example when you align the sides, middles, or top or bottom edges of objects. You can align them in relation to the entire slide, for example at the top or left edge of a slide. You can also align objects by using *guides* to align them visually, or by using the grid to align them with a corner on the grid as you draw or move the objects.

You can also arrange (or distribute) objects so they are equal distances from each other — either vertically or horizontally, or in relation to the entire slide.

Aligning Objects with Other Objects

When aligning objects with other objects, make sure the Relative to Slide option isn't selected. When this option is selected, objects will move in relation to the slide, not in relation to other objects.

To clear this option: on the Drawing toolbar, choose Draw, Align or Distribute. If Relative to Slide has a check mark in front of it, click Relative to Slide to clear the check mark.

Select the objects you want to align (such as placeholders, graphics, shapes etc). On the Drawing toolbar, click Draw, Align or Distribute and then click Align Left, Align Middle, Align Right, Align Center, or Align Bottom, depending on the alignment you require.

Positioning an Object in Relation to the Slide

In most cases, you just drag your objects to where you want them. However, to place an object in a precise position, use the following procedure:

Select the object you want to position. On the Format menu, click the command for the type of object you selected – for example, AutoShape or Picture – and then click the Position tab.

Select the options you want for your horizontal and vertical anchors in the From boxes and then enter the distances from the anchors in the Horizontal and Vertical boxes.

WordArt

You can insert decorative text by using Insert WordArt on the Drawing toolbar. You can create shadowed, skewed, rotated and stretched text, as well as text that has been fitted to predefined shapes. Because a special text effect is a drawing object, you can also use other buttons on the Drawing toolbar to change the effect – for example, to fill a text effect with a picture.

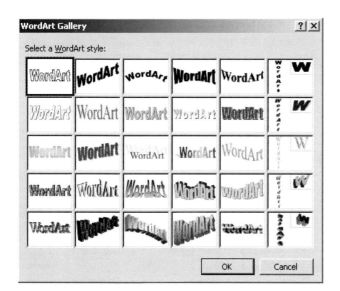

In the slide pane, click the slide on which you want to add a WordArt special effect.

Click on the Insert WordArt icon on the Drawing toolbar. Select the special effect you would like and then click OK.

In the Edit WordArt Text dialog box, type the text you want to format, select any other options (Font, Size and Style) you want and then click OK.

To add or change effects to the text, use the tools on the WordArt and Drawing toolbars.

Resizing and Cropping Objects

When you select an object, *sizing handles* appear at the corners and along the edges of the selection rectangle. You can resize an object by dragging its sizing handles, or you can resize it more precisely by specifying a percentage for the object's height and width.

If the object is a picture – a photo, bitmap, or clip art, for example – you can crop it and you can also restore it later to its original image.

Resizing Objects

Select the object you want to resize. Drag a sizing handle until the object is the shape and size you want. You can resize a placeholder the same way you resize any other object.

Resizing Objects by a Specific Percentage

Select the object you want to resize. On the Format menu, click the command for the type of object you selected and then click the Size tab. Under Scale, enter the percentages you want in the Height and Width boxes. To maintain the ratio between the object's height and width whenever you resize it, select the Lock aspect ratio check box on the Size tab.

Cropping Pictures

Select the picture you want to crop. On the Picture toolbar, click  Crop.

Position the cropping tool over a sizing handle and drag the handle.

WORKING WITH PICTURES

There are two types of pictures: those that can't be ungrouped – such as most imported pictures – and those that can be ungrouped – such as metafiles from the Clip Gallery. After you ungroup a picture, you can convert it to a drawing object and then edit it by using options on the Drawing toolbar.

You can change the look of graphics in your Microsoft PowerPoint presentations by applying a variety of enhancements, such as lines, fills, shadows and transparent colours. You can apply some enhancements to both drawing objects and to pictures, some only to drawing objects and others only to pictures.

The Clip Gallery

The Clip Gallery contains a wide variety of pictures, photographs, sounds and video clips that are ready for you to insert and use in your presentations. Most clip art is in metafile format, which means you must ungroup an image and convert it to a drawing object in order to enhance it. To add a clip to a slide, click Insert Clip Art on the Drawing toolbar.

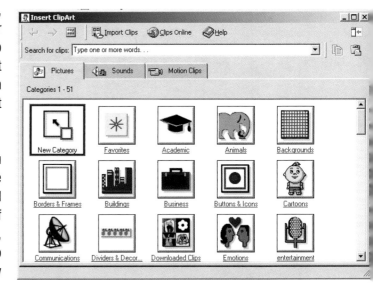

The Clip Gallery has a search feature to help you locate just the right clips for your presentation. To use the search feature, click the Search for clips box and then type one or more words that describe the type of clip you want. If you can't find the picture, music, sound, video, or animation clip you want, connect to Clip Gallery Live, a Web site where you can preview and download additional clips.

Inserting Pictures from the Clipart Gallery

- Display the slide you want to add a picture to.
- Click the Clip Art tool on the Drawing toolbar and then click the Pictures tab.
- Click the category you want.
- Click the picture you want and then click Insert Clip on the shortcut menu.
- When you have finished using the Clip Gallery, click the Close button on the Clip Gallery title bar.
- You can also drag a picture from the Clip Gallery to your slide.

Ungrouping and Modifying Clip Art

When you insert a Microsoft Windows Metafile from the Clip Gallery, you can convert it into Microsoft PowerPoint drawing objects. Then you can use the drawing tools to edit the objects, for example, you could add, delete, flip, rotate or rearrange the objects, or combine several objects into one. If the picture is a bitmap, .jpg, .gif, or .png file, it cannot be converted into drawing objects and ungrouped.

To ungroup a clipart object:

- Double-click the Clip Gallery picture that you have inserted into the slide.

- Click Yes when the message box appears.

- Click Draw and Group.

- Use the tools on the Drawing toolbar to modify the objects.

Inserting Imported Pictures

- Display the slide you want to add a picture to.

- Choose Insert, Picture and then click From File.

- Navigate to the folder that contains the picture you want to insert.

- Click the picture.

Do one of the following:

- To embed the picture into your presentation, click Insert.

- To link the picture in your presentation to the picture file on your hard drive, click the arrow next to Insert and then click Link to File.

> **TASK**
>
> **Open the two prepared presentations. Insert relevant pictures and manipulate as necessary. View all the slides in Slide Sorter view to see if further amendments may be required to the presentations before printing. Make any necessary alterations and mark these alterations on the original designs.**

PRINTING PRESENTATIONS

To print slides, notes, handouts or presentation outline:

Choose File, Print.

In the Print what box, click the item you want to print. The options are Slides, Handouts, Notes Pages and Outline View. If you select the Handouts option, you can also select a number of slides per page and whether the order should be horizontal or vertical.

Select any other options you want:

- Print to File prints the presentation as a disk file, which can then be used to print from at a later time.

- Print Hidden Slides prints all the slides marked *hidden* in the presentation.

- Black and White turns all colour fills to white and all patterned fills to black and white when printed.

- Collate Copies orders and collates the printed pages successively when printing multiple copies.

- Scale to Fit Paper Ensures that the printed slides will fit on the selected paper size (usually making them smaller, if necessary).

- Pure Black and White turns all colour fills to white, all text and lines to black and adds outlines or borders to all filled objects and greyscale pictures. Use this option if your printer can print in black and white only.

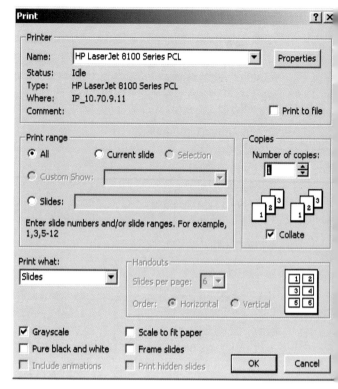

TASK

Create a printout for double glazing company for Handouts, 6 slides per page and Pure Black and White.

Printout the slides for the fun day out.

IMPORTING DATA FROM OTHER APPLICATIONS

The definition of 'import' is to place a file or data which has been created in one application into another application. Using import will enable you to import a whole document created in another application, such as Microsoft Word. Alternatively, the copy and paste functions can be used.

To import an existing Word document:

- Open PowerPoint and select Blank Presentation.

- Select File, Open from the menu bar, the Open dialog box will appear.

- Change the Files of Type to read All Files.

- Select a Word document and click Open.

PowerPoint will read the document and put the information into an order it thinks is appropriate. The presentation will appear in outline view. Some editing and formatting may be required.

Alternatively, import selected text only from the Word document:

- Open the word processing software.

- Open the Word document that you wish to take the selected text from.

- Open a new blank presentation in PowerPoint or open an existing presentation to import the text into.

- Highlight the required text from the Word document and choose Edit, Copy or click on the Copy button on the toolbar.

- Navigate back to the PowerPoint presentation and select the slide in which to insert the text.

- Choose Edit, Paste or click on the Paste button on the toolbar.

Some editing and formatting may be required.

RUNNING A SLIDE SHOW

Starting a Slide Show of the Current Presentation from PowerPoint

- Click the Slide Show button at the lower left of the PowerPoint window.

  Or on the Slide Show menu, click View Show.

  Or on the View menu, click Slide Show.

- Press the left mouse button to navigate through the slides.

Starting a Saved Presentation as a Slide Show

- Locate the file you want to open as a slide show In My Computer or Windows Explorer.

- Right-click the file name and then click Show.

- Press the left mouse button to navigate through the slides.

Saving a Presentation to Open Always as a Slide Show

- Open the presentation you want to save as a slide show.

- On the File menu, click Save As.

- In the Save As Type list, click PowerPoint Show.

- Press the left mouse button to navigate through the slides.

TASK

Run both of the presentations to friends and/or family, ask them what they think, glean their thoughts. On gaining the feedback make any alterations necessary – constructive criticism is useful!

e-Quals
UNIT 007 EMAIL

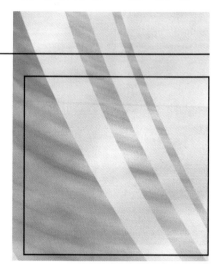

PERSONAL COMPUTER HARDWARE NEEDED FOR EMAILING

Firstly you have got to have a CENTRAL PROCESSOR UNIT (CPU) which lives in the plastic or metal casing (sometimes referred to as the cabinet). This is the actual computer which calculates, and marshals and shunts data around. It stores its data on a variety of disk systems hidden in the cabinet. Another essential is a MODULATOR-DEMODULATOR (MODEM), an electronic device in the cabinet which translates digital to analogue signals and vice versa. A modem is needed if the machine interfaces to the (analogue) public telephone system.

The KEYBOARD and modern GUI software (including Outlook and Outlook Express) is difficult to use without a point-and-click MOUSE.

It is still almost impossible to organise your office, or even emails, without a PRINTER for making hard-copies of outgoing and ingoing messages:

If you are going to send photographs or drawings as mail attachments to your respondents, or even things like planning facsimiles, then you will need a SCANNER to copy the pictures to computer disk in appropriately digitally-coded forms.

The Concept of Emailing

Emailing is an electronic letterbox system intrinsically not much different to old-fashioned Post Office packet mail communications. Instead of a paper letter in a paper envelope you type an electronic message which is stored on

your local computer disk as a magnetic recording pattern. When you are ready to send the message the magnetic recording is used to re-generate a coded electrical signal that is wired along to your respondent's computer over the telephone system. To allow for the fact that his computer may not currently be connected, intermediary large computers called servers, which could be anywhere, intercept your message, temporarily store it and forward it between each other. Eventually, your addressed message will arrive at your respondent's computer and be recorded in a file on their disk.

When they are ready, they can make their computer run a local email program to copy the magnetic recording to type on the screen and so read your letter. Of course, the recipient can also print your letter if they have a printer, delete it or reply using the same procedures, though not likely the same geographical route.

ACCESSING THE EMAIL PROGRAM – OUTLOOK EXPRESS

Outlook Express and the similar email program Outlook are Microsoft products intended to help you send emails (electronic letters) to other peoples' computers. These email messages are stored at the recipient's end for he or she to read straight away or later at their leisure.

Most of us buy Outlook or Outlook Express as 'free' incidentals packaged with paid-for programs like **word** (a word processor program for general-purpose report, letter and essay writing) or **excel** (a mathematical tabulation program useful for invoices, 'what if' models, etc).

By contacting Microsoft it is possible to obtain Outlook as a stand-alone program. The program will be sent to you through the post on a CD-ROM disk for you to transfer to your computer's hard disk.

Microsoft Outlook Express is freeware (you can have it for nothing) and it is perhaps most convenient to download from the Internet. If you are on the Internet and have some spare time and do not have to worry about possible metered call charges then you can download the programs via the public telephone system.

We will have a brief look at the Internet avenue and confining our attention to Microsoft Outlook Express 5.

Setting up the Email Program

To download Outlook Express go on to the Internet through your usual ISP (e.g. AOL, BT) and search for a suitable provider using the keyword sequence 'Microsoft Outlook Express download' in Google (*http://www.google.com*) Advanced Search.

Pick a good shareware broker. One option to be considered is to choose 5-star (*http://www.5-star-shareware.com/Internet/Email-clients/outlook-express.htm*).

Follow their link to download the email program. It is 469KB (about half a million text characters worth) in size so it could take a good hour to download over the telephone system to your hard disk, if you are still on narrowband. As they mention, a small set-up file will need to be downloaded first.

When I have got my Copy of Outlook Express

When you have downloaded Outlook Express you will need to obtain an email address. An email address labels a disk storage area on a web server, which is a complex of large computers that store and transfer Web

information. Email addresses are always associated with websites, which in turn are labelled by Universal Resource Locators (URLs).

Microsoft provides a basic, but free and convenient, email hosting site called Hotmail. You can access it at *www.hotmail.com*. When you enter this site you will be 'talked-through' obtaining your email address. You have purchased an 'Internet Package' which may include the use of an email address.

Your email address will have the structure:

alias@WebSite.com

or for example:

deaconbloxwich@hotmail.com

- 'deaconbloxwich' is an alias, a unique name identifying a particular email 'box'. A particular individual or group could have an unlimited number of such 'mail boxes'

- 'hotmail' is a domain name specific to a particular information storage partition (website) on the server system

- 'com' is a domain specifier, in this case denoting a global entity which is nominally a trading corporation

After you have registered your email address online it will be ready for use within minutes. Not only will you be able to use it to send emails, but your friends and colleagues will be able to use it immediately to send you letters and attached information, whether or not you actually have an email-reading program like Outlook Express, and whether or not you can use it!

Where can I find the Program I have just Downloaded?

You can invoke Outlook Express by clicking through the Start menu as illustrated in the screen below:

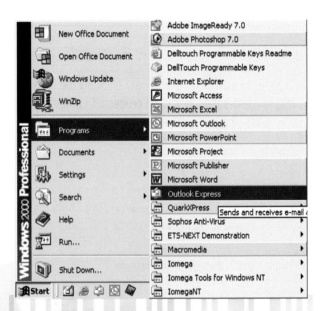

or, more conveniently, by double-clicking it's icon on your Desktop (provided you have set-up a shortcut icon).

Setting-up Dial-up Connection

The first thing we need to do now is establish a through connection via the public telephone system to the Internet. The exact steps vary depending upon which version of the Windows operating system you use: Windows 98, 2000, ME or XP.

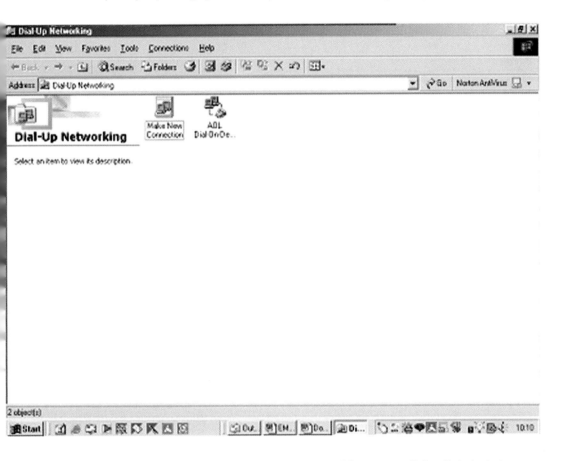

For all Windows users, the precise details can be read from your off-line Help text at:

C:\WINDOWS\help\msoe.chm::/mailtrb_not_connecting_to_ip.htm.

First, from the Desktop, click Start, Settings, Dial-up Connections or Dial-up Networking.

This is illustrated by the screen here. In this case, if you now click on the icon 'AOL Dial-on-De(mand)' you are immediately routed through to AOL and enter the logging-on process. Of course, if you use other ISPs their icons will appear in a similar place for you to invoke them with a click.

This whole Dial-up exercise is redundant for broadband users who are 'always connected to the Internet'.

TASK

To be able to carry out the tasks contained within this unit you will need to gather 5 e-mail addresses from family or friends (it is assumed that you have an email account already setup).

Email address 1 =
Email address 2 =
Email address 3 =
Email address 4 =
Email address 5 =

165

When I am in Outlook Express

When you are in Outlook Express you will see a screen like that below:

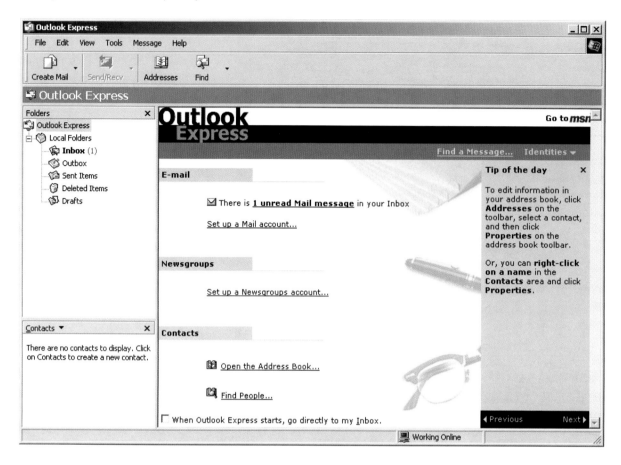

To close the Outlook Express program, choose File, Exit. Alternatively click on the cross in the top right hand corner.

EMAIL MESSAGE FEATURE OPTIONS

Message Addressee Options

From: Your email address.

To: This is the email address of the main (or only) recipient.

Cc: This is the one or more email addresses of the additional recipients. Multiple addresses on this line are separated with commas or semi-colons.

Bcc: If you list multiple addressees here, then each of them are kept in ignorance of the identities of the other addressees (if any).

Subject: This optional line lends a title to your letter which title is quoted in the recipients inbox. Omission of this title looks slovenly and may irritate the recipient or even lead to the message being deleted unread.

Font Style and Size: It is possible to choose the Font Style (i.e. artistic shape of the lettering) and the type symbols' Size as shown on the next page:

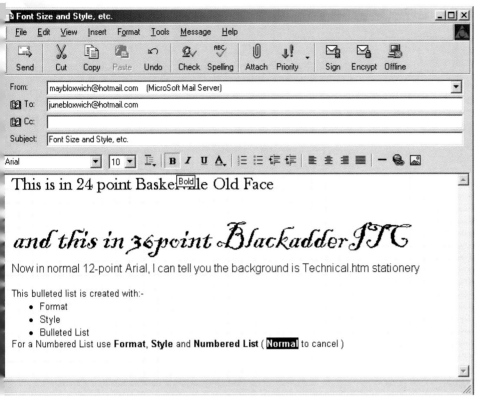

The screen also illustrates some of the other cosmetic and presentational features that can be incorporated in messages.

It is also possible to do extra things like modifying alignments and add bulleted lists.

CREATING AND SENDING EMAIL MESSAGES

Email combines many of the advantages of the telephone with many of the advantages we associate with written letters sent through the post but like both media it also has pitfalls that we need to watch out for.

Like the telephone, it is quite immediate, allowing our message to reach anywhere in the world in a matter of seconds, because telephone messages of any sort travel at the Speed of Light, and even in dense media like quartz or phosphor bronze this is many thousands of miles per second. Like packet mail, it is relatively cheap, an informative message costing pennies rather than pounds to send anywhere in the world.

Like packet mail, and unlike the telephone, it leaves us with a copy that we can compose, keep, review, change, and even duplicate to several people simultaneously.

Telephone can be a rather treacherous medium because it is difficult to judge the state of mind of our respondent as we depend solely upon auditory cues like tone of voice, accent and vocabulary to form an impression of his sub-text (if any). On the other hand, with email, as with packet letters, we depend entirely upon our respondent's grammar and choice of words for our understanding of the message. This of course means that unless we know the person it is very easy to misunderstand and be misunderstood, especially with controversial material or attempts at humour.

Because of the way in which an email can be 'fired off' more easily than a traditional letter, where there may be pauses for fetching paper, retracting bail bars and generally pausing for thought, we have to be particularly careful not to be too brusque, even unintentionally.

When the Outlook Express screen comes up you need to click Create Email on the toolbar. This will display the New Message screen.

To create an email message you need to supply these three essential elements:

1 Sender Address – this section will contain your email address.

2 Recipient Address – you need to type this by entering the email address in the To: textbox (the open book icon is a portal to an Address Book where you could store frequently-used addresses).

3 The Title (an indication of what the email contains) – This is entered in Subject:

4 The Message – This is typed in to the large text area below. As with other applications spell checking can be undertaken before sending to ensure professional looking emails (unlike the illustration).

The Cc: textbox is for nominating secondary addressees, but we will not use this at the moment.

Saving a Message

Choose File, Save As from the menu bar, the Save As dialog box will be displayed, the message can be saved into any disk directory (folder) of our choice; with a suitable filename.

In a likely case the computer will suggest that you save in the directory 'My Documents' (the default) and call the file by a suggested file name. We can change one or both of these conditions, but by clicking the Save button at lower right we will accept its suggestions for the filename and directory on this occasion.

Sending the Message

When you are ready to send the message, click on the Send button located under the File menu option and the message is dispatched instantly, because of interface mediation delays it can easily take half an hour for the email to reach a respondent.

Attaching Files to Email Messages

It is possible to include a variety of text document and image files with your email message. These extra files are known as attachments.

You can send emails to multiple recipients by putting the addresses in the Cc: line, using comma as a separator.

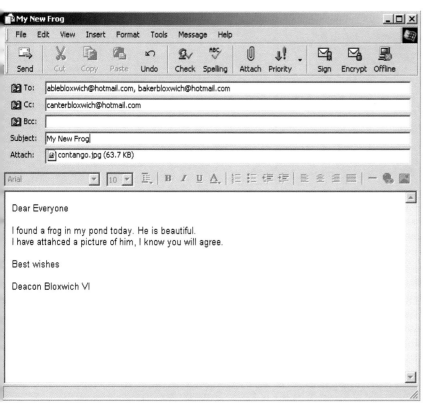

Choose Insert, File Attachment.

From this position you are offered a File Browser Window, navigate to the location where the file is stored. Select the required file.

Click the Attach button, the attached file is added into the Attach: text bar as shown:

To insert a picture into your message content (as opposed to forwarding it as an attachment) use Insert, Picture whilst you are entering data in the actual message.

And then browse for your picture in the succession of File Opening Windows, which you can then invoke.

Clicking in the Picture Window then inserts the picture into the message.

TASK

Create a new email and send it to email address 1 and cc it to email address 2. The content of the email can contain any suitable text requesting that the recipient reply.

Composing Messages Off-line in a Word Processor

It is possible to prepare text in a word processor or other editor program and later insert it into an email as the whole, or part of a message. This may be valuable if the material is of a lengthy or complex character and especially if it is a template standardised message.

For example, you could compose a poem 'Ode to Contango' in a Word document called ODEC.DOC stored in the My Documents directory and later insert the verse into a message. The file needs to be saved as a text file to be able to be inserted later.

To insert the off-line composition use the Create Mail and address entry stages. Choose Insert, Text From File.

The email program will only accept very basic text files or HTML (web language) files, so any fancy fonts or formatting I organised for my poem within the word processing program will be lost.

Clicking Text from File, Windows will invoke a File Browser Window. Navigate to the location where the poem is stored and click ODEC.TXT to load.

Obtaining a Digital Signature

A digital signature is an encrypted (scrambled) message which is attached to an email message as a means of 'authenticating' the identity of the sender. This is not a password in the usual sense and it cannot be stressed too highly that whatever the number-theoretical indications of security it is foolish to place too much faith in any security code.

Digital signatures can be ordered over the Internet from proprietary suppliers. Microsoft's preferred supplier is Verisign®.

Acquiring a digital signature is a lengthy procedure involving a lot of confidential personal information and it is a good idea to assign half a day to the process.

You will be made to search around a lot of cyberspace 'dead letter-boxes'. Do not attempt this process in a college, library or other semi-public place.

Attaching a Signature to Email Messages

When you have successfully acquired your digital signature tool you may implement it using Tools and Digitally sign before sending your message.

Attaching Stationery to Email Messages

Stationery includes pastel designer backgrounds set behind your message. Try not to use a Background colour that will clash with your text colour as this can be distracting.

For example, to implement the 'Nature' effect from the Message Window use Format, Apply Stationery, 1 Nature.

Using Templates and Default Layouts

In a more comprehensive sense, stationery involves not only designer backgrounds but also customised text font colours and margins.

To apply a comprehensive stationery template to all outgoing messages invoke Tools, Options and Compose from the Main Menu (not the message window).

All stationery-using messages need to be in Rich Text (HTML) Format, make sure HTML formatting is turned on using Format, Rich Text (HTML).

Create Email Messages and File them for Later Transmission

Compose a message in the normal manner and then use File, Save As in the Message Window to display the File Browser Window. Navigate to the folder that you wish to save the email, type in a suitable name and click Save.

Printing Email Messages

Select File, Print from the drop-down menu and click.

The Print dialog screen will be displayed, click OK or select suitable options from those available for a printout of the email message.

HOW TO READ AND ACTION YOUR EMAIL MESSAGES

Change of Identity

By default (i.e. unless you specify a different action), Outlook Express will start with a main identity (or managing user's folder). If other users share the local PC, then they can summon their work folders using File, Switch Identity and clicking their name in the Switch Identities box.

In the example on the next page, our sharers today are Francis and May; both Francis and May are members of the Bloxwich family. When May clicks her name her own folder screen appears and she is ready to open the mail (if any) from her own inbox. The email letters may have attached files, such as word-processor documents for lengthy, formatted reports, or maybe JPEGs containing photographs or indeed combinations of such.

Open and Read Email Messages

May has one email message lying unread in her Inbox. By clicking on *1 unread Mail message* on the Main Screen she can access this text.

May has received two identical messages. To open an email message double-click the title.

This will display a screen so that you can read the email, it also shows the details of the sender and the date and time of dispatch.

TASK

Read and reply to the response (click Reply) received from email address 1.

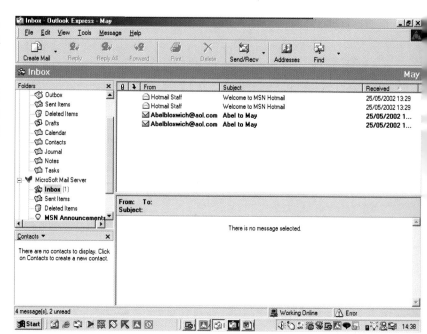

Deleting an Email

To Delete a message currently in view, click the red brush cross Delete key on the toolbar.

This leaves only the first message, and the software automatically reverts to May's **Inbox** listing screen; automatically opens the new last message, showing its content in the bottom right frame, and changes its list details from bold to grey to show it as read. (It may be difficult to see this with the blue highlighter over it).

Each email account provider has a different amount of storage space so be aware that deletion of unwanted mail is a necessity.

Viewing Attachments

An email with a symbol of a paper clip next to it indicates that the mail has been sent with an attachment.

Click on the larger of the two paperclip symbols in the extreme right of the screen centre between the inbox file list and the content preview window. Select the Save Attachments option to save the file to a specified location, for viewing later.

Double-clicking may open the file or display a wizard (a sequence of windows which then talks you through an operation) depending of the file type.

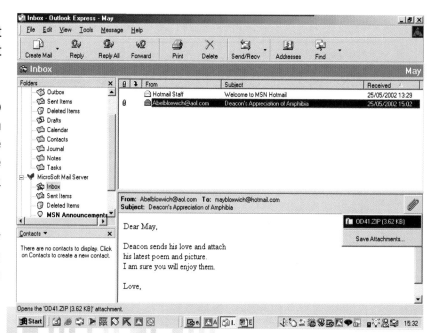

Some ISP servers will always compress multiple attachments, follow the on-screen prompts to save and view later. Many attachments sent by sophisticated popular ISP systems, will be 'self-decompressing' without you having to acquire special compressor/decompressor programs.

Printing Attached Files

Double-clicking the file within the message window will open the attachment (depending on file type), then just click on the Print button within the application. Alternatively, you may need to navigate to the application with which it was created and utilise the open procedure or navigate to the storage location of the file. Either method, the file will open in its 'native' software, click File, Print or press the Print button on the toolbar.

Forwarding Email Messages

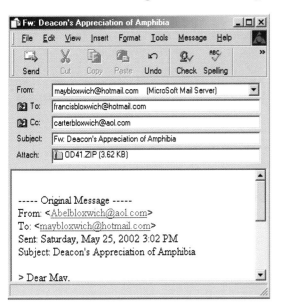

An existing message can be forwarded on, with any attachments, to one or more other email users.

To do this, click on the Forward icon on the toolbar.

This immediately gives the Fw: (Original Title) window.

Enter the address of the primary re-recipient in the text box To: and the addresses of secondary recipients (if any) in the Cc: box. Subject: is Fw: (Original Title) by default, but you can edit this before forwarding if desired. Attach: nominates the file(s) for passing on

Note the predicate in front of the passed-on message quoting the original author and the original recipient, together with the time and date of the original.

Editing Messages

Before you Forward or Reply to a message you may want to add your own comments and observations to it.

For example, after pressing the Forward or Reply button, you can edit the content of the original letter before forwarding the message to another recipient or returning the script to the sender. You can do this by clicking into the original text body (denoted with leading > signs) and typing your own material.

When satisfied, click Send.

Saving Messages

Choose File, Save As from the menu bar, the Save As dialog box will be displayed, the message can be saved into any disk directory (folder) of your choice; with a suitable filename.

In a likely case the computer will suggest that you save in the directory 'My Documents' (the default) and call the file by a suggested file name. We can change one or both of these conditions, but by clicking the Save button at lower right we will accept its suggestions for the filename and directory on this occasion. The message will be saved by default as a Microsoft email .eml file.

Blocking Messages from Particular Senders

You can Block messages from any sender you no longer wish to receive email from by clicking: Tools, Message Rules, Blocked Senders List and enter the email address of the person you would like to block in the text box of the Add Sender Window.

Another, Add Sender Window appears and is executed by clicking OK. Blocked senders can later be unblocked at any time.

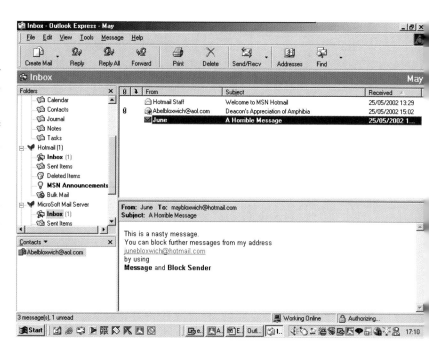

Setting up an Automated Reply to Respond to Email Messages

When you are away from your workplace ('Out of Office') you will probably want to send your respondents an automatic email reply apologising for your absence, explaining in brief and general terms why you are not in, and promising to action their correspondence by a given date.

For example, May is going on holiday for fourteen days and wants to send her clients this message:

> **Dear Client**
>
> **I am sorry but I will not be able to answer your emails until August 14th because I am taking some leave.**
>
> **But I look forward to giving your message my full attention when I get back.**
>
> **Regards**
>
> **May**

In Outlook, which is a paid-for full-function email utility, there is a regular menu function designed to expedite this feature. Outlook Express, however, is a 'free' and 'unsupported' product that does not explicitly offer this enhancement.

Message Creation

Use File, New, Mail Message to access the Message Window. Enter the desired message and click Save As. Save the file with a suitable name (such as 'Sorry').

Creat an Out of Office Rule

Select Tools, Message Rules and Mail.

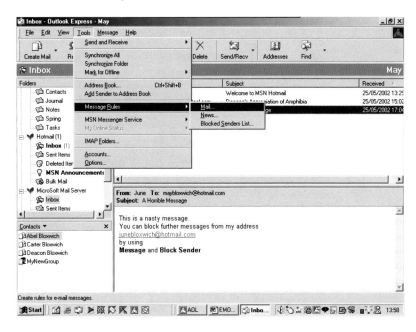

Select the New button to create a new rule. The New Mail Rule dialog box will be displayed.

1   Select For all messages.

2   Select Reply with message.

3   Click on the blue *message* in the Rule Description box, and locate the file with which you want to reply (such as 'Sorry') in the appropriate folder, accepting it with Open.

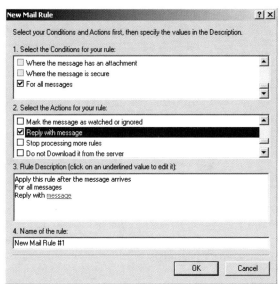

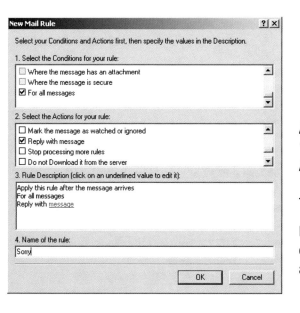

After naming the rule and clicking OK, select the *message* (such as 'Sorry') from the succeeding Message Rules window and click Apply Now.

Testing your Rule

Finally, pose as a respondent using a different email account, in order to test the functionality of your automated reply message. Or ask a friend to try it for you and let you know if it's working.

TASK

Create a new email add the subject line Trial. Send the email to email address 2 & 3 and blind copy it to email address 4. The context of the email should indicate how you are getting on and what you have learnt. Attach a file that you have previously created. Ask the recipient to reply and attach a file (any will do).

HOW TO FILE EMAIL MESSAGES

Creating Folders to store Email Messages

You can create folders (disk directories for storing groups of related files) through Windows Explorer or My Computer.

But you can also create them conveniently within Outlook Express.

Choose File, Folder, New from the drop-down menu.

Click New to display the Create Folder window. First you will have to select an existing folder in which to place your new folder (Local Folders has been chosen in the illustration). Now you can enter the name of the new folder (the illustration shows a folder called 'Spring' has been created) in the New Folder text bar and click OK.

Switching Folders

To switch folders simply click on the name of the folder in its list in the left-hand **Folders** window. The contents of the folder will then be displayed in the two right-hand windows.

Deleting Folders

To delete a folder, click onto the folder's name in the Folders list; and then click File, Folder, and Delete.

Moving or Copying Messages to other Folders

You want to copy a message from the Inbox to the new folder (such as 'Spring'). Select the file, choose Edit, Copy to Folder. The Copy window will be displayed click on new folder (such as 'Spring'). You now have the message in the new folder and also the original message in the Inbox.

If you wanted to shift the message to the new folder and then remove it from its original location you would select the Move to Folder option instead.

Retrieving the Emails from Folders

To retrieve a message from a folder, click on the folder name (such as 'Spring') in the **Folders** list, and then click on the **Subject** (or **From**) name in the messages list in the upper right window. Normally, the last message will be automatically displayed anyway, but others can be picked and will then display in an overlaid Message Window.

Storing Messages on a Mail Server

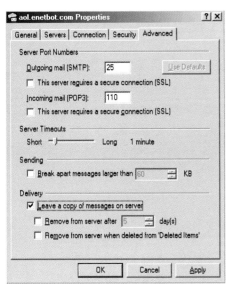

You will normally use a Mail Server for storing your messages if you read email from more than one computer. When you use a second computer you can download messages from the server. Most companies and organisations have such systems so that employees can access business email from home and of course mobile phone companies have similar systems for email downloads to handsets. There are different kinds of mail servers for the different messaging protocols: POP3, IMAP and HTTP.

Select Tools, Accounts. An Internet Accounts box appears. Click Properties, whereupon a Properties box appears. Now click the Advanced tab and look down to the Delivery section. Check Leave a copy of messages on server. There are further options for deleting stale messages from the server or those deleted from 'Deleted Items' within Outlook Express.

Click OK.

> ### TASK
>
> **Read the reply from the recipients and view the attachments. Create a storage location (folder) and save the email(s) into it.**

Creating Email Groups in an Address Book Facility

You can open the Address Book from the Main Screen by clicking Addresses on the toolbar; or alternatively Tools, Address Book.

To add all reply recipients to the address book automatically use Tools, Options, click on the Send tab, and then click Automatically put people I reply to in my Address Book.

Creating a Group of Contacts in an Address Book

Groups are especially useful if you have a group of people you email on a regular basis, rather than having to enter each recipient's email address each time a group can be created. When creating the email to go to the group the group name will be added to the To: box, this saves time and effort.

Within the Address Book, select New, New Group as shown:

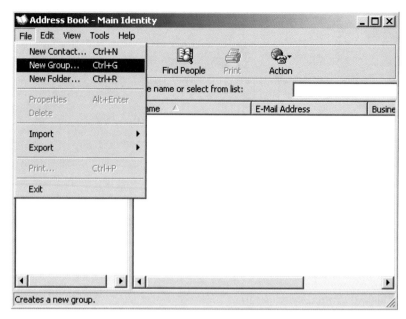

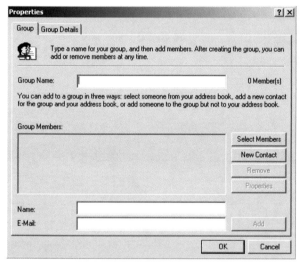

Enter a Group Name on the Group tab. Click OK.

Now to gather your chosen respondents into the new group click Select Members. Click on your contact's name and use Select to add them to the group.

TASK

Create a group to include email addresses 3, 4 & 5. Send an email to this group

HOW TO MANAGE AN ADDRESS BOOK

Adding a New Address

Within the Address Book window select New and New Contact. Now enter a friend/colleague's details in the Properties Window as shown (the title bar is updated to the persons name when you enter their details). Click Add and OK to confirm.

Editing Addresses

To edit details in order to clarify the personal and email identities of an individual and add a suitable nickname.

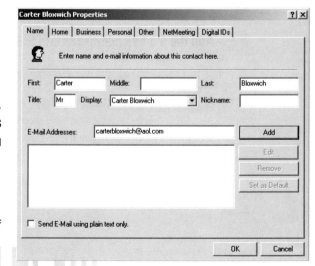

Click Name in the Address Book.

Select the Properties icon, followed by selection of the Name tab and make any revisions necessary in the appropriate text bars, such as:

First: Abel
Last: Bloxwich
Title: Mr
Display: (automatic update to 'Abel Bloxwich')
Nickname: Tasmania
E-mail Addresses: *Abelbloxwich@aol.com*

Click Add and OK to agree changes.

Deleting an Address

To delete an address within the Address Book click on the name of the person you wish to delete under the Name: column and then click the Delete: icon on the toolbar. An alert window will be displayed click Yes to accept permanent deletion.

Searching an Address Book

Within the Address Book click the Find People icon. In the resulting Find People window enter the name of the person you wish to find in the Name: text bar and click Find Now.

You can also search for people within groups by selecting the appropriate group name.

Creating Aliases

An alias is a single group name that represents a batch of contacts, it can be used to send a circular to each of the contained members.

To dispatch such a circular simply type the Group Name in the To: text box.

TASK

Add the 5 email addresses into the address book.

The Efficiency of Messaging

The efficiency of your email messaging depends upon three fundamental things:

- Speed

- Storage

- File and Directory Structures

In ordinary circumstances the speed of the computer and its attendant telephonic connections will be the dominant control. The speed is in turn resolvable into:

1   CPU Speed

2   Server Speeds

3   Connection Speeds

The CPU (Central Processor Unit) speed is the rated internal clock pulse speed of your computer. These days speeds of 1.6 to 2 MegaHertz (MHz) are commonplace. In theory, the greater this speed the better, but for email purposes the other, external, speed factors are very much more important. The operational speeds of the sender's and recipients ISPs and mail servers are in turn compounded by internal clock speeds, software efficiencies and congestion factors.

Lastly, the rated speed of the electrical, microwave or optical telephonic network connections is a major factor on email transmission speeds. Such transmission speeds are quoted in Mbaud or Mb (essentially millions of bits per second). For copper wire narrowband transmissions 56Mb is usual today, but this can be increased by a factor of ten using various broadband arrangements.

The Email Address

Email addresses have the following general format:

alias@UniversalResourceLocator

The alias is an arbitrary unique name without embedded spaces or punctuation which identifies a specific electronic mailbox attached to the website defined by the Universal Resource Locator (URL). The mailbox may or may not identify with an individual human: a certain person may have many mailboxes on many URLs, and some mailboxes may refer to functions or departments rather than people (e.g. *info@charlesworth.co.uk*).

In the email address:

deaconbloxwich@hotmail.com

'deaconbloxwich' is the alias and hotmail.com the URL.

THE ADVANTAGES AND DISADVANTAGES OF EMAIL

To assess some of the advantages and disadvantages of email it is useful to compare it with two of its close conceptual relatives:

● Packet Post sent in an envelope

● Telephone communications

With regard to the post it is:

- Much speedier, the message arriving in minutes rather than days

- Automatically generates a magnetic file copy

- Is easily edited, amended and forwarded without scanning or wholesale re-typing

- Also can be rendered as hard-copy if needed

- Does not require inconvenient carriage operations

- Is cheaper than postage

- Is accessible through websites

- Does not require the purchase and management of physical consumables like paper and ink

But on the other hand:

- Is difficult and expensive to make confidential

- Discourages thoughtful composition

- Needs special electronic machinery, connections and software

- Demands computing skills

- Is difficult to authenticate

When compared to the telephone, email offers these advantages:

- Suppresses abortive calls by automatically recording the address and message of respondents in your absence

- Prevents garbled or unintelligible message or contact content being recorded in any messaging system used in your absence

- Enables additional message material to be attached like enclosures in a packet letter

- A written record is automatically transcribed and filed

- Offers greater confidentiality than the telephone

- Is much cheaper than the telephone

- Is uncorrupted by background sounds

- Permits considered and unhurried delivery

On the other hand:

- Affective state of respondent is difficult to judge

- Computing and typing skills are needed

- Email is inconvenient in mobile applications

- Unsuitable for emergency use

In the majority of routine business communications email offers decisive advantages over either the letter or the telephone, but is not suited to critical legal or customer-facing applications.

ISPS AND PROTOCOLS

An ISP (Internet Service Provider) is a company which mediates computerised communication between the user and the telephonic Internet communications network. As part of this function, it will also permit a number of email aliases to be set up by a given user based upon its own website provision.

For example:

Abelbloxwich@aol.com

Is an email address for the alias 'abelbloxwich'. Of course Abelbloxwich is not the real name of the user.

There are many commercial ISPs: The most famous in Britain are AOL (America On Line), BT (with its OpenWorld and broadband services) and FreeServe. Like mobile phone companies they offer a range of domestic and commercial tariffs, depending upon whether you have a narrowband or broadband facility; the time of day you wish to use Internet connections and other deciding factors.

The usual way of establishing contact through an ISP is to load their software from a supplied CD-ROM.

It is quite possible to be your own email host, and set up a website with your own URL and a limited number of definable email aliases for example:

info@www.jamesrwarren.com

SECURITY AND ORGANISATION

Email Security

When you send emails beware that they cross a worldwide public telephone network, and that total security cannot be guaranteed. Nevertheless, it is possible to scramble (encrypt) the message content using a special program. This scrambling involves specialised password-like phrases called public and private keys. These keys are also used to re-constitute (decrypt) the received message back into plain text.

Encryption keys differ form ordinary passwords in that their component characters are not merely passively checked for matching an original record, but are actively exploited in the mathematical convolution process.

As a general statement, scrambling is expensive and inconvenient. It is easier to justify the use of an encrypted digital 'signature' whose only purpose is to validate the identity of the message sender, the actual message itself remaining in plaintext.

The Benefits of Offline Message Composition

It is often cheaper and more convenient to compose messages offline (i.e. when you are disconnected from the Internet).

This minimises call charges (if any) and also permits a greater range of software (e.g. WORD) to be used to compose the message, so offline working is particularly useful with longer messages. All attachments should be generated when you are off the Net, and have efficient use of the RAM memory and disk cache facilities which would otherwise be occupied by the memory-resident email program.

Checking for the Arrival of New Messages

The most straightforward way to do this is to use Tools, Options and select the General tab within Outlook Express.

You are then given the option of changing the frequency (in minutes) of message-checking and also the connective action to be taken (if any) should a message be detected.

There are, however, avenues of checking through directory services though from a non-corporate point of view some freeware email checking utilities such as AvirMail Version 1.70 are often attractive. Programs like this enable email to be visually inspected *whilst it is still on the server*.

Inserting Hyperlinks into Your Outgoing Message

A hyperlink is a line of text, perhaps just a single word, that your recipient can click on to invoke a website or other downloadable resource which you have associated with your message. For example, you have set up a website about newts called *www.newts.info*. (By the way, the system automatically recognises such links in many cases as presents them in underlined blue type like that). You want to send an email to *deaconbloxwich@hotmail.com* congratulating him for his artistry in presenting the frog picture and poem, and inviting him to visit your site about newts.

Just type the message normally via Create Mail. With a link of this format the computer automatically recognised it for what it is. But suppose that you just wanted to use the word 'newts' as the hyperlink. In that case you would highlight the word with your mouse cursor (dragging the mouse pointer over the word 'newts' whilst keeping the left mouse key depressed with your index finger) and then clicking Insert and Hyperlink.

Then complete the Hyperlink pop-up window with the appropriate Net reference.

When you Receive a Message

When you receive a message there are a number of things you may do with it:

(a) Delete it Straight Away
   This may seem strange, but it is the safest thing to do with messages of whose origin you are uncertain; or known junk mail (spam).

(b) File it
   If you know what the message is about and it seems lengthy or has attachments you may decide to file it for later reference.

(c) Print it

This can be handy for shorter emails that however need a considered or composed reply

(d) Read it Straight Away

You are likely to do this with briefer notes from trusted addresses.

Selecting Different Message Views

By selecting View, Current View it is possible to select the presentation of different message types.

There are options to show or hide messages of different status, to customise the message view or to group messages by conversational themes.

Downloading Files

Downloading is the act of making your computer copy the content of attached incoming files to a temporary files directory on *your hard disk*.

Downloads often involve large programs, reports or pictures.

Special care is needed with downloads:

● Their sheer size may tie-up your computer for a long time, in extreme cases provoking a server time-out

● Their content may not justify the time and money expended

● They may act as vectors for damaging viruses or trojans, not necessarily known about by the sender

When attachments are processed in this way always make sure they are segregated to a specialised temporary-downloads directory before inspection, and employ a reliable memory-resident virus-checking program during the downloading operation. Destroy anything the virus-checker queries and ring or mail your respondent about the problem.

Potential Problems with Automated Reply Methods involving Groups

Automated replies can be especially tricky if you venture beyond the simple 'Out of Office' format.

The very act of grouping your respondents implies that they have different conversational needs, and thought should be given to the nature of the content according to the nature of the incoming message.

For example, a well-organised email system may have different aliases for different categories of sender such as:

● *info@bloggs.com*

● *orders@bloggs.com*

● *vacancies@bloggs.com*

respectively for General Enquiries; placing an Order for Goods and Enquiring about Jobs.

Automated replies relevant to each group, and possibly returning a docket number, can be tailored to each sort of sender.

Automated Reply Methods involving specific Words

From The Outlook Express Menu Toolbar choose Tools, Message Rules, Mail.

You can then select New from the New Mail dialogue box to produce another dialogue box: New Mail Rule.

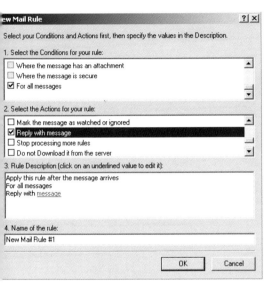

There are a number of different options that you can select, however for this example, in section 1, add a tick in the square next to the words:

'Where the Subject line contains specific words'.

In section 2, you can then add a tick next to the words:

'Reply with Message'

In section three:

Click the Hyperlink 'message' that is contained in the sentence 'Reply with message'.

You are now being prompted by the Open dialogue box to locate and select an email message that has previously been saved. This message is the one that will be used to automatically reply to emails 'Where the Subject line contains specific words'.

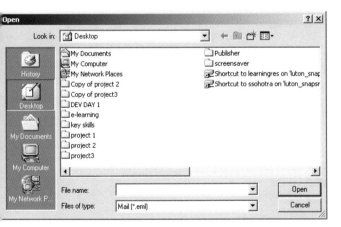

Once the email that you wish to use as your automated reply has been located and selected:

Click the Open button.

Back at the New Mail Rule dialogue box:

Click the hyperlink 'contains specific words' in section 3.

Now enter the words that will be used to activate the automated reply.

In this example the words 'market research' have been used.

Click the add button, then OK.

185

The Message Rules dialogue box now displays your new mail rules and in the window below, describes the values of the mail rules you have just applied.

Click OK.

For this example the words 'market research' were used, but you can decide to use any words you like.

You can also choose not to specify particular words and have an automated reply to all your incoming messages, maybe to say that you'll be out of the office for the day, or that you are on holiday, giving your return date in the automated reply.

Try setting up an automated reply as shown, and have your friends send you messages that receive automated responses.

DESKTOP PUBLISHING

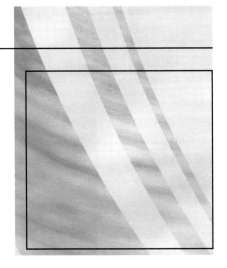

BEFORE YOU START

Checking Your System For Compatibility

Before you begin to design your DTP file, you need to check that your hardware is compatible. The monitor (Visual Display Unit) you have needs to be a colour monitor, not monochrome (black and white). This is so that you can see your DTP file in full colour and create eye-catching designs.

A CD-ROM drive is necessary to install the Microsoft Publisher software onto your system. If Microsoft Publisher is already installed, a CD-ROM may be necessary for additional clipart or photo galleries.

A mouse and keyboard are necessary to operate the software. Any PC compatible mouse or keyboard will be sufficient.

A floppy disk may be necessary if you need to transport your DTP file to another computer, or if you need to have your file printed at an outside commercial printers. A floppy disk holds 1.44MB of data, so you may need more than one if your DTP file is larger than 1.44MB in size.

If you would like to print your DTP file in full colour, you need to have a colour printer installed. Check your printer manual for print resolution, 360 dpi (dots per inch) should provide a good quality print. You may wish to check if your printer can take glossy paper, as this improves print quality at high resolution. Resolution and dpi are mentioned in more detail under Printing later in this section.

You will also need to check the RAM (Random Access Memory) of your PC. RAM is your computer's workspace. The larger the workspace, the more work can be achieved at one time. You will need more RAM to work more efficiently with photo files and high-resolution graphics. 32 MB is a minimum, and 64 MB or more is recommended for best results.

To check your system's RAM, right click on the My Computer icon on your desktop, select Properties.

Before you start check the RAM of your system.

This system has 128 MB RAM, which is recommended for working with MS Publisher.

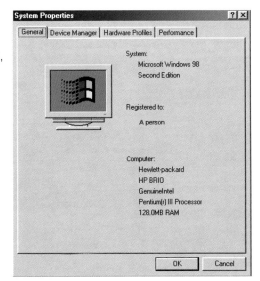

This system has 13.6 GB free disk space.

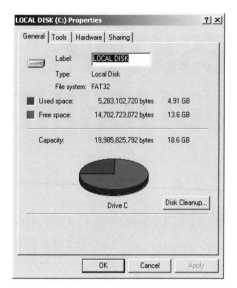

Your system's RAM will be displayed under the General tab

It is also important to check how much storage space you have on the hard disk where you are going to be saving your DTP file. This is to ensure that the file saves properly. Lack of storage space affects the overall performance of your system.

To check the amount of available storage space, double click My Computer on the desktop. Right click on your hard drive (usually C:\ drive) and select Properties.

A pie chart will display how much free space you have left on this drive. You should have around 500 MB free just to be safe.

TASK

Check your system and write down the RAM and available storage space on the hard disk you will be saving to.

RAM: _____

Hard Drive Space Available: _____

Check your printer and write down the name and model of your printer.

Name: _____ Model: _____

INTRODUCTION TO MICROSOFT PUBLISHER 2000

Microsoft Publisher 2000 is a desktop publishing software package that enables you to create, customise and publish items such as brochures, flyers, catalogues and websites easily and professionally.

LAUNCHING THE DTP SOFTWARE

Click on the Start button at the bottom left of the screen. Choose Programs and then click on the program you wish to launch i.e. Microsoft Publisher.

Alternatively, you may have a 'shortcut' to the program on your computer's desktop. If you can see an icon representing the program on the screen, double-click on it.

CREATING A NEW DTP FILE

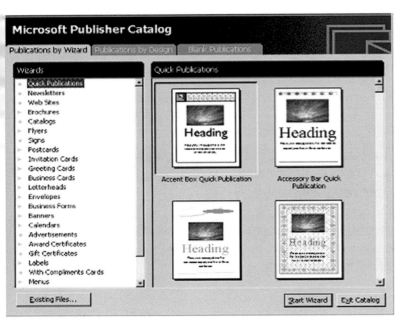

There are 3 ways of creating a new DTP file (also called a publication) in Microsoft Publisher using the Microsoft Publisher Catalog. The easiest way to layout a publication is to let Microsoft Publisher do it for you. However, you can also design your DTP file from scratch.

Publications by Wizard – create personalised publications using the wizards.

Publications by Design – create a set of publications, such as letterhead, business cards and a brochure, all with a common design theme.

Blank Publications – create a publication without using wizards.

Existing Files – to continue working on files you have already created.

Creating a New DTP File using the Wizard

When you start your publication or DTP file using the wizard, Microsoft Publisher inserts and positions the professionally developed design elements for you, letting you choose from the various design styles.

Choose File, New and then select the Publications by Wizard tab. In the Wizards window, click on the type of publication or DTP file you would like to create. In the right hand window, click on the type of design. Select Start Wizard. The wizard will now take you through a series of steps to change the layout, colour scheme or personal information in order to personalise your publication. Once you have decided on the changes click Next. Once all the changes are completed, click Finish. The wizard will take a few seconds to create your publication.

Once your publication has been created you can change the pictures and text with your own by clicking on the placeholders.

Using the Quick Publication Wizard with a Blank Document

Choose File, New and then select the Publications by Wizard tab. In the Quick Publication Wizard window click on the option you would like and then click Start Wizard. The wizard will now take you through a series of steps to change the layout, colour scheme or personal information in order to personalise your publication. Once you have decided on the changes click Next. Once all the changes are complete, click Finish. The wizard will take a few seconds to create your publication.

Once your publication has been created you can still change the pictures and text with your own by clicking on the placeholders.

Create a New DTP File using the Template

When you use a template for your DTP file or publication, Microsoft Publisher gives you a publication with the design elements already in place.

Choose File, New and then select Templates. Double-click on the template you would like to use for your publication; Microsoft Publisher will open up a copy of the template for you to make changes to. Make the changes you require to the open template to create a new publication.

Starting a new DTP File from Scratch

If you decide to lay out your DTP file from scratch, you need a design plan so that you are clear about how you want the file structured, where you'll place the text and graphics, and what colours you'll be using. You may want to sketch your design first, or use a design you have seen before and adapt it.

Choose File, New and then select the Blank Publications tab. Click on the type of publication you would like to use and click Create. If you do not see the type of publication you would like to use, click Custom Page at the bottom of the catalog, and then choose the options you would like from those given.

PAGE LAYOUT

Setting Page Margins, Columns and Gutters

A margin is the space between the edge of the page and where the text starts on the publication. To change the size of that space, you will need to change the size of the margins.

Choose Arrange, layout Guides to display the Layout Guides dialog box.

If you wish to change the size of the margins, use the spin buttons to adjust the margins. (The smaller the margin, the larger the work area and vice versa. Take note of the measurement unit (i.e. centimetres or inches) used.

The layout of columns is one of the main design elements in setting up a newsletter, but can be used in other publications too.

● One column layout is more often used for reports and technical documents. It has a more serious feeling.

● Two-column layout works well if you have a few long articles and can be easier to read than one column.

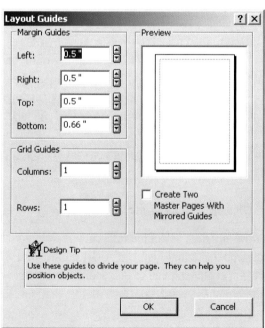

The Layout Guides dialog box displaying the Margin Guides, Grid Guides, Preview and Design Tip.

- Three-column layout is the most popular, as it is very flexible and it is easy to place text and graphics. Be careful of too much hyphenation when using three columns (see Text Wrapping).

- Four-column layout allows the most flexibility but requires the most care in design. This format works best if one column is left empty of text and is used for pictures or headings.

To change the number of columns, click on the Columns spin buttons to adjust the amount.

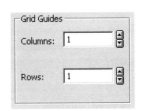

To make a large newspaper type format publication, you need to select the Two Backgrounds with Mirrored Guides option. This creates a newspaper effect with facing pages. This requires a Gutter Margin because facing pages need extra room between them for folding without losing any text.

To make a Gutter margin, first decide how much space the folding part of the newspaper will take. If the space required is an extra 0.5 cm, then set the margins on the inside of the facing pages 0.5 cm wider than on the outside. Only change gutter margins if you have clicked on the Two Backgrounds with Mirrored Guides option.

SETTING PAGE SIZE, PUBLICATION LAYOUT AND ORIENTATION

To change the size of paper from the default or to change the layout of your publication to labels or envelopes, choose File, Page Setup. This will display the Page Setup dialog box.

To change the publication layout click on the radio buttons within the Choose a Publication Layout at the top of the dialog box. The publication layout you choose will change the publication size options.

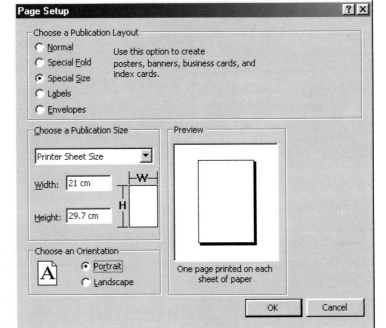

However, further options are available from the drop-down box within Choose a Publication Size section and these differ depending upon the layout choice.

The paper orientation you choose determines whether your publication will be printed cross-wise or lengthwise on a sheet of paper. You can choose either portrait, which is the regular, taller-than-wide orientation, or landscape, which is the wider-than-tall orientation.

Selecting the appropriate radio button in the Choose an Orientation section can change the orientation of your publication. When you change the orientation, the preview shows how this affects the height and width of your publication, as well as the number of sheets needed to print it. Check the Preview and click OK to confirm selection.

Changing the Page Size

The Print Setup dialog box displayed here indicates that the EPSON Stylus Photo 700 printer has been selected, paper size A4 and set to Portrait.

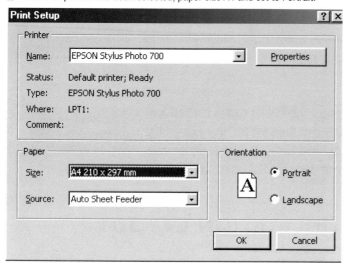

To change the size of the paper you would like to print on, choose File, Print Setup. This will display the Print Setup dialog box. To change the paper size, click on the arrow next to the size box and choose from the options given. The default paper size is A4; A5 is half the size of A4. Options for envelopes are also given here. Once you have selected the page size you require, click OK.

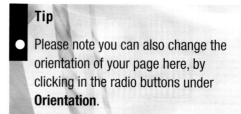

Tip

Please note you can also change the orientation of your page here, by clicking in the radio buttons under **Orientation**.

SAVING A DTP FILE

It is a good idea to save your DTP file often as you make changes, as you may lose your file if there is a power cut or your computer crashes. You can set Microsoft Publisher up to remind you to save your work if you think you are going to forget to save regularly.

Get a Reminder to Save your DTP File

Choose Tools, Options from the menu, select the User Assistance tab.

Click the Remind to save publication box to add a check mark. Type the number of minutes you want between reminders.

Click OK to confirm. Publisher will now periodically ask if you want to save the publication you're working on.

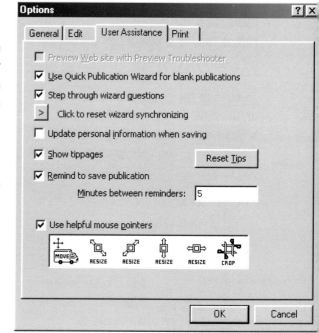

The following reminder will pop up after the time you entered has passed.

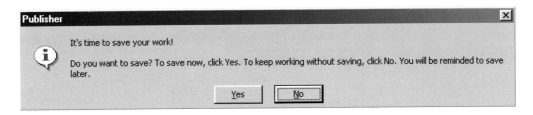

Save a New DTP File

If you wish to keep the publication, so that you can use it again, you will need to save it. Saving your documents is important if you ever want to retrieve them later.

To save a new DTP file for the first time, choose File, Save.
In the Save In box, select the folder where you want to save the new publication.
In the File Name box type a name for your new DTP file.
Click on the Save button to save your file.

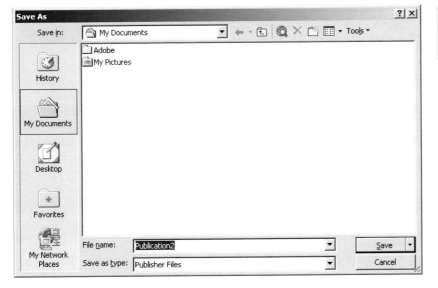

The Save As dialog box displaying the contents of the My Documents folder. Double-click to move into other folders.

*Remember where you have saved the file and what you named it!

Save an Edited DTP File without changing its name

To save an edited DTP file, you have two options:

1 Click on the Save icon on the toolbar 💾

2 Choose File, Save and select the Save button in the Save As dialog box. You will not need to rename your file.

Save a DTP File under a New Name

You may have saved your DTP file and want to keep the original file as it is, but save the changed file under a new name. This will ensure you have an original and a changed version.

Choose File, Save As. Enter an alternative name for your DTP file in the File Name box and click on the Save button to save the changed file.

You can use the same save procedure if you want to save your file to another location, for example a floppy disk. Simply change the Save in location to display an alternative location.

TASK

1 **Open Microsoft Publisher and create a new DTP file from scratch, without using a wizard. Choose the Full Page option. Save this new file as Exercise 2 – DTP. Make the following changes to the Page Layout:**

Left Margin	**2cms**
Right Margin	**2 cms**
Top Margin	**4 cms**
Bottom Margin	**4.25 cms**

2 **Divide the page into 3 columns.**

3 **Change the paper size to A5, and the orientation to Landscape.**

4 **Save the changes to your file and close.**

OPENING AN EXISTING DTP FILE

You may need to retrieve saved publications, to view, print or edit. Click on the Existing Files button on the Microsoft Publisher catalog.

Alternatively, choose File, Open. The Open dialog box will be displayed.

The Open dialog box displaying the contents of the My Documents folder. Double-click to move into other folders.

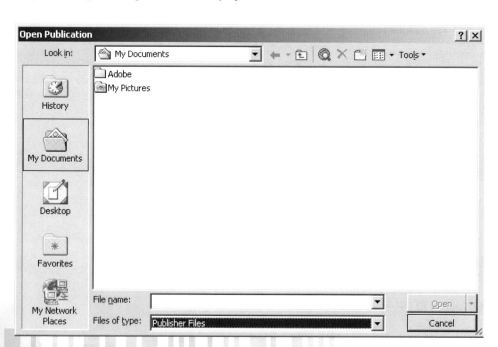

Open the drop-down list by Look in and navigate to the folder that your document is stored in (folders are indicated by the yellow icon). Double click on a folder to move into it, or use the Back or Up One Level buttons to move up out of a folder.

Locate the document you wish to open, click on it and then click on the Open button at the bottom right of the dialog box. (Alternatively, you can double-click on the file).

If you cannot see your publications in a folder, make sure the Files of type list at the bottom of the dialog box is showing the correct file types. Publisher recognises publication files because they have a .pub filename extension. This filename extension may not be visible if it has not been set in Windows Explorer.

MANIPULATING TEXT IN A DTP FILE

The text in your DTP file plays a very important part in defining the style of your file. The look of the letters gives your file personality and feeling and can affect the readability of the file. The style of the text (or font) has more visual influence than any other element. It is therefore important to think carefully about what you want your file to say, before choosing the font. Start with some basic fonts that put across the idea of your file, and then add fonts that are good for that particular type of publication. The font also affects the compactness of your file – so if you want a lot of information to fit into a small space, choose a more compact font.

Entering and Editing Text

To insert text into your DTP file, click on the Text Frame Tool on the toolbar to the left of the screen. Your cursor will change to a cross as you pass it over the blank file. On the blank file, draw a box by clicking and dragging the mouse in the desired area on the blank file. This will be the text area into which you can type your text. The text area is visible because of the dotted grey border and handles surrounding the text frame.

Text
Frame
Tool

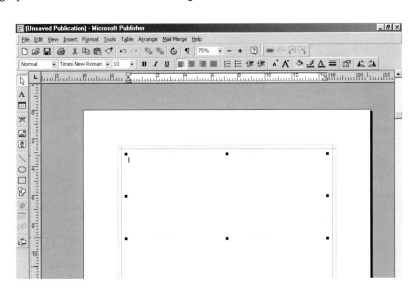

Selecting Text

To move, copy, or delete text, change the font, font style, font size, font colour, or apply any formatting to the text, you first need to select it. This is simple – click to the left of the text, or the starting place of the text, and left click and drag across the text. Selected text will be highlighted in black. To select all the text in a DTP file, simply press the Ctrl+A keys on the keyboard.

Moving Text

To move text, simply select it, and then drag it to the new position on the page. You can move text to another textbox on the page in this way.

Alternatively, select the Cut ✂ icon on the toolbar, click in the new position where you would like to place the text and select the Paste 📋 icon on the toolbar to paste the text into the new position.

NB   Your original text will have been deleted when you cut it.

Copying Text

To copy text, simply select it by pressing and holding the Ctrl key and then drag it to the new position on the page. You can copy text to another textbox on the page in this way.

Alternatively, select the Copy 📋 icon on the toolbar, click in the position where you would like to copy the text and select the Paste 📋 icon on the toolbar to paste the text into the new position.

Your original text should still be in place.

Deleting Text

To delete text, simply select it and then press the Delete key on the keyboard, or select the text, right click over the text, and click Delete Text on the sub menu that appears. To delete the text box, select it so that the handles appear, and then right click over the text box and click Delete Object on the menu.

Applying Formatting to Text

To apply formatting to text, choose Format, Font. This will display the Font dialog box. Any changes made to the text will be previewed in the box at the bottom called Sample. This allows to you to see how your changes will look before applying them.

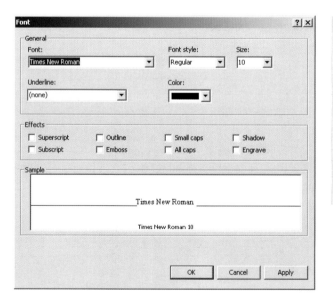

The Font dialog allows changes to be made to the Font, Fonts Style, Size, Underline, Colour and Effects. The results from the selections are displayed in the sample box, this ensures changes can be viewed before being agreed.

To alter the Font, Font Style, Size and Underline select the relevant drop-down arrow and choose from the options available.

To change the colour of your text, click on the drop-down arrow next to Color. This will bring up a menu of the most recently used colours. To choose from a wider range of colours, click on the More Colors command box. This will display a palette of colours to choose from. Click OK to agree selection.

To add Effects to your text, such as All Capitals, Subscripts, Superscript, click in the check box to change the text.

To agree changes to the text click Apply and OK.

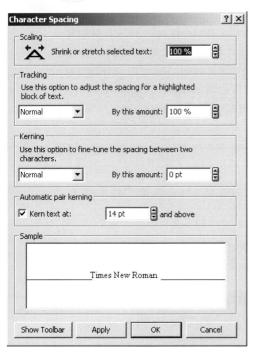

Character and Line Spacing

You can adjust the spacing of letters or characters in your text for a single line, or for a whole paragraph. This can help to improve the readability of small font sizes, or fit more characters into a smaller space thereby improving compactness. Microsoft Publisher also puts some vertical space between single-spaced lines, and this is usually adequate for most files, but you may need to increase the line spacing to make your file easier to read, especially if you are using sans serif fonts like Arial or dark fonts like Impact.

To change the spacing between letters or characters, choose Format, Character Spacing. You can stretch the text, make the spacing very loose or tight, and change the kerning. Kerning allows you to change the space between characters. The Sample box displays the effects of the changes made. Click Apply and OK to agree selection.

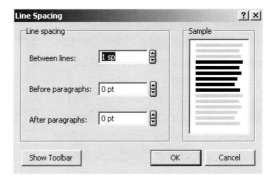

To change the spacing between lines, choose Format, Line Spacing. This dialog box allows changes to spacing between lines from single spacing (1 sp) to one and a half line spacing (1.5 sp) to double line spacing (2 sp). It also gives the option of choosing spacing before and after each paragraph. The Sample box displays the effects of the changes made. Click OK to agree selection.

Justifying Text

This is also known as 'alignment'. It is easy to change the alignment of the text in your document, by selecting it and clicking on the relevant icon on the toolbar. The icons are shown below with a brief description.

Left Aligned: All text lines up against the left margin, with the right edge of text uneven or 'ragged'. This alignment is recommended for body text because it's the most readable. This paragraph is set to left alignment.

Centred: Text is aligned from the centre of the page, and both left and right edges are uneven or 'ragged'. This text is not as easy to read as left-aligned text, but this alignment is often used for headings, invitations and announcements. It also offers a formal feeling to the file. This paragraph is set to centre alignment.

Right Aligned: All text lines up against the right margin, with the left edge of text uneven or 'ragged'. The eye struggles to find the beginning of each line with the alignment, so it is not often used. It is good to use for labelling a picture, or for an address on a letter. This paragraph is set to right alignment.

Justified: Text is aligned to both the left and right margins. Only use justified alignment if the font is regular or small and if there is quite a lot of text, otherwise it may create gaps in the body text, which affects readability of the file. If you are going to use Justified alignment a tip is to turn Microsoft Publisher's automatic hyphenation on so that words break evenly, and to prevent too much white space in your file. To do this choose Tools, Language, Hyphenation and click in the check box to turn automatic hyphenation on (or off!). Make sure there are not too many end-of-line hyphens in a paragraph. This paragraph is set to justified alignment.

Applying Fill Styles to a Selected Area

You can save yourself a lot of time and effort and easily keep your layout consistent by using style. This is especially useful if your DTP file has many pages.

A text style is a set of formatting characteristics that you can quickly apply to text on a paragraph-by-paragraph basis. A style contains all text formatting information: font and font size, font colour, indents, character and line spacing, tabs, and special formatting, such as numbered lists.

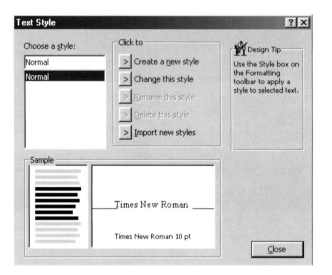

Publisher installs some default styles, such as Normal style. This style formats text as Times New Roman, 10 point, left aligned.

Other text styles can come from a variety of sources. You can define your own styles in Publisher, import text styles from other publications, or use text styles you have saved in a template.

To create a new style, select Create a New Style.

To change the current style selected, select Change this Style.

To import a style from another publication, or use text styles created in a template, select Import New Styles.

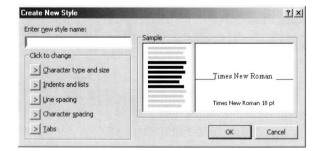

To create a new style, choose Format, Text Style. The Text Style dialog box will be displayed, giving you the options to create a new style, or change the existing style. Select Create a new style.

The next dialog box will give you the option to name the style and choose the formatting to apply to that style. Once all the formatting has been chosen, click OK.

Once you've created a style, you can apply it to a paragraph in either a text frame or a table in one step. The formatting changes affect the entire paragraph. Simply click on the Style box on the Formatting toolbar to change the style.

Positioning Text

You can position text within a text box by using the justify options, and you can position the text on the page by moving the text box around using the handles. It is also possible to place more than one textbox on a page, and this will allow you to position text more freely.

Using the Wrap Settings

To make your document or DTP file easier to read or to format it for a particular type of publication, such as a newsletter, you may want your text to wrap around an object or graphic. This can be achieved through changing the wrap settings.

Click on the WordArt or picture frame to select it. Choose Arrange, Bring to Front and then drag the picture over the text in the text box. Select the Wrap Text to picture ▣ icon or the Wrap Text to Frame ▣ icon on the Formatting toolbar.

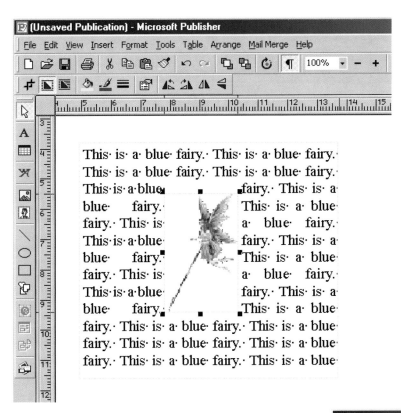

To wrap text squarely around the object, click on the Wrap text to Frame icon.

To wrap text tightly around the object, click on the Wrap text to Picture icon.

When wrapping text to the picture you will receive a confirmation dialogue box, click Yes if you wish to alter the wrapping, click No if you do not.

Once the wrapping text to the picture has been applied you may wish to adjust the wrap boundary. To do this, choose Format, Edit Irregular Wrap or click on the Edit Irregular Wrap ▨ icon on the toolbar.

Position the mouse pointer over a handle you want to move until it changes to the Adjust pointer. Drag the handle to change the outline of the picture. To add additional Adjust handles, hold down Ctrl key on the keyboard and

click where you want a new handle to appear. To delete a handle, hold down the Ctrl+Shift keys on the keyboard and click the handle.

NB Text contained in a table cannot be wrapped around a picture or WordArt.

Another way to change the wrap settings is to select the text frame and choose Format, Text Frame Properties. The Text Frame dialog box will be displayed. Click in the Wrap Text Around Objects check box.

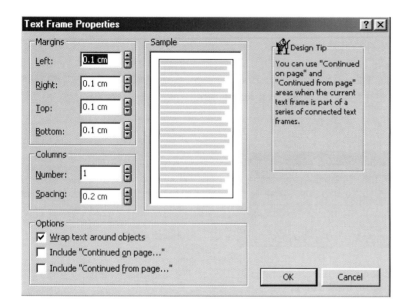

Choose the space between the object and the text by changing the margins.

Wrap text around graphics or WordArt by clicking Wrap text around objects.

Placing a Border around Text

Placing a border around text can define specific areas within the publication. To put a border around text in a text box, select the text box.

Choose Format, Line/Border Style. A sub menu will appear showing the most commonly used borders. If the border style, thickness or colour that you require is not shown, select More Styles.

The Border Style dialog will be displayed, select options for style, thickness and colour of borders. Once you have selected the border you want, click OK.

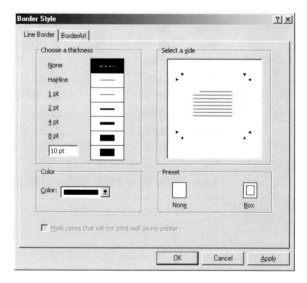

TASK

1 Open the file **Exercise 2 – DTP.**

2 Change the page size to **A4** and the orientation to **Portrait.**

3 Enter a heading for your newsletter: **Your Name CyberNewsletter**, which must be 2 cms high and span across all three columns. Choose a suitable font, size, and colour to suit your publication. Centre your heading on the page.

4 Change the background colour to add emphasis to your font colour.

5 Make sure your font is appropriate for a newsletter heading and that it fits the size of the heading as given in step 3.

6 Under the heading, enter the date right aligned, and formatted as follows:
30th May 2002

7 emboldened, with the date using superscript for the 'th'.

8 Place a hairline border in a suitable colour around your text.

9 Save the changes you have made to your file and close it.

USING WORDART

WordArt Frame Tool

Every publication should have display text – headings or headlines – which should catch the reader's attention by being distinctive or different from the rest of the text (body text). As a general rule, display text is big, colourful and eye catching. Display text works differently in different types of publications, for example a newsletter or flyer may look different to a heading in a report. You will need to identify the purpose of your document before you choose how to design your display text.

In Microsoft Publisher you can set the display text as plain text for publications such as reports, which are more formal; but for advertisements, flyers or informal invitations you can use WordArt. WordArt provides splashy effects, which can heighten contrast between display and body text. But in this case less is definitely more – limit your usage of WordArt to around a maximum of half a dozen words, and do not use too much on one publication or you'll lose emphasis.

To insert WordArt, click on the WordArt Frame Tool on the toolbar to the left of the screen.

Choose the WordArt style you would like for display text from the Gallery shown.

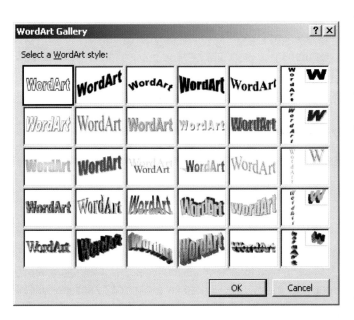

Your cursor will change to a cross as you pass it over the blank file. On the blank file, draw a box. This will be the WordArt area into which your WordArt text will go.

The WordArt Gallery dialog box will be displayed. Choose the style of WordArt you would like and click OK.

Microsoft Publisher will automatically run the WordArt wizard, which will prompt you to insert the text you want as display text, and give options on how the text will be displayed on the publication.

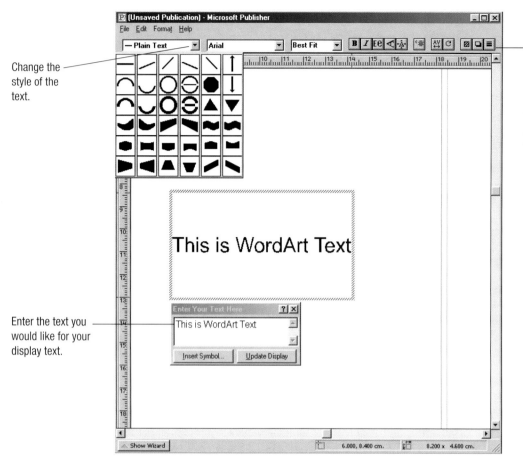

These buttons allow you to change the formatting, direction and kerning (spacing of characters) of the WordArt text.

You can also add shading, shadowing and borders with these buttons.

Change the style of the text.

Enter the text you would like for your display text.

GRAPHIC OBJECTS

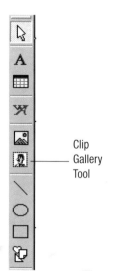

Graphics (pictures) are one of the best ways to attract your readers' attention. Use graphics to reinforce the message you want your readers to see, feel and understand. Once you are clear about your reader audience and the message you would like to put across, you will need to choose pictures that are appropriate for your publication or DTP file, and place them on the page so that they make your message as clear as possible. There are different types of pictures to choose from, each with a different use.

Clip Gallery Tool

Types of Pictures

Illustrations: These are useful to put across a feeling. They are open to interpretation and can be very powerful. Scientific or technical illustrations can show detail not captured in photographs. Microsoft Publisher comes with it's own set of illustrations under Clip Art, and more can be viewed on the Microsoft Publisher Clip Gallery Live website.

To insert an illustration or ClipArt, click on the Clip Gallery Tool on the toolbar to the left of the screen. Your cursor will change to a cross as you pass it over the blank file. On the blank file, draw a box. This will be the Clip Art area into which your illustration will go. MS Publisher will automatically open up the Clip Art Gallery, offering a gallery of illustrations to choose from.

Click on the category picture to display all the illustrations in that category. Once you have selected a suitable illustration, click on the Insert Clip ![icon] icon on the sub menu that appears (or double-click the picture) to insert the illustration.

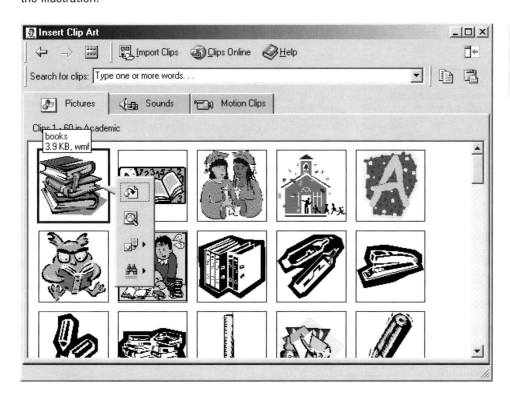

The Insert Clip Art dialog box displayed here shows the books image selected with the sub menu options.

An alternative method of inserting clipart is to choose Insert, Picture on the menu bar. A sub menu will appear to the side, select Clip Art. The Clip Gallery will open as before.

Photographs: Photographs are good to use when you want a realistic depiction of an object (e.g. a house for sale) and can also be very good at putting across the feeling of your publication. Photographs can be imported from the Internet, from the Microsoft Publisher Clip Gallery Live, or from a photograph or picture scanned and saved on your hard drive.

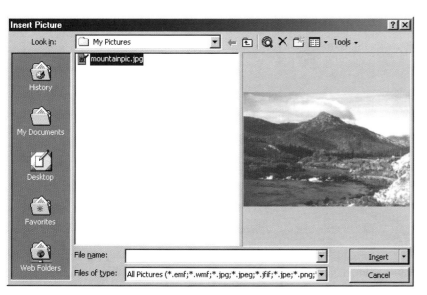

To insert a picture from a file (previously downloaded, scanned, saved picture or photograph) click on the Picture Frame Tool on the toolbar to the left of the screen. Your cursor will change to a cross as you pass it over the blank file. On the blank file, draw a box. This will be the Picture Frame area into which your picture will go. Double click in the picture frame area. MS Publisher will automatically open up the Insert Picture dialog box.

Navigate to the location where the file was saved from the Look in drop-down box. Select the image from the list, and then

click on the Insert button. The picture will be placed in the picture frame area, and this frame will be adjusted to suit the size of the picture or photograph inserted.

An alternative method of inserting a picture from a file is to choose Insert, Picture, and From File on the menu bar. The Insert Picture dialog box will open as before.

Photographs can also be inserted directly into Microsoft Publisher from a scanner or digital camera. The scanner reads a printed picture as a series of dots and translates (digitises) those dots into a bitmap file that the computer can display and print. Bitmaps take up a large amount of disk space on your hard drive and you may not be able to fit your publication onto a $3\frac{1}{2}$ Floppy disk. Large bitmap pictures can cause your printer to print very slowly, or not print at all.

The most effective way to keep the file small is to keep the scanning resolution as low as possible. Resolution is the number of dots per inch making up the picture or photograph. The higher the resolution, the better the quality of the picture. You can control the number of dots per inch (dpi) that your scanner records as it digitises the picture. The more the dpi, the more information is stored about the picture and the bigger the file becomes. It is important to know the dpi that your printer can print at, so that you scan at the same dpi level. Otherwise you have more information (dpi) than you can use. But you can scan a photograph at a lower resolution, and get a good quality photograph.

To scan a photograph into Microsoft Publisher you will need to have a scanner. Turn on your scanner and place the picture face down onto the glass surface (or as recommended by the scanner user manual). If you haven't done so already, create a picture frame as mentioned above. If the frame already exists, click to select it.

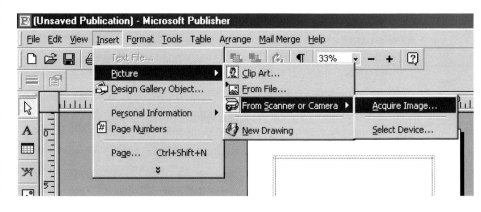

Choose Insert, Picture, From Scanner or Camera and then Acquire Image. Using the scanning program, start the scanning process and make any adjustments you want to the scanned image (follow the user manual instructions). When you're finished, exit the scanning program. The scanned image is then automatically added to your publication. If you're printing your publication at a commercial printing service, it's best to have your printing service scan images for you.

MANIPULATING GRAPHIC OBJECTS

Selecting, Moving, Copying, Positioning and Deleting Graphic Objects

To move, copy, position or delete a graphic object, you first need to select it by clicking on the graphic object, so that the handles (little black squares) are visible. To move a graphic object, select it, and then drag it to the new position on the page. You could also click on the Cut icon on the toolbar and then Paste the object into the new position. To copy a graphic object, select it and then click on the Copy icon on the toolbar and then click Paste. Your original graphic should still be in place, and the copied object will be placed on top. You can move the copied

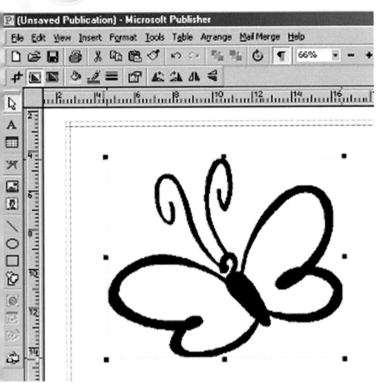

object to a new position. To position an object on the publication, simply move the object frame around the page until you find a suitable place for it. To delete a graphic object, simply select it and then press the Delete on the keyboard or select the object, right click over the object and click Delete Object on the menu that appears.

Changing the Size and Shape of an Object

Select the object to be changed. Move the cursor (mouse) to a handle. The outside/corner handles resize the object in proportion and keep the object the same shape; the middle handles skew the object making it longer or wider. Left click and drag the handle outwards to increase or inwards to decrease the size of the object, without distorting it.

Changing the Border or Background of an Object

To change the background colour or border of the object, select the object to be changed. Right click on the object and select Change Frame.

To change the *background colour*, click Fill Color: the previously used fill colours will be displayed. If the colour background you want is not shown, select More Colors. This will display a palette of colours to choose from. Click on the colour you would like and then click OK.

To change the *border style*, click Line/Border Style. The most common styles are shown here. If the border style you want is not shown, select More Styles. This will display a palette of styles to choose from. Click on the style you would like and then click OK.

To change the *border colour*, click Line Color. The previously used line colours will be displayed. If the line colour you want is not shown, select More Colors. This will display a palette of colours to choose from. Click on the colour you would like and then click OK.

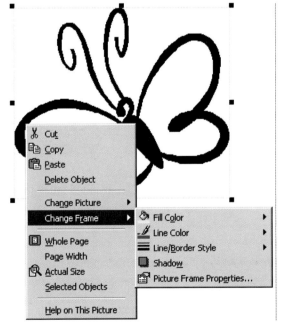

You can also add a shadow to your object by clicking Shadow. The above-mentioned options are also available by choosing Format on the menu bar, and selecting the appropriate option from the menu.

205

Rotating, Flipping, Scaling and Cropping an Object

To rotate (turn around clockwise), flip (turn upside down), scale (change the size proportionately) or crop (trim the object) the object, you must first select the object. The above-mentioned options are available on the toolbar once the object is selected, as shown below.

Crop Picture, Rotate Left, Rotate Right, Flip Vertical, and Flip Horizontal Icons.

Drawing Tools

Drawing Tools

It is possible to draw lines, boxes and circles in Microsoft Publisher using the drawing tools, which are on the toolbar to the left of the screen.

To insert a straight line click on the Line Tool, to insert a circular shape, click on the Oval Tool and to insert a box shape click on the Rectangle Tool. Once you have decided which object to draw, click on the appropriate tool icon. The cursor will change to a cross as it passes over the DTP file or publication. Left click and drag the mouse to create the object you require. The object may be resized or reshaped using the black handles at the corners and sides of the objects.

To change the colour or thickness of the line drawn or to fill in the object with a particular colour, right click on the object and then follow the same process as for the graphic objects or choose Format, Fill Color to change the colour of the object or Line/Border Style to change the style, thickness or colour of the border.

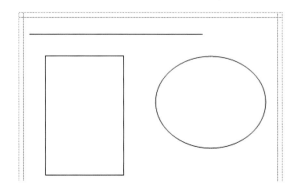

Combining Text and Graphic Objects

To place text within a graphic object, draw a text box, as shown before, inside the graphic object box. Select the text box, choose Arrange, Send Backward. This will merge the text box and the graphic object box, so that the text appears to be part of the graphic object. Make sure you have placed the text box exactly where you want it, as it is difficult to select after arranging it.

TASK

1   Open the file **Exercise 2 – DTP**.

2   Select a suitable image from clipart and insert in into the bottom of the first column. Make sure the clipart is a suitable shape for the frame and adjust the size to fit into the frame. Be careful the clipart image is not distorted when you make it larger to fit.

3   Select the clipart object, copy it and move the copy to the third column on your publication. Flip the clipart in the third column horizontally, so it mirrors the image in the first column.

4   Delete the image from the first column.

5   Add a hairline border to the clipart.

6   Save your changes and close the file.

TASK

1   Copy the following text into your newsletter, keeping each column of text separate.

2   Resize the text so that it fits into each column as shown below. (Use the Best Fit feature).

The Opening of a New Cyber Café

A big, warm welcome to the new Downtown Internet café, which recently opened in the high street.

The café offers a delicious cup of freshly brewed coffee on the house, while you sit and enjoy the Internet facilities.

There is also a selection of cakes and sandwiches for the hungrier surfers as well as coffees for you to take home.

What to Do?
You can surf the web on their broadband line, play multi-network games, video conference with people around the world, send email to relatives and use their productivity software.

Users pay access to all of the above facilities using a pre-determined rate table, which works out at around 8 pounds per hour.

Open Day
They are having an Open Day on June 15th from 12 noon to 6pm so go down and have a look.

Downtown Internet Café
The High Street
Richmond
TW9 1XP
Tel: 020 8345 6789

Or visit their website at:
www.downtown.co.uk

207

TASK CONTINUED

3 Justify the text in the columns, except for the name and address of the café, which must be centred.

4 Make sure the text is formatted as above, i.e. that headings are bold, italic and underlined, subheadings are bold and italic etc.

5 Move the picture you inserted into the middle of column 2. Wrap the text around the picture, so that it fits tightly. Resize the picture so that text can flow around it.

6 Arrange the picture and text so that they are both visible on the newsletter.

7 Change the picture for another appropriate one. Recolour the picture to match the background of your heading.

8 Change the background colour of the first and third columns to match the background colour of your heading.

9 Put a box with a hairline border around the name and address of the café.

10 Save the changes and close the file.

PRINTING YOUR DTP FILE OR PUBLICATION

Previewing your File before printing

- To check that your publication is going to print, as you would like it to, you may want to preview the file first before printing to check layout and correct any spelling errors. This will also save on ink and paper!

- Choose View, Zoom and then click Whole Page. This will allow you to see how your full page will look when printed.

- If your publication is more than one page, you can view two pages at a time by choosing View, Two-Page Spread.

- To hide any special characters or boundary lines (pink and blue borders), choose View, Hide Special Characters or Hide Boundaries and Guides.

Printing a Draft Copy

Before you print your DTP file in colour and with all the options required, you may want to print a draft copy, with lower resolution graphics, to check for any spelling or layout errors. A draft copy may also be required if you are producing a publication for a third party, so that they can check to see that the publication is what they want. Before you begin this procedure, be sure the publication is set up for commercial printing (Tools, Commercial Printing Tools, Color Printing) and that the printer driver for your printer is installed.

Choose File, Print. Select the output device that you wish to print to from the drop-down box in the Name box. Select the Advanced Print Settings button. On the Publications Options and Device Options tabs, click the options you want for example, print lower resolution graphics and then click OK.

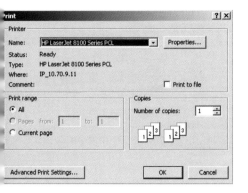
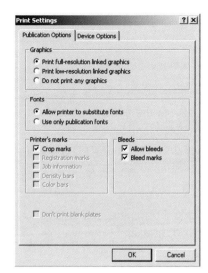
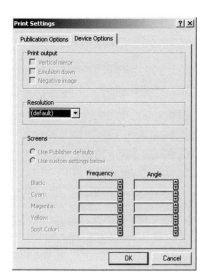

Printing Final Output

After checking your document for errors on screen and checking a draft copy, you will be ready to print a final copy of your DTP file or publication.

Choose File, Print. The Print dialog box will be displayed which gives you options to change the number of pages to print, as well as which pages to print if you do not want to print all pages. The resolution of the graphics can be changed within the Advanced Print Settings, Publications Options tab. The drop-down menu will give the options of 150 dpi, 300 dpi, or 600 dpi, depending on the quality of printer installed.

TASK

1 Open the file called **Exercise 2 – DTP.**

2 Preview the file for printing. Check for layout and spelling errors.

3 Print a draft copy of the leaflet and call it Newsletter1.

4 Check the draft copy for errors. Highlight any errors found, and make the changes to the file.

5 Print a final copy of the file and label it Newsletter2.

6 Close the file, saving if prompted.

PACKING YOUR DTP FILE

You may want to pack your file in Publisher format to print later, to take to a professional printing service, or to take to another computer on a network.

To pack your file to take to a printing service, choose File, Pack and Go and then Take to a Commercial Printing Service.

- The Pack and Go Wizard takes you through each step of the packing process. Click **Next** to move to the next step.

- If you haven't saved your publication already, the wizard will ask you to save it.

- If you're taking your publication on disk to the printing service, choose $3\frac{1}{2}$ Floppy or A:\drive when prompted for a save location. If you're putting your files on an external drive, on a network, or on your computer's hard disk, click Browse, choose the drive and folder you want, and then click OK. Click Next.

- To embed TrueType fonts, include linked graphics, and create links for embedded graphics, click Next, or click to remove the check mark for options you don't want. Click Next.

- Click Finish.

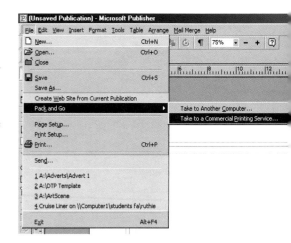

If MS Publisher cannot find a linked graphic while packing your publication, click Retry after you insert the disk or CD-ROM containing the original graphic into the appropriate drive; click Skip to leave the current link and replace the graphic later, or click Browse to locate a graphic that has been moved or to select another graphic and link to it.

If MS Publisher notifies you that you used fonts that cannot be embedded, click OK. Be sure to talk to your printing professional about getting any fonts that were not embedded.

Insert another disk if Publisher prompts you, and then click OK. It's a good idea to number the disks so your printing service knows which disk to insert first when they unpack your files.

To print composite and separation proofs of your publication, click OK.

Some important points:

- The files are saved in the directory you choose during the packing sequence. Publisher names and numbers your packed files and adds a .puz extension. For example, the first file will be named Packed01.puz, the second file will be Packed02.puz, and so on. A Readme.txt file and Unpack.exe program also are included with your packed files. The Readme file contains instructions for using the unpacking program to unpack your files. Unpack.exe is the program you use to unpack your files.

- If you make changes to your publication after packing your files, be sure to run the Pack and Go Wizard again so the changes are part of your packed publication.

TASK

The editor of the newsletter has decided that it would be better quality print if it were taken to a printing company. Pack up the publication, so that it can be taken to a commercial printer. Save the file to a Floppy disk and call it Commercial Print Newsletter. Close any open Publisher files. Close the Publisher application.

e-Quals
Index